MIKE FIGGIS: COLLECTED SCREENPLAYS I

# MIKE FIGGIS
# Collected Screenplays

## VOLUME I
*Stormy Monday*
*Liebestraum*
*Leaving Las Vegas*

*faber and faber*

This collection first published in 2002
by Faber and Faber Limited
3 Queen Square London WC1N 3AU

Typeset by Faber and Faber Ltd
Printed in England by Bookmarque Ltd, Croydon

*Liebestraum* first published in 1991 by Faber and Faber Limited
© Mike Figgis, 1991

*Leaving Las Vegas* first published in 1996 by Faber and Faber Limited
© Initial Productions SA, 1995
The author of the screenplay wishes to thank Lila Cazès, producer of
*Leaving Las Vegas*, and Initial Productions SA for their courtesy in
permitting this publication. Photo from *Leaving Las Vegas* by
Suzanne Hanover © United Artists

This collection, *Stormy Monday* and Introduction © Mike Figgis, 2002

Photo on p. vi by Suzanne Hanover. Photo from *Stormy Monday* courtesy of
Red Mullet. Photo from *Liebestraum* © MGM/Initial Entertainment Group

The right of Mike Figgis to be identified as author of this
work has been asserted in accordance with Section 77 of the Copyright,
Designs and Patents Act 1988

A CIP record for this book
is available from the British Library
ISBN 0–571–21012–0

2 4 6 8 10 9 7 5 3 1

# CONTENTS

Introduction
*Stormy Monday* and *Liebestraum*: an interview
with Mike Figgis
vii

Stormy Monday
I

Liebestraum
115

Leaving Las Vegas
195

Afterword to *Leaving Las Vegas*
by Mike Figgis
294

# INTRODUCTION
*Stormy Monday* and *Liebestraum*


WALTER DONOHUE: *You once said that* The People Show *was the best apprenticeship for film-making that you could think of.*

MIKE FIGGIS: I joined *The People Show* in 1970, having spent the year after I left college playing in France in a rock 'n' roll band, and deciding that I wasn't going to be a teacher, which is what I qualified to do. When I was a student I had moved to the Abbey Art Centre in London, which was where *The People Show* had been started in 1965 by Jeff Nuttall as a sort of 1960s version of a Happening. He called it *The People Show* because he collected seven people who happened to be there – drama students mainly – and put together a show, which he called *The People Show*. And afterwards, they just kept the name. They carried on for a few years doing his work, but eventually he drifted away, so they started doing their own scripts and working out their own structures.

*And you just sort of drifted in.*

Yeah. I was working with a free jazz group called The People Band, so named because they often worked with *The People Show*. I did a couple of shows at the old Arts Lab in Drury Lane as a musician and liked the work a lot. But, at a certain point, I got politically involved in the middle of a huge dispute between the musicians and the actors. The musicians felt that they weren't being given enough room to be truly improvisatory and were being held back by what they felt were the too rigid structures of the performance element of the show. I felt that if you elected to be in that situation, there were certain rules you should obey, otherwise the anarchic element would ultimately destroy what was good about the combination. There was a huge fight one night, a split occurred, and The People Band walked out. I felt very strongly that they were wrong, so I stayed. I then joined *The People Show* as its musician.

*But you weren't content simply to be a musician. You wanted to be involved in a much broader way, didn't you?*

Because *The People Show* was the kind of group that never had a director – never had a production designer – everybody did everything. You were expected to cross over into every area. So, although I was mainly there to do the sound, I also very quickly became a performer. I remember my first performance was at the Come Together Festival at the Royal Court Theatre in 1970 in front of a very hip, very aware audience. It was terrifying. I had to wear a dress. Both Mark Long and I wore the same dress. The show was about Bix Beiderbecke and Mark Long's mother. Within ten minutes of the show starting, it went very well. It was very funny, and short enough so we didn't get into trouble. I didn't look back after that. Because it worked, no one really then questioned the idea of whether you were a performer or not, whether you could act or not. You just carried on.

*Did being a performer also mean writing your own material?*

Each performer in *The People Show* was responsible for his own lines, so I became very actively involved in the writing of the scripts.

*Writing meant what? Writing speeches?*

No speeches were ever written. Our method was, basically, locking the door and the three or four performers sitting together and not coming out of the room – other than to sleep – until you had unanimously decided that the structure was correct. It meant hours and hours of talking about structure. Someone would suggest an image at the beginning of the process. Someone would say: I have this image. And it would usually be a painterly image. It would be: broken glass or a rose. In fact, they sound rather bland. Usually, it would be a strange image. There would be a surreal quality to the image. But it would be an image in isolation. This image would trigger off other images, and then one would find a connecting image, and so on. Then, through a natural process of selection, certain images would be put on the shelf, perhaps for another show. Everyone kept notebooks. So, the whole notion of a

notebook became crucial as a reference for this process of
work. Then, having assembled a certain number of images, the
hard work of actually connecting those images and coming up
with a dramatic structure – which was a sort of storyline,
which would also involve characters – would begin. Maybe,
one of the images suggested in the first place would literally be
a character. Mark Long would say: I want to do this in a red
face, and I'm going to wear these clothes. That's my character.
And my obsession is cleaning windows. Now, that might
change as we talked, but the red face would probably remain,
and he'd have this very strong sense of character. With Mark, it
was always a very strong sense of character.

*And with you?*
With me, it was more an overall sense of how 'red face' and
'broken glass' could connect. I became the main notebook
writer; in a sense, the person who co-ordinated the images.
Not exclusively. Everyone did it. But by the time I left *The
People Show*, a situation had naturally evolved whereby on the
last day of the meeting I would come in and say: OK, here's
the order. Because I was the person who made the sound
tapes, the timings of which would be used as triggers for certain light cues, and the appearances or disappearances of
characters – these sound timings providing the skeleton of the
show – it seemed natural to be the one who came in and said:
OK, here's the order. Mark and I would then work closely
together to get the lights cued up. And of course Mark, as a
performer, was very much in the front. So his sense of character was very important. My sense of character always evolved
much more slowly, as a result of the performances. I would
tend to, in the more successful shows, write myself as a kind
of watching character who would just stand at a bar and
drink, and then do small things, and have an overall view. In a
sense, like a director.

*This idea of having images be the starting point – in terms of the
films which you have written yourself, has this been the process?*
No. The starting point tends to be ideas, not visual images.

*So, the image of the couple sprawled on the floor at the end of*
Liebestraum *was not the starting point of the film.*
No. But when I look at the stills from *Liebestraum*, I suddenly
realize exactly what they are: they're images from *People Shows*.
The image of the couple on the floor at the end is an image
from a performance I did in a basement. I was still with *The
People Show*, but it was one of the first things I did on my own.
There's a striking similarity. And there are other images in
*Liebestraum*. There's one from *Redheugh*. It was an image to do
with earth, with being buried in earth.

*Where does that occur in* Liebestraum?
It's the image of the store covered in dirt. Also, the image at
the end: the couple lying in dirt, lying in soil, ambiguously
dead or alive. These images tend to recur.

*Like in* The House: *the soldier lying, covered in snow. You're not
sure whether he's dead or alive.*
Also, the lovers in *The House*, lying in the room covered in
cobwebs.

*So, for a number of years you worked with* The People Show.
I was with *The People Show* for ten years, but then the group
started to change. The advent of what was called *The Cabaret
Show* took *The People Show* in a whole new direction. It was a
bit more commercial, very funny, very entertaining, but much
less surreal, much less confrontational. The situation on the
fringe was changing. It was hard to get grants, venues were closing, and, in a sense, one had to adapt. I have to say, with complete admiration, that *The People Show* still exists, and that is
probably because of their ability to adapt. I had ambitions that
we could adapt in a different way. So, I decided that probably
the best thing for me to do was to stand back and do something
else for a while, and by then I'd become very interested in film.

The National Film School had opened a few years before; it
sounded like a really good place, so I applied to go there. I
read the prospectus and it seemed that, in a sense, I was their
most perfect student. I'd done everything they wanted one of
their students to have done, i.e. I was between the age of

twenty-five and thirty-five, and I'd had a wide experience of a number of film-related things: lighting, acting, directing, writing, music, etc. So, I assumed I'd get in. I probably even told people that's what I was going to be doing for the next couple of years. But when I went for the interview it went very badly.

*Why?*
I think because I assumed I'd get in, and they probably picked this up as a form of arrogance. Coupled with this, I think, was their natural suspicion of theatre, particularly experimental theatre. You know, the idea that you can't cross over, that there is not a strong connection between the two, and that it's an arrogant assumption to think that there is. David Putnam was on the panel, as well as Colin Young. Romaine Hart was very sympathetic. There were also a couple of well-established television and film people. I found them very hostile, and I then in turn became aggressive. In all honesty, I was surprised at their attitude, which was: You've had no experience in film, so what makes you think you'd be any good at it? I said: Well, I think it's self-explanatory. The work that I've done is so closely related to film that I don't see that it's going to be a huge leap. The only thing I don't know is camera technique. I made the mistake of saying 'and it can't be that difficult'.

*The National Film School tends to be seen as an avenue to get people into the industry, so probably what they're looking for is people who can fit into the industry.*
I think so. They kept using the expression 'teamwork', that film-making is essentially a team process and that I didn't seem to be expressing a team attitude. Yes, of course, you can't make a film without a team, but I don't actually think it is a team process. I think it's a singular vision. And I think that probably worried them a little bit.

*In a way, the perfect product of the Film School is Michael Caton Jones. There isn't a single vision in any of his films.*
I was very surprised. It was literally my first experience with film people, and in a sense it was a very accurate taste of, certainly, the British attitude to film-making.

*Which is?*
The old boy network. You have to pay your dues. It's not a
thing you can jump into and be clever with very quickly. It's
something where you have to swim through mud to get to the
point where they'll give you the toys.

I mean, everyone said: Keep your mouth shut. You can do it
if you keep your mouth shut. Your credits are sound credits, so
say you want to be a sound recordist, and then you can change
once you've got it. But it seemed to incense the panel that I
wanted to do directing, and also camera. They said: Why do
you want to do both? And I said: If you don't understand camera, how can you direct a film? So, to cut a long story short,
the application was rejected. Putnam said: If you don't get in,
what are you going to do? And I said: I'll make a film anyway.
He said: But you've already said that you can't use a camera.
And I said: Yes, and I've already said that it can't be that difficult. I'll work it out. So, I decided that that would be my goal.
I'd make a film. Which I then did.

*Which was?*
*Redheugh.*

*I thought that was a theatre piece?*
I'd written a film script which was basically a forty-minute film
about the war. My father had died a couple of years before.
He'd been a pilot in World War Two, and it had been my
observation that he – and most of his generation – had never
recovered from the war, emotionally recovered. Anyone who
was seventeen or eighteen when the war started and was there-
fore twenty-four or twenty-five when it finished – those crucial
years when you're gently meant to be growing up – if you grow
up in three weeks in a war situation and then spend the next
couple of years – as my father did – drinking heavily to get over
your fear of flying, when the war finishes, what are you fit for?
You've missed out on a whole psychological period, and he
spent the rest of his life trying to deal with it. So, I wanted to
make a little film about a pilot who gets shot down in the north
of England. But then, to make it ambiguous, it could have
been in Germany or England, he could have been dead or

alive. There was very much a kind of 'is this really happening' feel to the piece.

I obviously wasn't going to get the money to make it as a pure film, so I formed a theatre company, with myself as the director. I got a writer's grant from the Arts Council, and then wrote to the Mickery Theatre in Amsterdam to Ritsaert Ten Cate, who'd been a firm supporter of *The People Show*, told him I was writing my own first piece, and would he be interested in it. He said he would. Ultimately, they came in as the main producers with the ICA, and he put up £6,000 to make the film – which was very brave of him. I then went ahead and made the film up in Northumberland at the house where my father had died. I brought the material back to London, edited it, and ended up with a forty-minute film which then became the central part of a live performance involving four classical musicians, an opera singer, three other actors, and a fairly complicated technical set. But the film was the starting point for the performance; in other words, the live performance elements all came from elements within the film. The film also functioned by itself as a film.

This also coincided with the beginning of Channel Four. I was aware of the fact that Channel Four was opening. Very quickly word got round that Channel Four was commissioning films, and that they were interested in people who had not been in the industry before, and that they were going to help new people. I had my *Redheugh* film, as well as added pages of script that had originally been taken care of in the live performance. So, my proposition was: Here is half a film. With very little money we could complete the film, add a score, and so on, and you'd have a complete film. That was really the extent of my ambition.

I remember coming to the meeting at Channel Four and there was David Rose, and yourself, and probably Karin Bamborough, and pitching this very complicated, rather experimental idea, and leaving a video cassette of the film, as well as a sound cassette of the songs that had been written for the film. I came back for the second meeting and you, I think, said: Look, I don't think this is going to be so interesting for us. It's something you've already done. We'd be much more interested in commissioning something completely original, written especially for the channel, not something that's half-done and then adapted. So, I was suddenly in one of those situations in which you occasionally find yourself, where someone says: Do you have anything else? In fact, this is where the notebook pays off. If you do keep a notebook, then of course, you always have things half-cooking. And I did have one idea which had been commissioned, but hadn't, in fact, materialized. It was for a festival in Paris. The idea was that six different performance artists were each going to be given a house in which to make a performance. The piece had to be about a house. I had come up with the idea of a house which was an English house, but it wasn't in England, it was in the middle of Europe. So, the whole philosophy and approach would be different; the idea of the English being an island race would be challenged by putting them in a different environment. I already had a map with England in the middle of Europe, which was a striking visual image. I then handed this over, saying: Yeah, I have an idea. David Rose immediately picked up on it and said: That's an interesting idea. Yes. I think we can talk about this. So, between you and David, it got kicked off. The next stage was the crucial one: who was going to write it? I remember being very nervous about that and suggesting to you that Jeff Nuttall be brought in since he was a writer I knew. What's interesting is that I was intimidated, in the sense that because it was a film, it had to have a more conventional approach to it. There should be lots of words on a page. And you said: Well, why don't you write it? I said: No, I can't write it. And you said: Well, why don't you just do the first draft. If it's terrible, we can then talk about what writers we could bring in. In fact, when I brought in the first draft, from then on in, the conversations were solely about the script, not about bringing in a writer. I'm sure everyone goes through that paranoia about whether they can write or not. Film writing is such a different thing from theatre writing.

*Different in what way?*
It's a much more minimal thing. You have far more tools to play

with in a film, such as the visual elements, and all the other
things that come in post-production which make a film work
and which aren't actually the script or the dialogue as a dominant thing above everything else. I mean, you need dialogue.
But if you choose your actors well, they're usually pretty good
at dialogue. If you give them an indication of what you want,
give them dialogue as a guide, and work with them in an interesting way, they'll come up with their own speech patterns
which are more authentic anyway than anything you could try
to write for them. There are areas where things have to be said
briefly and they're usually to do with plot and you don't really
want to spend more time on that than you need to. You should
write those in as precise a way as possible and stick to that. But
writing is not nearly as intimidating a thing as I thought it
would be. And the transition from thinking of oneself as not
being capable of doing that to suddenly accepting that you are a
writer of films was, in this particular instance, totally painless.

*In a sense the film was more like your theatre pieces. It didn't have a
conventional narrative in any way. It was much more poetic.*
Yes. As a transition from theatre to film, it was perfect because
I was allowed to work in a theatrical way. There was a lot of
voice-over. The main dialogue in the film is Stephen Rea's
voice-over as he is dying in the snow.

*And what is the film about?*
It's about trying to return to one's home. In this particular
case, it's an England which is set in the middle of Europe, with
Stephen Rea as an English soldier who is returning from a
failed campaign in which the English army has tried to invade
the neighbouring state of Latvia.

*For what reason?*
For reasons of late nineteenth-century imperialism. In fact, in
the story, Russia has stepped in and signed an alliance with
Latvia, using it as an excuse to counter-invade England. So, it's
New Year's Eve and a party is taking place in a country house.
There's a bishop there, and a general, and a rather degenerate
aristocrat whose house it is, and his very young wife who is

grieving over the death of their child in an accident when the child fell down the stairs. They're all talking about the rumours of whether the Russians are coming.

At the beginning of the film you see a soldier, the Stephen Rea character, who is the main character of the film, and who is in the house as a ghost, but we also see him walking through the snow in a blizzard. He collapses and is so tired that he decides just to die in the snow. So, the voice-over that goes through the entire film is his thoughts, his recollections of the campaign in Latvia – where he has just been – of this house, and of the affair that he had with the woman in the house. He struggles for a while in the snow, and then just lies there. And the camera then tilts up over the next hill and you see that he's only about a quarter of a mile from the house, but he can't see it. The camera then zooms in on the house, and then the interior stuff of the film begins and we go into the party. In the course of the one hour that the film takes, the house ages and begins to fall apart and get tattier. Similarly, as the party pro-

**EUROPE 1884**

gresses, they get more and more drunk, and they end up in the opium room completely out of it as the Russian soldiers come in – along with the Communist elements of the English army who have revolted – and start burning and looting the house.

*The soldier is a ghost in the house, but he also has recollections of the house he was billeted in in Latvia when he was part of the conquering army. Isn't there a danger that having these different levels of reality could lead to confusion in the audience?*

Well, it goes back to *The People Show*, and a mentality where the ability to juggle a lot of ideas at the same time is highly developed and seems like a natural thing. It's certainly characteristic of the French films that came out in the 1960s and 70s, like *Hiroshima Mon Amour*, *Last Year at Marienbad*, *Providence*, and, in a different way, the work of Jean-Luc Godard. So, with something like *The House*, which in the space of an hour certainly presents a lot of very complicated ideas in conflict and in parallel with one another, I spent very little time worrying about whether the audience would understand it or not. I just spent all my time trying to make it as seamless as possible as a piece of work so that even if they didn't consciously understand it, at least their subconscious would click in and people would start to understand it at that level. So, what is dictated to by their ego – which is the need to apparently understand something, which often confuses and gets in the way of the way people look at art – can be overridden by a kind of sophisticated style. I believe that if someone is enjoying something, and is taken on a journey by something, then they will let go.

One of the strongest moments in *The House* was when the soldier and the young wife make love in the abandoned nursery. From her point of view, the sexual element is very much a grieving; for him, it coincides with this story he is telling as a dying soldier about an affair he had with a woman in the occupied town he was in, which then becomes part of a story about walking down a hill behind an old man and having the urge to kill him – just experiencing the sense of power of being a conquering soldier and how that destroyed him, having to confront the fact that it existed in himself as a human being. All this coincides with him walking down the stairs behind the young wife who is going down to rejoin her husband, and the camera does this incredible move right round in a circle and comes back up on to the soldier who is watching. Meanwhile, his voice-over is telling a different story, which builds up to a point where he suddenly sees the ghost of the child. He's talking about death, and the child suddenly appears and throws himself down the stairs and kills himself, in a flashback, at the soldier's feet. Now, if you had asked someone who had watched this to explain it, he probably couldn't have. But because all those different elements coincided at that time, there was a very strong emotional impact.

When you make your first film – and I think I have this in common with every film-maker – you think you might never make another film. So, you cram so much into it. In *The House*, in the space of one hour, I had so many ideas and images going through it. It's only when you get a little bit more secure, as you carry on working, that you realize that you don't need to put every single idea in your head into the film you're making at the time. You can have fewer ideas and expand them more.

*So, what happened next?*
I got into a commission situation with Enigma. Putnam had seen a preview of *The House*, and I got a call from his producer, Susan Richards, who said: David and I have seen *The House* and we're terribly excited. We're looking for new film-makers, so come and have a drink with us. It was all very nice and exactly the way one would always like it to be.

*Did you remind David Putnam about your previous encounter with him?*
No. He claimed never to have met me before, and I didn't argue with him. I'd learned something. They were ecstatic about my idea. I had written a short film called *Mindless Violence*, about a gangland execution which took place in Newcastle right underneath the bridges I used in *Stormy Monday*. I had sent it to the BFI, trying to get it made as a short film, but it was rejected. They found it visually stimulating, but politi-

cally vacuous – I think that's what the letter said. It was a long
tracking shot down a hill as a man was taken to be executed.
So, I had this idea of a gangland thriller in Newcastle. I
pitched that, and they loved it and said: Do that for us. Don't
talk to anyone else about it. We'll definitely make this film. So,
that was great. I went away with the idea that I was going to
make this feature film. And then nothing happened. I ended up
teaching again at Middlesex Poly in their film course, and also
keeping my theatre work going. I started another piece called
*Animals of the City*, elements of which ended up in *Liebestraum*:
a lot to do with architecture, cast-iron buildings, and things
like that. So, I waited, and nothing happened. I never heard
back from David Putnam. I don't think he even read the treatment. Susan Richards would say: I think you need to do more
work on the treatment, and I kept saying: You can do treat-
ments for ever. It's not until you actually try and write a script
that you start to understand what your problems are. Just commission a script. But they didn't.

*So, how did* Stormy Monday *get made?*
I was in Soho one day in my car in a little connecting street
between Wardour Street and Dean Street, and I saw a skip full
of sound tapes. I was working at the Polytechnic, and they
were running out of money, and I looked in the skip and there
were maybe a thousand five-inch reels of tape being thrown
out. They'd been used maybe once. I thought this was crimi-
nal. So, I opened the boot of the car and was unloading all this
stuff out of the skip when Nigel Stafford-Clark, who had pro-
duced *The House*, walked past. He asked me how it was going.
And I said: Not very well, as you can see. I think Nigel was a
bit embarrassed to be having a conversation with a person who
was obviously unloading a skip, so I stepped out of the skip, we
walked to the other side of the street, and I told him what had
happened. He said: Well, let me see the treatment. So, I got
him the treatment the next day. And within a day – all credit to
Nigel – he rang me back and said: Look, I have three or four
points about your treatment. I think it's too complicated, but
basically I think it's a good idea and, if you're prepared to take

on board my suggestions, I'll commission a script. He then
went to Channel Four and got it as a Film on Four, for part of
the finance. On the strength of that, he took it to British
Screen and got well over half the finance for the film, which
was budgeted at £1.3 million. So, we still needed to raise just
under half of the money. But on the strength of that, he got the
script commissioned. It went through its first and second
drafts, and then it was really just a question of getting the
finance from the Americans. Simon Relph was consistently
supportive from the very beginning, even at a time when the
finance fell through in America.

*Was the presence of American characters in* Stormy Monday *done
primarily to raise the American finance?*
No, I wanted that. I think the best parallel would be a musical
one. If I'd been writing a piece of music and someone said you
can have whoever you like to play on this, I would have
brought in some American musicians. I think American actors
are better film actors by and large, and certainly having the
spice of some American actors in a British film, particularly a
film set outside London, in a place like Newcastle which I
knew was gritty and had a kind of American quality anyway,
was something I found very attractive.

The whole point of the film was the Americanization of our
culture. The willing take-over. We certainly haven't fought the
Americans, or tried keeping them out. I think it's because we
always wanted that in our culture. It was an exciting infusion
into British music, and certainly into film. I've never felt that I
was an English artist, anyway. So, purely from the point of view
of: you can have whoever you'd like to work with in the film –
Melanie Griffith would have come pretty near the top of my list.

*What's interesting about your films is the level of acting in them.
Sting, Richard Gere, Kim Novak have never given better performances. In* Stormy Monday *you had Hollywood stars, rock stars,
fringe-theatre actors, as well as a wide range of actors with different
degrees of film experience. Yet all of them appear to be seamlessly a
part of the same world. How do you achieve performances which are
so natural?*

When you start to direct a film – I mean literally directing it – I think you have to let your unconscious instincts dictate a lot of what you are doing. One of the first things is that you have to be so aware of people's nervousness and their ability – and the combination of these things – that you can decide how to apportion your time, in terms of who you are going to help. Obviously, the more people there are in a scene, the more difficult that becomes. Like with Sting. He's a nice man; he's not at all a confrontational, aggressive man. There's a scene in the film where Sean Bean turns up at his house to warn him about a plot against him. This was the first scene Sting shot. He's sitting at the breakfast table. I let him do the scene, but basically what he did was, he decided he needed cigarettes as a prop. So, he took a cigarette out, put it in his mouth, offered them to Sean Bean, who declined, then he lit the cigarette, and tapped it on the table. There was a lot of this kind of little finger acting going on. So, after we rehearsed it for a while, I had a cup of coffee with him and said: Look, there's a couple of things I want to say, and I hope you won't be offended, but you're being very busy with your hands, and I think that if you just kept very, very still it would be much stronger. Do you mind me saying this? And he said: No, no. I can't tell you how grateful I am for someone telling me how to act. I'm comfortable acting, but I have no sense of what I'm doing with my body. And if you could tell me that, I would be very grateful.

Other actors, however, when you start to pick on mannerisms and things like that, would be fearfully offended and feel that somehow you were attacking their performance. More trained actors, of course, study themselves in the mirror, and those little mannerisms are crucial.

*How do you find a way of maximizing an actor's good points and minimizing the weaknesses they have?*
Well, you watch, of course. It really goes back to *The People Show* and the whole idea that most of the creative work comes from notes, rather than literally from rehearsals: you do the rehearsal and then just use that as a basis for talking. My big thing when I'm shooting is that I don't allow anyone to make

any noise for the two minutes immediately following a shot.
The only time I would ever be angry or lose my temper was if
people abused that. You forget very, very quickly the details.
So, I like to come in immediately after a rehearsal or a take
and say: OK, that hand movement didn't work, hold the hand
down, don't look up, say the line, just keep looking down –
moving very quickly. It then may take half an hour before we
can do the shot again because things have to be adapted, but I
want to get my notes in straightaway.

So, that's one thing. The second thing, I think, is creating an
atmosphere on the set, participating to such an extent with
enthusiasm and with your spirit that you never dissociate yourself. The minute you dissociate yourself from what's going on,
the actors become insecure. If you're in there making a fool of
yourself as much as you're asking them to, then they'll go
along with you. If it's working well, you'll end up with such an
atmosphere on the set that even the less able actors will give
something and be natural.

*A lot of* Stormy Monday *takes place at night. Was that a problem?*
The start date got delayed and delayed and delayed. So, we
ended up shooting bang on mid-summer in the north of England where night starts – in real dark terms – about 11 o'clock
at night, and dawn begins at about 4 or 4.30. So, you might
have five hours maximum to shoot a whole night scene. You'd
start shooting a scene, and you'd be doing one angle, and
you'd suddenly realize that you weren't going to be able to turn
around because it was going to be dawn. There'd be this
dreadful moment when the birds would start to sing and you'd
know that that was it. Those things were very frustrating. In
fact, one of the best things in the film was shot after one of the
worst nights of the film. The scene when Tommy Lee Jones
and Sting are walking across the bridge at the crack of dawn,
we grabbed that on the run after a night of filming, in the rain,
the final scene outside the nightclub. All communication had
broken down, everyone was in a bad temper, nothing worked –
it was just desperate.

*In that end scene Melanie Griffith and Sean Bean disappear up the*

*steps and Sting is the last character you see. Somehow you miss a
final moment between the two lovers.*

I think so. I remember when I was cutting it, longing for that
last moment. It was a very strong lesson in how important an
ending is, the last image you leave everyone with. I felt it was
weak. I felt I would have liked to have stayed with our lovers,
and had that extra moment.

*Well, you said that was the worst night of the shoot.*

It was. And there is that awful reality when you make films,
that the budget is a real thing, the schedule is a real thing, and
you have to make the best of what you have in the cutting
room afterwards. So, you find yourself using every trick, every
artistic device you can engender, to make the film flow to the
end in such a way that you minimize the fact that the ending
was a little inadequate for the emotion that had been set up
just prior to the ending. If I'd have had the power to do it, I
would have got back on to the streets with a camera, got
Melanie Griffith and Sean Bean back, and shot another scene
the way Woody Allen is able to. But the reality is, you can't do
that. Not only can you not do that, they start saying: And
you've only got another two weeks left to edit. It's got to finish.
I mean, this is a budget of £1.5 million. It doesn't buy you anything.

*Liebestraum is your own script, and yet it's also a thriller and it's
also set outside England. I would have thought it would have been
more personal.*

My most comfortable performances as an actor in *The People
Show* were always ones in which I was slightly removed from
the action and was watching it. The characters I tend to write
tend to be outsiders who come into a situation and react,
rather than come in and create things that other people react
to. So, I tend to write things where people return to some kind
of structure that represented a home, or some kind of approxi-
mation of a house or womb-like environment, and they find
that things are different. I'm interested in how they react to
that whole thing. Like the soldier in *The House*. In *Stormy
Monday*, the Sean Bean character is coming through town, he's

not really a part of it, but he happens upon a series of events that then draw him in. And then he carries on. Basically, it's a sense of always passing through something. A journey. And never quite resolving that journey. In all of the endings I've written, the characters are unresolved. In *Stormy Monday* Melanie and Sean Bean have shared something, they're still together at the end of the film, but you don't get the feeling that they'll stay together. The characters will then move on.

*But at the end of* Liebestraum *you do get the feeling that something has been resolved because they have consummated the relationship.* I think *Liebestraum* is important for me, in that it's a growing-up script in the sense that only by the two of them getting together do they give themselves the potential to carry on and go somewhere else – not keep returning to the house, not keep returning to that mother/father situation.

*The fact that Paul doesn't shoot them allows them to go beyond the situation. The gesture he makes is quite important, isn't it?* Yes. I think his gesture is as important as theirs. His story is as interesting as theirs, even though he is a secondary character. I found him immensely sympathetic – the kind of husband who can't quite make it work.

*Isn't that partly a tribute to Bill Pullman's performance?* Absolutely. Bill Pullman gave levels to that performance and that character which were beyond my expectations. With a lesser actor I would have accepted a lesser interpretation because he would have fulfilled the crude requirements of the part, which is to be a pivot, to be something you were fright-ened of and who you thought would come back and repeat the violence of the past. To get more dimensions from an actor, and to get a sympathetic reading to that extent, gives you so much more ambiguity. It's better for me, but for a general audience, I'm told, it makes things more complicated, and maybe not as satisfying because they don't know where their sympathies should lie. But for me, you're getting more for your money.

*Certainly, as far as Kim Novak is concerned, you are definitely get-ting more than you ever would have expected.*

Kim Novak is one of those actors who means it. If she goes for
something, she means it. As a director you have to work very
closely with her. With Kim Novak, the problem was holding
her down to a believable state of terminal cancer. She's one of
the healthiest women I've met in my life, with colossal reserves
of strength. She has this energy and enthusiasm to do something, but, at the same time, not a great technique.

*You mean that in the course of making all those films, she didn't
develop a technique?*
She wasn't allowed to. One of her problems is that she is aware
that she was used as a sexual iceberg image. It was a complete
surprise to me when I discovered this incredibly sensual extro-
vert. Not at all the cool, frigid blonde. Nothing could be further from the truth. But, basically, she was put into sexy
clothes and told to stare blankly into the camera. So, she has
this tremendous frustration that she wants to be an actress; she
wants to be a great actress. Given an opportunity like *Liebestraum*, where she's got a role where she's dying and she wants
to express herself, then this urge to act and to do this death
justice is overwhelming.

The energy that came out of her was not at all compatible
with my view of this terminally ill woman who, I felt, barely
had the strength to speak and then had to gasp for breath. Getting her in each scene to the level of exhaustion and pathos –
because pathos is not a natural characteristic of Kim Novak;
she's a fighter – required a great amount of patience. Just sticking with a scene until it was right. After you've been in a small
hospital room, with her in bed, for three hours doing one
scene, and she's done it quite well – your instincts are to say:
Look, let's get out of here, let's move on to the next scene. But
there's another part of you saying: No, it could be better than
this. So, you say: We'll go again. And then everyone starts to
look at their watch and you start to feel all those pressures that
you're somehow holding everyone up. That's the funny thing
about making a film. That's why you're there. But, at the same
time, you sometimes have the feeling that the reason you're
there is to move on to the next scene.

*Was there any problem about getting her to use the coarse language required by the script?*
No. There was a very funny moment – there's only a remnant of it in the film – where she finds out from reading the newspaper that she's in the town where the murders originally happened; she'd been so doped up she hadn't been aware that the hospital was in the same town. So, she has a fit and tries to get out of bed. And then her son walks into the room, and at that moment, especially because of the physical resemblance, she focuses on him as if he were her husband and starts to scream at him. In the original script it said a stream of filthy language comes out of her. She said to me: I'm having difficulty getting into this. I don't really know quite how to do it. And she tried it and it wasn't really working. And then I had this idea. I said: Is there anybody in your past, perhaps in your film career, who you feel totally exploited you, and who you've never forgiven? And suddenly her eyes opened and she said: All right. Don't say anything else. So, we did the scene and this incredible stream of violent, repressed anger came out of her. It was almost too hard to watch.

Liebestraum *is suffused with sex and death.*
The link between sex and death is a very strong and fascinating one to explore. When people close to us die, the sexual urge becomes very strong as an affirmation of being alive. In *Liebestraum*, the character Nick finds himself in a situation where he is visiting his mother, a mother he's never met before, a mother who is obsessed with sexual guilt and jealousy for her husband/son. So, he finds himself in a situation where he's presented with the chance to be promiscuous: he doesn't really know why, but it's a fascinating world to be drawn into. So, what I tried to do in the film is not to play it in a particularly sexual way, but to try and charge the atmosphere.

There is also the fatalistic aspect of sex. People are fated to get together and it's not necessarily to do with a kind of 1960s idea of sex being good, clean fun. The cleaner and more wholesome you make sex, the less interesting it becomes. It also demeans it as the strongest and most basic instinct we have, and separates it into a containable compartment – which American film has done.

*Obviously, that was brought home to you when you had the preview in the US and the film was deemed too offensive.*

The script in this volume is the script of the film that I took to a preview in New York. I was convinced that it was the finished film. It was the closest I could get in editing, post-production, dubbing, music, and so on, to the vision I had of the film, based on the material I had collected throughout shooting. Obviously, I had got very used to the imagery, having written it, shot it, and edited it. To me it was just normal. I knew some of it was shocking for a first-time viewer, but not that shocking. I thought there was a seamless quality to the way the film was put together, that it flowed, and that the flow of the film would get you across what were the bumps – the shocking scenes.

The scene in the whore-house, as scripted – although it functions, in a sense, like a one-act play and can be lifted, as it has been, completely out of the film – had an enormously important role to play psychologically, for the leading charac-ter, Nick. His experience with these prostitutes – which had to do with the smell of women, the taste of women, and the establishing of his character in terms of how he behaved in the situation – was not at all like something out of *Tom Jones*. In other words, it was not a rollicking yarn where a 'real man' would go in and roger those prostitutes and come out and say: I managed to fuck ten of them, how did you do? Nick was very submissive and intimidated by these strong women, who also confronted him with the flip-side of the coin of how men would like women to behave, which is as demure rape victims. No, these were women who came forward and said: What would you like? They were very aggressive. And I thought it set a tone in the film which was sort of outrageous, from which the character then had to live through the rest of the film, and go through a sort of romance, and deal with his mother, and ultimately come to terms with an image which had already occurred in that scene. But at the preview the audience were horrified by the scene. They were so offended and uncomfortable, and made so hostile by having to watch this scene, that it was impossible to watch the rest of the film. It turned into a complete circus, with people shouting and leaving. There was this incredible aggression coming from the audience.

*So, what did you do?*
Well, first I recut the film, keeping the scene in. I tried to make the scene stronger. I tried to make it more obvious why the scene was there. But, on viewing that myself, I felt very dissatisfied. Suddenly, the scene did seem incredibly crude, which I had never seen it as being before. So, there were two choices. Either go back to the previewed film and keep it exactly as it was – at least I was happy with it. Or to radically recut the film, and take out the whore-house in its entirety. Which is what I did.

*What is interesting is that although your first three feature films are all very different, they also seem to inhabit the same world.*
I get attracted to material that is very different to what I've done before, but then, very quickly, find the darkness in it and start to work on that as the key thing in the plot. So nothing would ever remain light completely. I think that any film I make will have an element of darkness in it.

# Stormy Monday

# CAST AND CREW

## MAIN CAST

| | |
|---:|---|
| KATE | Melanie Griffith |
| COSMO | Tommy Lee Jones |
| FINLAY | Sting |
| BRENDAN | Sean Bean |
| TONY | James Cosmo |
| PATRICK | Mark Long |
| JIM | Brian Lewis |
| ANDREJ | Andrzej Borkowski |
| BOB | Derek Hoxby |
| COSMO'S BODYGUARD | Clive Curtis |
| PETER REED | Heathcote Williams |
| MRS FINLAY | Prunella Gee |

## MAIN CREW

| | |
|---:|---|
| *Directed by* | Mike Figgis |
| *Written by* | Mike Figgis |
| *Produced by* | Nigel Stafford-Clark |
| *Associate Producer* | Alan J. Wands |
| *Original Music by* | Mike Figgis |
| *Cinematography by* | Roger Deakins |
| *Film Editing by* | David Martin |
| *Production Design by* | Andrew McAlpine |
| *Costume Design by* | Sandy Powell |

## BRENDAN

*Brendan is the kind of boy who is too old for his peers and yet too young for the older people that he is more attracted to.*

*His heroes are deliberately chosen from outside the mainstream: Hemingway, Charlie Parker, Edward Hopper and the American existentialists.*

*Brendan, through a conscious choice of 'image', has set himself up as an outsider. He dresses in the style of the American 1950s student: tight Levis, football jacket, loafers, button-down shirts.*

*He is attractive in an odd way. I think of the young Orson Welles.*

*Brendan's room is of great importance to him. It is a self-portrait. On the walls are photographs of Charlie Parker, a reproduction of Edward Hopper's* Nighthawks, *the photograph of Francis Farmer being dragged out of court, a huge blow-up of a page from a Marvel comic, a New York skyline of the 1940s. A selective, romantic view-point. The room is neat. A mattress on the floor, two chairs and a table. A large collection of LPs, a turntable and a valve amplifier and two hand-made speaker cabinets. A music stand with a book –* A Tune a Day for the Alto Saxophone. *A saxophone case. A stack of comics. Book shelves made from bricks and shelving wood with books by selected American writers.*

## FINLAY

*Finlay is a tall man of forty-five. He dresses smartly in outlandish suits and shoes. His face is lined like Eddie Constantine.*

*In his youth Finlay has been a rough man, the leg man who has injured many and enjoyed his work. He has also mixed with people of all classes. Rich people who like to mingle with low life. Girls who like to sleep with gangsters. Finlay is still quite capable of cold-blooded action, as when he has the London hoods' arms broken.*

*Finlay is from the North East but spent time in London and in his early twenties became involved with jazz clubs and musicians on the London scene. He has a genuine love for music, a romantic attachment to the myths and styles of jazz music.*

*On his return to the North East Finlay starts his own jazz club, the Quay Club. This is a short-term success and he is able to open a nightclub. All this is happening at the time that Newcastle is enjoying the boom. Two other nightclubs are added to Finlay's circuit and he is a wealthy man.*

*Finlay is married to a middle-class woman, older than himself. They live in a large detached house in the suburbs. He has three children. The family is completely separate from the club business. His eldest son is the same age as Brendan. The other children are twelve and fourteen. Finlay has girls who work in the clubs.*

*The jazz club does not make money. Finlay subsidizes it totally from the profits of the other clubs. He refuses to close the club or in any way change its format. Suddenly he changes his mind. His philosophy, his outlook, is closely linked to the way he looks at his music. He is not naive; romantic up to a point, but not naive.*

*He sees that 'jazz' is now dead as a form and wants to, by bringing the appropriate musicians, play out the music to an end.*

*Thus the Polish avant-garde group are his last band. He knows that this is the end.*

*When the band turn up early (three days early) he doesn't hesitate to put them in the best hotel in town.*

*When Brendan enters Finlay's world, he comes in on the last moments. Finlay, for his own reasons, has decided to sell the club but plays the game through.*

*He likes Brendan, but is distanced from his own son.*

*The closing of the club is the end of his own youth. He is more involved with big business than he would admit.*

*From here on in his life will be harder, simpler, more to do with money and corruption of local politics.*

COSMO

*Cosmo is a smooth, ruthless American of about the same age as Finlay. He is from New York. There is an impression that he may have links with organized crime, but now he is in the process of becoming a legitimate businessman. In England his natural charm and ruthlessness makes him seem special, exotic, like a film star. He carries with him an entourage of quiet, hard Americans. He is interested in the charisma of the powerful. Personal relationships are of little importance to him. He has no sentiment. He can recognize power in others and adjust, as he eventually does with Finlay. He has contempt for the English and their small ways and lack of dynamism.*

KATE

*Kate is an American girl of about thirty. She is living in the town at the expense of Cosmo in an apartment owned by him as his mistress.*

*She works at night in a restaurant on The Side.*

*She is from the Midwest of America, of Polish origin. She has the air of melancholy admired by Bergman, but is not thought of as American.*

*She thinks of herself as an actress between jobs.*

*She is tall and boyish. Long legs, small breasts.*

*She has a hard attitude to relationships. Her relationships have invariably been with older men. Married men.*

*Unlike Brendan she is a realist. She does not have a highly developed sense of fantasy. She clearly sees, for example, that the relationship with Brendan has no future, and yet she does fall in love with him.*

*Like Brendan she is an outsider. At thirty plus she is single and without a long-term relationship.*

*At first Brendan is attractive to her because he is no threat. She is lonely.*

*She would not choose to be an outsider, preferring to be part of the conventional world.*

SUBTITLE: LONDON — 3 A.M. — THURSDAY

*Blue letters against a black background.*

EXT. SOHO STREET — NIGHT

*Two men, Patrick and Tony, are walking down Frith Street towards Soho Square. They are each carrying a briefcase and an overnight bag. It has been raining. The streets are still quite wet. Tony and Patrick are London 'heavies' in their early forties.*

*In Soho Square they stop next to a bright red Jaguar E-Type which is parked. The car is in perfect condition. Patrick opens the driver's door, throws his things into the back and gets in. Tony gets into the passenger side. Patrick opens the glove compartment and takes out a pair of driving gloves. As he does so, we catch a glimpse of a gun. He starts the car, turns the lights on and drives off. As the sound of the car recedes on the soundtrack, the film title music comes in. It is Otis Redding singing 'I've Been Loving You a Little Too Long'.*

    CUT TO:

OPENING CREDITS *which are seen with the following images:*

*The Jaguar driving up Edgware Road passing a sign for the M1 motorway.*

*The Jaguar on the M1 motorway at speed.*

*The Jaguar on the motorway in the rain. Exterior and interior.*

*The Jaguar in a service station. A close-up of the engine being checked for oil. The engine is spotless.*

*The Jaguar on the motorway as dawn is breaking, passing a sign for Newcastle.*

INT. JAGUAR — DAWN

*The Otis Redding music is finishing. On the motorway the traffic is*

*suddenly starting to slow down. Patrick changes gear. The Jaguar
slows down. A siren is heard. A police car flashes past on the hard
shoulder. The traffic slows down even more and stops. The Jaguar
has stopped about twenty cars short of the brow of a hill and so it
isn't possible to see the cause of the hold-up. The Otis Redding music
finishes and we hear an American DJ. The sound is coming from the
car radio.*

INT. BRENDAN'S ROOM – DAY

*The daylight is streaming in through a gap in the curtains. There is
a pause in the DJ's dialogue and then the radio alarm next to Brendan's bed goes off and the DJ continues.*

*We see the geography of Brendan's room. His 'American' images on
the wall. Brendan is awake but doesn't get up.*

EXT. MOTORWAY – DAY

*Long lens shot of two policemen appearing over the crest of the hill,
walking down the line of cars looking at them.*

*The policemen see the Jaguar. One of them takes out a walkie-talkie
and speaks into it.*

INT. KATE'S APARTMENT – DAWN

*Kate is asleep in bed. She is having a nightmare, turning her head
from side to side.*

INT. JAGUAR ON MOTORWAY – DAWN

*The policemen walking around the front of the Jaguar to the driver's
window. Patrick winds down the window. One of the policemen
bends down and looks in.*

*In long shot we see the policeman talking to Tony and Patrick. It is
clear that he is admiring the car.*

AMERICAN DJ (V.O.)

. . . Movies, movies, MOVIES. Every movie theatre in
town is showing American movies – SO WHAT'S NEW?

– Not just *any* American movie but the *great* great movies.
Now you're gonna have to check the tabloids for time and
place but remember to wear your 'I love America' badge
and you'll get into most places for half price. *Right.*
Tonight you can see . . . *Oklahoma, West Side Story, On the
Waterfront, The Girl Can't Help It, Jailhouse Rock, Invasion
of the Body Snatchers, Cat on a Hot Tin Roof, I the Jury, The
Asphalt Jungle, Casablanca, The Absent-Minded Professor*
OR *The Magnificent Seven.*

INT. KATE'S APARTMENT – DAWN

*Kate gets out of bed. We see her reflected in a Clark Gable poster.
She opens the curtains.*

INT. JIM'S GYM – DAY

*Several hard-looking men are doing weight lifting. One of them
deliberately drops the weights. They bounce on the floor, making a
loud noise.*

INT. KATE'S APARTMENT – DAY

*On the kitchen table, the coffee is percolating, the toast pops up.*

INT. KATE'S APARTMENT – DAY

*In the shower Kate turns off the hot tap and counts to twenty before
emerging.*

AMERICAN DJ (V.O.)
Tomorrow, that's Friday, you can take your pick from . . .
*Some Like it Hot, The Jazz Singer, The Grapes of Wrath,
Chinatown, In the Heat of the Night, French Connections* one
and two, *Godfather* one and two, *The Blob, A Night at the
Opera, The Big Country* . . .

INT. BRENDAN'S ROOM – DAY

*Close-up of typewriter with note in it.*

*Brendan's hand picks up a Walkman. He gets up slowly and puts a kettle on. He turns on the cold tap and puts his head under it.*

AMERICAN DJ (V.O.)

. . . Saturday, that's the last day of American week, you have . . . Walt Disney festival, *Bambi, Snow White and the Magnificent Seven, Mickey and Minnie, Donald Duck, Pluto, The 99 Dalmations, Lady Is a Tramp* and so on . . . Then there's *Citizen Kane, Giant, Bonnie and Clyde, Saturday Night Fever, The Long Goodbye, Easy Rider* and the first road movie – *Stagecoach.* If you don't like movies . . .

INT. KATE'S APARTMENT – DAY

*Kate eating breakfast, reading a copy of* The Times. *Fruit juice, coffee with honey, toast.*

AMERICAN DJ (V.O.)

. . . that's no sweat because Thursday afternoon at St. James' Park – there's a lark. A real American rodeo followed by the US Marines band with their tribute to J. P. Souza. After that the US Marines strike unit in 'Combat emulation'. The Science Museum is running an exhibition of American space technology – 'A Giant Step for Mankind?' Is that a question mark? No, it's not. There's American football every evening on the town moor, as well as baseball, volleyball, handball, basketball – it's a ball, kids. There's the history of the American patchwork quilt at the Womens' Institute, and the City Gallery has American Art – Hopper to Pollock – sounds like a train Hopper to Pollock, Hopper to Pollock. And finally shopping-wise – don't forget that *any* shop displaying the American week sticker will sell you at half price *any* item made in the USA if you are wearing your 'I love America' badge. News coming up in two minutes direct from KTO New York. Meanwhile, here's something good from Harvey and the Moonglows.

*Music.*

INT. KATE'S BEDROOM — DAY

*The telephone rings. Kate hesitates, reluctant to pick up the phone. She finally does pick it up.*

                              KATE
                        (*after a pause*)
Hello.

                              BOB
                        (*American voice*)
Kate?

                              KATE
Who is this?

                              BOB
Kate . . . this is Bob. We haven't met yet. I just took over
from Elliot Johnson.

                              KATE
So what happened to Elliot?

                              BOB
He's back in New York . . . it was a sudden thing.
                        (*pause*)
Listen, Kate, I've been trying to contact you since last
night.

                              KATE
I was at work.

                              BOB
You have another job? I have no record of this. No contact
number.

                              KATE
Elliot has my number.
                        (*pause*)
What was it you wanted?

                              BOB
Mr Cosmo rang. He has a job for you. It's tomorrow. He

says to buy a new outfit. Everything new.

> KATE
> (*interrupts*)

I can't do it. It's too short notice, I'm working tomorrow.

> BOB
> (*cool*)

Kate, I understood from Mr Cosmo that you were one of the team.

> (*silence*)

Is this not so, Kate?

> KATE
> (*after a pause*)

I guess so.

> BOB

That's what I thought. That's what Mr Cosmo said. 'Kate works with us, right?' . . . RIGHT?

> KATE
> (*quietly*)

Right.

> BOB

So, Kate, this is what you do. Go shopping, you'll enjoy that, a new outfit. Use the credit cards. Mr Cosmo says everything new. Dress, shoes, underwear, perfume, make-up, everything. Mr Cosmo is flying up from London this morning. He wants to meet you at the Central Hotel at one o'clock. You got that, Kate?

> KATE
> (*flat sarcasm*)

Got that, Bob.

> BOB

One o'clock at the Central Hotel. I'll be there also. I look forward to meeting you in person. Have a good day.

*The phone goes dead. Kate replaces the phone thoughtfully. She pushes her half-eaten breakfast away. On an impulse she picks up the phone again, opens her address book, looks up a number and then dials it.*

> TELEPHONE VOICE (V.O.)
> Hello, Exclusive Travel, can I help you?

> KATE
> Yes, can you tell me about availability on flights to New York?

> TELEPHONE VOICE (V.O.)
> From?

> KATE
> From now.

> TELEPHONE VOICE (V.O.)
> If you give me your number, I'll call you back. It may take some time.

EXT. BRENDAN'S HOUSE – DAY

*Brendan, wearing headphones, is leaving the house and turning left. He walks a short distance to join a bus queue.*

EXT. MOTORWAY – DAY

*The traffic starts to move again. The camera keeps pace with the red Jaguar, its radio still playing. Just over the crest of the hill is the accident. We see a badly smashed-up Ford Transit van and an almost unrecognizable smaller car. The vehicles have been moved over on to the hard shoulder. A body is covered with a red blanket on the grass. A man with a cut head is walking aimlessly about in a state of shock. Police, firemen and ambulancemen are in attendance. On the side of the van is written 'The* TRANSATLANTICS'. *On the side of the road are objects from the van. A suitcase has burst open scattering a lurex suit and matching shoes, hundreds of audio cassettes, parts of a drum kit and a smashed-up tenor saxophone.*

EXT. NEWCASTLE AIRPORT — DAY

*The Frankfurt–Newcastle jet touches down.*

EXT. MOTORWAY — DAY

*The red Jaguar passing a sign for Newcastle at speed.*

EXT. MAIN STREET NEWCASTLE — NORTHUMBERLAND STREET — DAY

*Yellow double-decker bus clears frame and we see Brendan.*

*(Polish jazz music still playing.)*

*Brendan begins to walk down the street from left of frame to the right.*

EXT. NORTHUMBERLAND STREET — DAY

*Kate walking up the street (from right to left). She goes into a dress shop.*

EXT. NEWCASTLE AIRPORT — DAY

*The passengers emerging from the Frankfurt–Newcastle jet. This is our first glimpse of the Polish band. Most of the passengers are businessmen and women. In sharp contrast the band are shabbily dressed and are carrying items in old polythene bags plus their instrument cases.*

INT. DRESS SHOP — DAY

*Kate trying on clothes, looking at herself in the mirror, scowling at herself.*

EXT. NORTHUMBERLAND STREET — DAY

*Brendan entering the newsagents next to the dress shop.*

INT. NEWSAGENT — DAY

*Brendan buys a local paper. He turns immediately to the 'jobs vacant' section and begins looking. He is still listening to the head-phones. He takes a pen from his pocket.*

*Close-up of small ad being ringed: 'Cleaning person wanted for nightclub. Hard work, good money, contact N. Finlay, Quay Club, after 10.00 a.m.'*

*Brendan looks up at the wall. The clock shows 9.50 a.m.*

INT. CLOTHES SHOP — DAY

*Kate signing the counter credit slip. She puts her credit card away and picks up her parcels.*

INT. NEWCASTLE AIRPORT — DAY

*The Polish band is going through passport control.*

> PASSPORT OFFICER
> Passports please.

EXT. NEWSAGENTS — DAY

*Brendan, still examining the jobs section of the paper, absentmind-edly walks out of the shop. Kate, at the same time, is coming out of the dress shop, also absentmindedly. She is also wearing her head-phones. Kate and Brendan collide with each other. Kate falls to the ground, dropping her parcels. Her dark glasses smash. She is very upset and at first doesn't attempt to get up. Brendan is horrified by what he thinks he has caused.*

*Kate pulls herself together. Brendan pushes his headphones off and the music stops. He helps Kate up. Her headphones have also fallen off. She looks pissed off.*

> BRENDAN
> I'm sorry.

> KATE
> It's all right.

*Kate is picking up her stuff, still looking for something.*

                          BRENDAN
What are you looking for?

                           KATE
My sunglasses.

*Brendan finds them. They're broken.*

                          BRENDAN
I'm sorry.

                           KATE
I never used them much.

*There is a silence. Brendan looks at Kate. He is very taken with her. Her face, her voice. He is also aware of his own clumsiness.*

I mean . . . the sun doesn't shine very often here. I have to go. It's been nice bumping into you. Bye.

*Kate walks away. Brendan watches her carefully. She turns briefly and smiles, and then is lost in the people. Brendan looks at the paper again.*

*Close-up of small ad: 'Contact N. Finlay, Quay Club, after 10.00 a.m.'*

INT. AIRPORT BAR — DAY

*The Polish band are ordering drinks. The bar is modern. Stainless steel and glass. Through the window, an aircraft can be seen taxiing. Through an interior glass partition we see Andrej, arguing with the customs officer. They are standing next to the Poles' luggage and some of the instruments.*

*The bar staff are slightly nervous of the Poles. Their scruffy belongings are scattered around the room.*

                 PUBLIC ADDRESS VOICE (V.O.)
British Airways apologize for the late arrival of the London Heathrow flight. This is due to fog at Heathrow. This flight is now expected in approximately forty-five minutes.

CUT TO:

*Medium close-up of Andrej. He takes out a notebook, opens it, picks up the telephone and dials a number.*

*Close-up of Andrej's notebook. There are various things in Polish but a red ring around 'N. Finlay, Quay Club 655112.'*

*On the soundtrack we hear the sound of the engaged tone.*

EXT. DEAN STREET — LEADING TO THE SIDE — DAY

*Brendan is walking down this very steep street leading to the quay-side.*

*He passes three huge American billboards for Coca-Cola, Marlboro cigarettes and Levis. A graffiti artist has written:* LEVIS–ELVIS–LIVES.

*Brendan passes bars, restaurants and strip clubs. There is a lot of neon artwork. Each window has a neon sign for a different American beer: Schlitz, Budweiser, Pabst, etc. Music, mainly jazz and blues, comes out of each doorway, blending in and out of the sound-track as Brendan descends. Some of the bars are being cleaned, chairs on the tables, sawdust on the floor. Outside a strip club three girls are talking. One of them whistles at Brendan as he passes. He looks at them. They laugh at him. On the side of the road, English and American cars are parked. Different vintages.*

*A Chinaman with a pigtail and a Charlie Chan moustache, wearing traditional costume and carrying a huge sack, passes Brendan.*

*On the intersection of Dean Street and The Side is a Chinese market, colourful fruit stalls. Behind the market is a block of Chinese restaurants and shops.*

*Brendan reaches the block that the Quay Club is in. A small crowd of people are gathered around an angry young black man. Several policemen are next to him. Brendan joins the crowd. They are stand-ing outside a record shop selling second-hand blues records. Two workmen have stuck up a notice saying:* 'ACQUIRED FOR RE-DEVELOPMENT'. *They are attempting to board up the window. The black man is trying to stop them. The workmen show the policemen an official document. The policemen allow them to continue. The black man picks up a crowbar and speaks to the policemen.*

BLACK MAN

I think you'll agree that I'm within my rights.

*He smashes his own window.*

*Brendan asks someone where the Quay Club is. He walks down a narrow alley and sees the Quay Club sign.*

*He enters a hallway. Facing him is a ticket-office for the club with an arrow pointing to the left. A small flight of stairs leads into the club. To the right a flight of stairs leads to the next floor. On the wall is a painted sign for 'JIM'S GYM'.*

*Brendan walks down the stairs and into the club.*

*The club has its lights on. A piano tuner is hunched over the piano, tuning it. At regular intervals there is the dull thud of weights being dropped on the floor of Jim's Gym. Behind the bar Finlay's secretary is washing glasses. She is quite conventional and looks out of place.*

*Brendan is uncertain what to do. He stands near the bar.*

BRENDAN

Is Mr Finlay in?

SECRETARY

He's on the phone. What was it about?

BRENDAN

I've come about the job.

*The secretary gives Brendan a strange look.*

SECRETARY

Just a moment.

*The secretary comes out from behind the bar. She knocks on a door marked 'Private' to the left of the bar. Without waiting for a reply she opens the door and goes in. By moving, Brendan can see Finlay behind his desk talking on the phone.*

FINLAY

. . . Roy . . . Roy . . . don't get me wrong, the man's a good

alto player. The other guy Pete . . . er Pete . . . Yes, him, a
very fine pianist – gifted. Individually they're all good
blowers but the drummer, he's a fucking English drummer. He wants to be in the front line. What's happened to
the ensemble, Roy . . . hang on a sec, Roy . . .

*He caps his hand over the phone and looks at his secretary.*

SECRETARY
It's someone about the job.

FINLAY
Oh, show her in.

SECRETARY
Well, actually it's a . . .

FINLAY
(*back on the phone*)
Roy, we'll have to continue this later. I'll call you. Yeah. . .
(*laughs*)
. . . talk to you later.

*The secretary shows Brendan into the office. Finlay is writing some-
thing on a calendar behind the desk.*

Be with you in a moment.

*Finlay turns around smiling. The smile vanishes.*

Who are you?

BRENDAN
I'm . . . Brendan. I've come about the cleaning job.

FINLAY
It said 'cleaning person'. If I'd wanted a bloke I'd have
said so.

BRENDAN
I didn't realize. Sorry . . .
(*grins*)
. . . 'Farewell Blues'.

FINLAY

'Farewell Blues'?

BRENDAN

Dave Tough . . . with Eddie Condon. Wild Bill Davison.

*Finlay is very surprised.*

FINLAY

Who's on bass?

*Brendan thinks carefully.*

BRENDAN

Jack Lesberg.

*The phone rings. Finlay looks at Brendan and picks up the phone.*

FINLAY

Finlay, Quay Club . . . Who? . . . Slominski! Mr Slominski, you're not supposed to be here until Saturday morning . . . Well, I'm sorry to hear that, but couldn't you have stayed over in Frankfurt . . . I see . . . Well, we're going to have a problem finding you a hotel, most of them are booked, there's a festival on, American week . . . that's how I feel about it too, Mr Slominski . . . look, get into a cab or two and get here, I'll pay at this end and . . . What do you mean? . . . Jesus Christ . . . OK, put him on.

INT. AIRPORT – DAY

*Andrej hands over the telephone to the customs officer.*

CUSTOMS OFFICER

Hello . . . Mr Finlay? . . . How do you do? Mr Brown of Customs and Immigration here. Mr Slominski here assures me that he and his colleagues have a contract to perform for one night at your nightclub, but unfortunately he doesn't have any documentation or other proof and I cannot release their baggage without . . . official documentation . . . There's no carnet you see . . .

(*pause*)
. . . I'm afraid that will not do, Mr Finlay. Someone will
have to bring documentation to me here at the airport
before I can release the baggage . . . thank you, Mr Finlay
. . . Goodbye.

INT. FINLAY'S OFFICE — DAY

*Finlay slams the phone down.*

FINLAY

Jesus Christ.
(*looks at Brendan*)
What did you say your name was?

BRENDAN

Brendan.

FINLAY

Can you drive?

BRENDAN

Yes.

FINLAY

Right! You have two jobs. You can clean the club, a dubi-
ous privilege, but first I want you to go to the airport and
pick up a band.

BRENDAN

The Krakow Jazz Ensemble?

FINLAY
(*surprised*)
You know them?

BRENDAN
(*touching his headphones*)
No, I just heard them on the radio.

FINLAY

Not too way out for you?

BRENDAN

No, I liked it.

FINLAY

Me too . . .

(*shouts*)

. . . Jean!

*The secretary comes in.*

Jean, the frigging Poles have turned up early. Where the hell are we going to put them?

SECRETARY

Well, not with me this time, and I can tell you now, the only hotel in town with any space left is The Central, and the rooms start at fifty pounds a night.

*Finlay pulls a face.*

FINLAY

What the hell . . . do it. Give him the keys to the Transit bus, and do a Xerox of the contract for him. He'll need some petty cash for petrol.

(*to Brendan*)

Get a receipt for anything you have to pay for.

EXT. TYNE BRIDGE – DAY

*A dramatic high-angle shot of the red Jaguar crossing the bridge.*

EXT. THE SIDE – DAY

*The secretary is with Brendan by a white Ford Transit bus. She hands him a brown envelope.*

EXT. INTERSECTION OF MOSELY STREET AND DEAN STREET

*The red Jaguar is turning left and proceeding slowly down the hill, the same route as Brendan just took.*

INT. FORD TRANSIT — DAY

*A profile shot of Brendan carefully starting the engine. Camera pulls focus as the red Jaguar drives slowly past, the two men looking for the club. They see it and accelerate away.*

CUT TO:

*High shot of The Side.*

*The white Transit and the Jaguar driving away from each other.*

INT. AIRPORT BAR — DAY

*The bar has filled up considerably with people waiting to board or meeting the London plane delayed by fog.*

*Close-up of the electric clock. We see that the band has been drinking for an hour. Andrej is trying to keep them in check but he too is drinking and his efforts are half-hearted.*

*In one corner of the bar there is a small bandstand with a white upright piano. The pianist has been eyeing the piano for some time. He edges towards it, sits on the stool.*

CUT TO:

*The bar manager watching him.*

CUT TO:

*The piano. The pianist opens the lid and very thoughtfully plays one note.*

CUT TO:

*The bar manager. He wags his finger and shakes his head.*

*The pianist chooses not to see him and begins playing a series of moody chords.*

*The camera follows the bar manager as he glides out from behind the bar and makes his way to the piano. He taps the pianist on the shoulder. The pianist ignores him.*

*The music has attracted the attention of the people in the bar. They*

*welcome this unscheduled distraction from their boredom/nervous-*
*ness.*

MIDDLE-AGED MAN
(*well-spoken*)

Let him play. Sounds jolly good to me. Makes a change
from that damned muzak.

(*turning to his neighbour*)

I like a bit of jazz, once saw Oscar Peterson at the City
Hall. Absolutely marvellous, you could always hear the
melody . . . (*etc., etc.*)

*This support effectively takes away the power from the manager.*
*Shaking his head resignedly he returns to the bar and begins polish-*
*ing glasses, a hurt expression on his face.*

*The rest of the band, observing this small victory, take it as a green*
*light and one by one they open their instrument cases and begin*
*playing.*

NOTE ON THE MUSIC: *The essence of the scene is musical. The*
*pianist begins melodically. He is joined by the bass player, then one*
*of the horns. It gradually becomes faster, freer, more anarchistic.*
*When the police arrive it goes through a transition and ends as a*
*parody of Dixieland jazz.*

*Early on in the music there is a PA announcement.*

PUBLIC ADDRESS VOICE (V.O.)

British Airways flight 601 from London Heathrow will
arrive in five minutes. We apologize for the delay.

*Half-way through the sequence we see Brendan arriving. He*
*watches the band with amazement and pleasure.*

*The bar manager calls the airport police in, but they allow the music*
*to continue. Their appearance does, however, cause the band to begin*
*winding things up and go into their Dixieland parody.*

*The music climaxes with a strange impersonation of Louis Arm-*
*strong.*

*The music stops. The band bows to the audience very seriously. The audience applauds heartily and disperses cheerfully.*

*Brendan approaches the band. None of them speaks English, but Andrej, realizing who Brendan is, introduces himself.*

ANDREJ

Excuse me, but are you Mr Finlay from the . . . Kyoo-Ay Club?

BRENDAN

I work for Mr Finlay. I have your contract. That was really good.

ANDREJ

Thank you so much.

*Andrej turns to the band and speaks in Polish. They gather around.*

What is your name?

BRENDAN

Brendan.

ANDREJ

Brenda! . . . Let me introduce the members of the ensemble. Zygmunt is our percussionist . . . Tadeusz plays bass, violin and piano, Melchiar is on piano, trombone and cello . . . Jerzy plays bass clarinet and alto saxophone . . . Marek plays the tenor saxophone and sometimes the baritone . . . Stanislaw plays all of the reeds but mainly the soprano . . . and Wiktov here plays the trumpet and sings. This is Brenda, Mr Finlay's partner, who is here . . .

*Andrej laughs at the blank expression on the faces of the band and goes into Polish again.*

(*to Brendan*)

Can we take the contract to the customs officer?

*Brendan and Andrej go to the customs office. The band is putting away instruments.*

INT. AIRPORT — DAY

*Travelling shot of Mr Cosmo walking through the airport bar with the other London passengers. The camera stays with him as he walks through the building. He is beautifully dressed. A good-looking middle-aged American, part senator, part gangster.*

*Bob and another American meet him. They are wearing pale light-weight suits and steel-rimmed sunglasses.*

*Without pausing the three men walk to the door, the third man taking Cosmo's case (but not his briefcase).*

*They go through the exit and into a black 'stretch' Cadillac waiting outside. They get in and the car drives off.*

NOTE: *What is vital here is that a sense of smooth unhurried speed is conveyed. The pecking order of Cosmo, Bob and the third man. The third man walks just behind the other two.*

INT. CADILLAC — DAY

*Cosmo, Bob and P.A. in back, driver and bodyguard in front.*

> COSMO
> Have the London boys showed up?

> BOB
> Not yet.

> COSMO
> (*shakes his head*)
> Great . . . Did you talk to Kate?

> BOB
> She'll be there at one.
> (*looks at his watch*)
> We're going to be late.

> COSMO
> She'll wait.

EXT. AIRPORT BUILDING — DAY

*Brendan is putting the last of the cases into the back of the Ford Transit. He closes the door, gets into the driver's seat, starts the engine and drives off.*

INT. FOYER OF THE CENTRAL HOTEL — DAY

*There is a bustle of activity as preparations for the Anglo-American luncheon take place. Flags and bunting are beginning to give this traditional English hotel the look of a typical American 'convention' hotel.*

NOTE: *At this first hotel scene the transformation is beginning but not advanced. We must see the two extremes.*

*Cosmo and his two men arrive. Cosmo looks critically at the scene. The luncheon organizer Peter Reed, a nervous young man, joins the group.*

> BOB
> Mr Cosmo, this is Peter Reed, who is responsible for the overall planning.

> COSMO
> How do you do, Peter?

*They shake hands.*

> Peter, it's looking good.

*He puts an arm around Reed's shoulder.*

> More flags, Peter, more flags. What do you say we put on that wall there . . . a huge photograph of the President . . . and over there another of your own Prime Minister.

> REED
> Great idea.

*Cosmo slaps him on the back.*

> COSMO
> Good man. Do it.

*He turns to Bob.*

Let's look at the ballroom.

*As Cosmo and his group walk across the foyer and down the corridor that leads to the ballroom . . .*

*. . . Brendan and the Krakow Jazz Ensemble come in through the main entrance.*

*Brendan and Andrej go to the reception desk. The band slump into the smart armchairs. (The band have the ability to make any space look untidy.)*

*The receptionist, a young, attractive, ordinary girl, clearly disapproves of the band. Both Andrej and Brendan smile but fail to make any impression on her.*

ANDREJ
Good afternoon, Miss. We are the Krakow Jazz Ensemble. Could you tell us our room numbers and give us our keys? Please.

RECEPTIONIST
(*cool*)
Do you have reservations?

BRENDAN
Yes, Mr Finlay, from the Quay Club. He phoned about an hour ago.

RECEPTIONIST
One moment please.

*The receptionist walks over to the manager. The two of them have a whispered conversation.*

INT. FOYER ENTRANCE — DAY

*Kate enters the foyer carrying parcels.*

*Kate's eye is drawn to the Poles and then she notices Brendan.*

CUT TO:

KATE'S POV OF BRENDAN

*Brendan and Andrej are sharing a joke about the hotel. Brendan laughs. Kate sees him as attractive.*

*A piece of music is heard which repeats later as a theme for Brendan and Kate.*

*Brendan does not see Kate. The receptionist returns, puts on a very cold smile and confirms the booking. Without her seeing, Brendan and Andrej smile at each other in imitation.*

CUT TO:

*Close-up of Kate smiling. She turns and walks in the direction of the ballroom.*

*The music continues.*

*The camera follows Kate into the ballroom. The four men are standing in the middle.*

> COSMO
> . . . And don't forget the cranberry sauce. It's a very important detail, Peter. OK . . . Is everybody coming? Nobody turned down the invitation?

> BOB
> So far only three people.
> > (*takes out a piece of paper*)
> Let's see . . . the chairman of the housing committee . . .

> COSMO
> That bastard, good. Who else?

> BOB
> . . . Alderman Thorpe is in hospital.

> COSMO
> Nothing serious I hope.

> BOB
> Terminal . . . and Mr Ferguson is on holiday.

COSMO

Ferguson?

BOB

The union guy. The helpful one.

COSMO

Right . . .

*During this conversation Kate has slowly walked into the ballroom, first putting her parcels down. As she reaches the group of men Cosmo, who has his back to her, speaks.*

You're late.

KATE

I've been here for an hour. I went out for some coffee.

*Cosmo suddenly smiles warmly, a complete transformation of mood. He turns to Kate.*

COSMO

Then it is I who must apologize, Kate. We were held up at Heathrow. Fog. It's all part of the great English tradition. Let me look at you.

*Kate is wearing a new pair of dark glasses. Cosmo lifts them off her face. He cups her face in his large hands.*

You look great, Kate. Bob here tells me you've been having a good time. New friends, different faces. Oh, of course . . . you haven't met Bob before . . . Kate, this is Bob. Bob, this is my little Kate.

BOB
(*shaking her hand*)
I was trying to picture you from your voice.

COSMO

She's as pretty as a picture, isn't she, Bob?

BOB

She sure is, Mr Cosmo.

COSMO

Bob here's taken over from Elliot.
(*shakes his head*)
Elliot fucked up. Elliot did something very stupid. Elliot
went to bed with a journalist. Bob here's taken over and
Bob . . . always sleeps alone. Don't you, Bob?

BOB
(*chuckling appreciatively*)
Yes, sir.

COSMO

Don't misunderstand me, Kate. The man's no faggot, are
you, Bob?

BOB
(*considerably embarrassed but laughing*)
No, sir.

COSMO

Bob's a full-blooded American.

*Cosmo has enjoyed the discomfort he has created.*

KATE

Can I talk to you?

COSMO

Sure.

KATE

Alone.

COSMO
(*looks at his watch*)
Bob. What time are we seeing the fat man, what's his
name?

BOB

Councillor Perry. He'll be waiting for us at the office now.

*Cosmo puts an arm around Kate and walks a few steps with her.*

COSMO

Kate, can it hold until tomorrow, till after the luncheon,
then you and I can go somewhere nice and intimate and
talk . . . and talk . . . and talk.

(*big smile*)

OK.

*Without waiting for Kate's response Cosmo heads for the door.*

Mustn't keep the fat man waiting. See you tomorrow,
Kate.

(*to Peter Reed*)

More flags, Peter . . . Talk, talk, talk.

*Cosmo and his party exit, leaving Kate alone in the ballroom. She is
upset. She has worked herself up to this confrontation with Cosmo, to
ask for her freedom.*

*She holds herself in check. Gathers her parcels and leaves.*

CUT TO:

*A wide-angle low shot of Cable Cale House, emphasizing its height.*

INT. CABLE CALE HOUSE − TOP FLOOR − DAY

*The camera tracks with Cosmo and Bob as they come out of the lift
and walk through a general office area.*

COSMO

What's the guy's name again?

BOB

Councillor Perry.

COSMO

No, his first name.

BOB

John.

*They enter Cosmo's office. It is sparse and modern. By the window
is a scale model of the riverside redevelopment. A fat man is sitting
in a low leather chair. He struggles to get to his feet as Cosmo*

*glides past and goes behind his glass desk.*

COSMO

Stay where you are, John, we sit on ceremony in this
office.

*On the glass desk is a single folder.*

CUT TO:

*Close-up of folder. On it is written 'Riverside redevelopment scheme
– IMPEDIMENTS, OBJECTIONS.'*

*Cosmo picks it up, flips through it and tosses it back on to the glass
top.*

COSMO

Bob has filled me in on the report. It sounds good, John.
Excellent work. I'll read it carefully tonight.

*Cosmo sits on the desk close to the councillor and looks at him.*

John . . . is it going to be a problem with the housing committee?

*The councillor moves to an upright position and clears his throat.*

COUNCILLOR

I'm absolutely sure the vote will go in favour. The job re-
creation angle is enough to ensure it. There were three or
four who were holding out against it, but we've done a little deal with them over central heating in tenement buildings. I think it will be a blanket vote.

COSMO

You're sure of this, John?

COUNCILLOR

Absolutely sure.

*Cosmo looks at Bob, who nods.*

COSMO

That's good work, John. Anything negative at this stage
and the project becomes another British 'almost hap-

pened', and the company takes off for Antwerp or Rotter-
dam.

COUNCILLOR

Quite so, Mr Cosmo. I'm sure it will never come to that . . .
(*cautiously*)
And is our friend still being difficult?

COSMO
(*ignoring the question*)
Bob, damnit, let's have some champagne . . .

*Bob goes next door.*

. . . Cigar, John? They're Phillipino . . . almost as good as
Cuban . . . but without the . . . guilt.

*They both laugh.*

John, I really appreciate what you're doing for us. I never
forget a good deed. Tomorrow, at the luncheon, I have
something special for you.

*Bob enters with the champagne and glasses.*

Ah, the champagne.

*The P.A. comes in.*

P.A.

There is a call for you from a local call box, Mr Cosmo.
The gentleman says it's about a co-production.

COSMO

Would you ask him to call back at . . .
(*looks at his watch*)
. . . at eight this evening. I'll be here.

*Bob has opened the champagne and poured three glasses. Councillor
Perry struggles to his feet, and Cosmo takes them all to the window
and looks with great satisfaction at the river view and then the
model.*

Gentlemen . . . to the project.

*The three men raise their glasses and clink them.*

EXT. A DESOLATE STRETCH OF THE RIVER — DAY

*Near the Redheugh bridge. The red Jaguar is parked near a public telephone box. Patrick is just coming out of the box.*

INT. KATE'S APARTMENT — DAY

*The phone is ringing. Sound of the key in the lock. Kate comes in. She puts her parcels down and answers the phone.*

> KATE
>
> 657478.

> TELEPHONE VOICE (V.O.)
>
> This is Exclusive Travel. You phoned us this morning about flights to New York.

> KATE
>
> Yes, that's right. Have you had any luck?

> TELEPHONE VOICE (V.O.)
>
> I'm afraid not. There are no spare seats on any flight to New York until next Wednesday, and that would be first class.

> KATE
> *(disappointed)*
>
> Oh . . .

> TELEPHONE VOICE (V.O.)
>
> I'm sorry.

> KATE
>
> Thanks for trying. 'Bye.

*She puts the phone down.*

INT. QUAY CLUB — DAY

*Brendan is hoovering the club. The noise of the hoover is very loud. He switches it off and as the noise dies down we hear Finlay talking on the phone.*

FINLAY

Wonderful, isn't it? They can't understand how someone
can refuse so much money . . . they can't, can they? . . .
Wonderful . . . Well, just say no and wait and see what
happens next . . . No . . . No . . . No deals . . . Well, tell
him to go fuck.

*He puts the phone down.*

*Brendan sticks his head into the office.*

BRENDAN

I've done the floor, Mr Finlay, what's next?

FINLAY

It's the bogs, Brendan. I'm afraid someone has puked in
the gents. Dettol first, freshener afterwards.

INT. GENTS TOILET — DAY

*Brendan gagging as he swills a bucket of water over the floor.*

INT. LADIES TOILET — DAY

*Brendan going into the 'ladies', cleaning the mirror, sweeping out the
cubicles, looking at the feminine graffiti. There is the sound of someone else coming in. The door of the adjoining cubicle opens and
closes. There is the sound of clothes rustling, someone starts peeing
and there is a sigh of relief.*

GIRL'S VOICE (V.O.)

Another minute and it would have been too late. I came
up the stairs cross-legged . . . that's better. How are you,
Jean?

*Brendan is extremely embarrassed and starts to creep out, but the
lavatory flushes and the cubicle door opens and the girl comes out
pulling her pants up. She and Brendan look at each other.*

BRENDAN

I'm the cleaner.

EXT. WEEGEES DINER — IN THE SIDE — EVENING

*A flashing neon sign proclaims 'The happy hour'. The restaurant has brick walls with framed photographs by Weegee. Stripped pine floors. Tables and chairs with 1940s-style lampshades above each table. Along one wall there is a long reading table with many American magazines:* Look, Life, Time, Travel, National Geographic Magazine. *In the centre of the room there is a scale model of New York's waterfront with a crane lifting a model 1940s American car out of the water. It is quite busy. The camera is looking through the window.*

INT. WEEGEES DINER — EVENING

*The manager is sorting through a selection of audio cassettes. He selects one, puts it into a cassette player and turns it on. It is a recording of New York street ambience: sirens, cars, subway rumble.*

*On a shelf is a collection of video cassettes. He selects one and puts it into a VHS machine. There are two monitors in the restaurant. The video tape is a recording of an American football match, complete with American commercials every four minutes.*

*Kate enters the restaurant. She is out of breath. She comes up to the manager.*

> KATE

Hi.

> MANAGER

You're late.

> KATE

I'm sorry. I had to dump some stuff off at my apartment and then I couldn't get a cab, so I came by bus.

> MANAGER

I told you last week if you can't make it on time . . . leave! It's a job. Turn up on time. Don't give me some crap about a cab, OK? This is the happy hour, we're busy. Get changed. Make it quick.

*Kate sets her face.*

INT. CHANGING ROOM IN THE RESTAURANT — EVENING

*Kate is changing into her 1940s-style waitress outfit. Pencil skirts and round-collared blouses with short black cardigans. Half hats worn on the back of the head.*

*One of the other waitresses comes in.*

> WAITRESS
> Hello, Kate. Has he been nasty?

> KATE
> He tries. Have you been covering for me?

> WAITRESS
> It's no problem – see you in there.

INT. QUAY CLUB — EVENING

*Brendan has finished cleaning. He goes to Finlay's office. The door is half open. Finlay's writing something. He looks up.*

> FINLAY
> Finished?

> BRENDAN
> Yes.

> FINLAY
> . . . Go and have a drink, Brendan, I'll be with you in a moment.

INT. WEEGEES DINER — EVENING

*Kate is serving a table. A man is looking down at the menu.*

> KATE
> Are you ready to order?

*The man looks up. It is Tony. He has a frightening face. He smiles.*

TONY
I'll wait.

INT. QUAY CLUB — EVENING

*Brendan is having a drink at the bar. The barmaid is the girl he met in the ladies' toilet. Several of the men from Jim's Gym are drinking there. Finlay joins them.*

FINLAY
Brendan, let me introduce you to Carrol.

CARROL
We've met. He was eavesdropping in the toilet.

*Brendan is quite embarrassed.*

I'm only joking.

FINLAY
Did you want something, Brendan?

BRENDAN
I was wondering if I could have an advance.

*Finlay reaches into his pocket and takes a wad of money out.*

FINLAY
Is twenty OK for tonight? We'll talk about money tomorrow. If you want to come to the club tonight there's a good tenor player on.

*Finlay attracts the attention of José, one of the Jim's Gym crew.*

José, this is Brendan, he works here now.

BRENDAN
I'll go and eat first and then come back. Thanks very much.

EXT. THE SIDE — DUSK

*A series of establishing shots showing the night feel of the street. The neon signs are now switched on. American cars cruise up and down the street. Music is heard coming from the bars. A group of sailors in white drill are walking down the street.*

*Brendan, looking for somewhere to eat, watches the activity with interest. The feel of it is very 'cinema' American.*

INT. WEEGEES DINER – DUSK

*Brendan looks into the restaurant from outside. He comes in and sits at one of the two empty tables by the window. He looks at the menu on the table. Kate comes to serve him. Brendan, concentrating on the menu, does not see her.*

> BRENDAN
>
> Can I have the . . . clam chowder please.

> KATE
>
> I wouldn't, it's awful.

*Brendan recognizes Kate's voice and looks up.*

> BRENDAN
>
> Hello.

> KATE
>
> Hello.

> BRENDAN
>
> I'm sorry about this morning – are you all right now?

> KATE
>
> I'm fine.

*Brendan looks at her.*

> BRENDAN
>
> What do you recommend?

> KATE
>
> The steak is safe.

> BRENDAN
>
> Right, I'll have a steak.

KATE

English?

BRENDAN

What do you mean?

KATE

Burned.

BRENDAN

Medium.

KATE

French fries and spinach?

BRENDAN

Yes, please.

KATE

Side salad?

BRENDAN

Yes.

KATE

Thousand island, French or vinaigrette?

BRENDAN

French.

KATE

Beer or Californian wine?

BRENDAN

Beer, please.

KATE

Bud, Pabst, Colt, Carlsberg . . . Heineken? . . .

BRENDAN

Guinness?

KATE

Nope.

BRENDAN

Bud.

KATE

It'll be about ten minutes. I'll bring you your beer first.

BRENDAN

Thank you.

KATE

It's my pleasure, sir.

*There is a strong flirtatious element in this exchange.*

*Kate walks away, watched by Brendan. Through the window we see the red Jaguar pull up on the opposite side of the street.*

*Patrick gets out, crosses the street and enters the restaurant. Kate brings Brendan his beer and some nuts. Patrick joins Tony at the table next to Brendan's. Kate goes to serve them. Patrick is looking at the menu. He does not acknowledge Kate's presence. Tony stares at Kate, looking at her body. She is uncomfortable. Tony smiles, revealing discoloured teeth.*

I'll come back in a minute.

PATRICK
(*looking up*)
No! Just wait. The clam chowder, is it hot?

KATE

It can be.

TONY

Is it big?

KATE

Well . . . I can bring you double portions.

PATRICK

Do it. And a couple of double scotches, ice, no water. Bring 'em straight away.

*Tony is still staring at Kate as she tears off the receipt, puts it on*

*their table under the ashtray and walks away. While she is still
within earshot . . .*

                          TONY
You can sit on my face any time you like.

CUT TO:

*Brendan's face watching the men. A mixture of anger and fear.*

CUT TO:

*On another table a bald man and his wife have turned to stare at
Patrick and Tony.*

                          TONY
What's the problem, baldy?

*The couple hurriedly avert their eyes.*

*Kate brings Brendan his steak. Tony watches her serving.*

                          KATE
                        (*quietly*)
It's my lucky day.

*She walks away. Tony continues to stare at Brendan. Brendan looks
up and their eyes meet, Brendan looks away.*

CUT TO:

INT. WEEGEES DINER – KITCHEN – NIGHT

*Kate picking up two bowls of clam chowder from the cook.*

                          KATE
They want it hot.

*The cook hands Kate a bottle. Kate unscrews the regulator and
pours a large amount into each bowl.*

INT. RESTAURANT – NIGHT

*Kate serves the clam chowder. The two men begin eating. They make
no reference to the food.*

TONY

You got through to the Yank.

PATRICK

It's tomorrow afternoon.

TONY

And we hit him at the Quay Club.

PATRICK

He's always there in the afternoon.

CUT TO:

*Brendan's face. He has picked up on what they are saying.*

TONY

Hurt him or kill him?

*A party of six people at a nearby table begins laughing at a joke and the rest of the conversation is obscured. By the time it has died down Tony is talking again.*

> . . . I hate the fuck-ing north . . . the fuck-ing pits . . . the fuck-ing poverty . . . the fuck-ing Geordies . . . The fuck-ing Finlays of this world . . . I'll *hurt* him.

*The camera moves on to Brendan's face. He does not look at them but is listening intently.*

*One of the other waitresses passes their table. Tony smiles; she smiles back. Tony flicks his tongue like a snake; she is shocked. She joins Kate.*

WAITRESS

God, who are those guys?

KATE

Jerks, but they'll tip well.

WAITRESS

I don't think so.

KATE

They will leave . . . five pounds.

> WAITRESS

I'll bet you five they don't. Who's the young guy? He looks cute.

> KATE

Yes, he is, isn't he?

> WAITRESS
> (*as she walks away*)

Not quite rich enough for you, Kate.

*Kate looks at her. The two men have finished eating. Kate goes over to clear their table.*

> KATE

Is there anything else I can get you?

> PATRICK

No. How much?

*Kate puts their cheque down on the table.*

*Patrick takes a roll of notes from his pocket. He puts a twenty-pound note on the table.*

> PATRICK

Keep the change.

*Tony belches extremely loudly and long. The two men leave.*

*Kate, passing the waitress, holds up the twenty-pound note.*

> KATE

You want to pay now or later?

*Kate puts Brendan's cheque down on his table. Brendan is watching Kate. He is very attracted to her. He comes to a decision, takes a pencil from his pocket and writes something down on one of the cheques.*

*Kate picks up Brendan's cheques and begins adding them.*

CUT TO:

*Close-up of Kate's hand with cheques.*

*On one of them Brendan has written: 'Will you have a drink with me later?'*

*Kate says nothing in response.*

KATE

That's six twenty, please.

*Brendan has only the twenty-pound note that Finlay gave him. He gives it to Kate.*

(coolly)

I'll get your change, sir.

*Brendan blushes. Kate returns with his change and the bill on a saucer. She walks away. Brendan picks up his change, leaves a pound tip. He notices something in the bill.*

CUT TO:

*Close-up of the bill. Kate has written: 'I finish at 11.30.'*

*Brendan looks up. Kate is on the other side of the room. They catch each other's eye. Kate smiles, a little uncertainly.*

EXT. ENTRANCE OF THE QUAY CLUB — NIGHT

*Brendan comes to the entrance.*

*José, the doorman, recognizes him and waves him past. The music from the club can be heard: very bluesy, aggressive tenor saxophone playing.*

INT. QUAY CLUB — NIGHT

*Brendan comes into the club. It is a quarter full.*

*He goes to the bar and attracts the attention of the barmaid Carrol.*

BRENDAN

Where's Mr Finlay?

CARROL

He's gone. He's at his other club tonight, the Dolci Vita. It's just around the corner on the quayside.

EXT. SHOT OF THE SIDE — NIGHT

*A tracking shot of Brendan walking through the Chinese section, arriving at the entrance to the Dolci Vita club. The club has a well-lit modern façade. Two large men in tuxedos guard the entrance. Brendan approaches them.*

> BRENDAN
>
> Excuse me, would it be possible to go in and talk to Mr Finlay for five minutes?

> BOUNCER 1
>
> Are you a member?

> BRENDAN
>
> No.

> BOUNCER 1
>
> Then I'm afraid you can't go in. It's members only tonight.

> BOUNCER 2
>
> Besides which you're not wearing a suit or a tie so we wouldn't let you in anyway.

> BOUNCER 1
>
> Incorrectly dressed to be precise.

> BOUNCER 2
>
> So fuck off.

> BRENDAN
>
> You don't understand. It's *very* important that I talk to Mr Finlay. I work for him.

*The first bouncer puts a large hand on Brendan's shoulder.*

> BOUNCER 1
>
> Are you going?

> BOUNCER 2
>
> Or is he going to ploat you?

BRENDAN

I'm going.

BOUNCER I

Good.

(*to his partner*)

I hate violence.

BRENDAN

What time does the club close?

*They glare at Brendan.*

I just wondered.

BOUNCER 2

One o'clock.

EXT. WEEGEES DINER — NIGHT

*Brendan is waiting for Kate. He is leaning against a wall to the side of the restaurant. He is a little on edge.*

*Kate comes out of the entrance, looks around a little uncertainly and then sees Brendan. They walk towards each other cautiously.*

KATE

Hi.

BRENDAN

Hello.

KATE

What shall we do?

BRENDAN

Would you mind . . . if we just go around the corner for a drink. Something's just come up . . . I have to see a man . . . my boss . . . so I'll have to wait . . . till he comes out sort of thing. If you don't want to, it's OK.

KATE

It sounds very complicated.

BRENDAN
(*grins*)

Sorry.

KATE

Would you like me to come?

*Brendan nods.*

OK. Let's go.

EXT. HOPPER BAR — NIGHT

*A wide shot of the bar showing its relationship to the Dolci Vita. The street is deserted. The Hopper Bar is based on the painting Nighthawks by Edward Hopper. The sound of a piano and voices comes from the club. Brendan and Kate enter left and right of the frame. They stop and look at the bar. They look at each other. As they walk towards the bar, the camera tracks in with them. This is the beginning of their relationship. The bar is a world they enter together.*

INT. HOPPER BAR — NIGHT

*As the door opens, the noise of the bar floods into the soundtrack.*

*During the bar scene the camera is always busy moving from character to character, sometimes on Brendan or Kate. In one sense the camera is Brendan as he absorbs the images and looks at Kate and she at him. The sound is intimate.*

*At the bar a drunk is telling the barman the misunderstood husband's tale.*

*Around a table a group of young Norwegian sailors are drinking in competition with each other and having arm-wrestling competitions.*

*In a corner a man is writing in a notebook and nursing a drink.*

*At the bar a man is talking to two girls. One of the girls is his companion and is trying to persuade him to come home. The other girl is trying to persuade him to buy her a drink.*

*The music is provided by a piano, bass and drums trio. The pianist is old and the music introverted.*

*Two sailors dance together.*

*Kate and Brendan sit on stools at the bar. Brendan positions himself so that he can watch the entrance to the Dolci Vita. They are very careful with each other.*

KATE

I don't know your name.

BRENDAN

It's Brendan. What's your name?

KATE

Kate.

BRENDAN

It suits you. What would you like . . . Kate?

KATE

I'd like a whiskey. Malt if they have.

*Brendan attracts the barman's attention. The drunk continues undeterred. The barman raises his eyebrows resignedly.*

BRENDAN

What malt whiskeys do you have?

BARMAN

Glenfiddich, Glenlivet, Islay Mist, Laphroig, Glen-morangie . . . Knockando, Glen Grant.

KATE

Glenlivet.

BARMAN

Two?

BRENDAN

Yes.

BARMAN

With ice?

KATE

No, thanks.

BRENDAN

No, thanks.

*Brendan prepares to pay, but the barman ignores him and writes it down on a slate.*

*Kate and Brendan take their glasses and Kate drinks half of hers. She shivers.*

KATE

That's better. I like it here. I'm glad we came. It's the first time I've felt good for days.

*Brendan smiles and looks around.*

BRENDAN

Yes, it's good.
(*pause*)
Have you been here before?

KATE

Do I come here often?
(*quietly*)
Once before. It wasn't so nice then.
(*she clinks his glass*)
You're nice, Brendan.

*Brendan looks at Kate as she takes a packet of cigarettes out of her bag. He is not sure of his luck – as if she might vanish at any moment. Kate offers him a cigarette.*

Do you?

BRENDAN

Sometimes. Thanks.

*Kate lights the cigarettes.*

KATE

What a day.

BRENDAN

I'm sorry I knocked you over.

KATE

So you did. Actually – that's very British, 'actually' – actually that was one of the nicer things.

BRENDAN

What was bad then – those guys in the restaurant?

KATE

No, I'm used to guys like that. In some ways they're the easiest to deal with.

BRENDAN

They were . . . abusive.

KATE

(*finishing her drink*)

Sure, but they only had eyes for each other.

*Brendan catches the barman's attention and holds up two fingers and points at the glasses.*

BRENDAN

Well, if wasn't me or them, what was it?

KATE

(*pensive*)

It's complicated. I'll tell you some other time. Cheers. I have another job. It's become a bit heavy. I want to quit but I'm under . . . contract in a way and it's difficult. That's enough about me. What about you? What do you do?

BRENDAN

I work for the guy that runs the Quay Club.

KATE

I've never been. What do you do?

BRENDAN

I look after the group and sort of help out in the club.

KATE

Have you been there a long time?

BRENDAN

Oh yes.

KATE

How long?

*Brendan grins and looks at his watch.*

BRENDAN

Oh . . . fourteen hours or so. I don't know how long it will last. I'm the cleaner but I'm also looking after this Polish group for a couple of days.

KATE

The Krakow Jazz Ensemble?

BRENDAN
(*surprised*)

That's right.
(*the penny drops*)
You were listening to them on your headphones.

KATE

Yes. They sound crazy.

*Brendan suddenly sees someone coming out of the Dolci Vita. For a moment it could be Finlay, but then it isn't.*

Is that him?

BRENDAN

No, it's not. Sorry.

KATE

I don't mind. Why do you have to see him, or is it a secret?

BRENDAN

No secret. Those two men in your restaurant . . . Maybe I got it wrong . . .

*Kate looks at him.*

. . . I heard them talking. They're from London I think . . .
and . . .

KATE

And what?

BRENDAN

The guy that runs the Quay Club, my boss, his name is
Finlay . . . and they were talking about hurting someone
called Finlay . . .

*Something registers on Kate's face, but Brendan doesn't notice.*

KATE

Did they mention anyone else?

BRENDAN

Just Finlay . . . oh, and someone called the Yank.

*Brendan smiles at Kate.*

The town's full of Yanks. You're a Yank. What part of Yank-
land do you come from?

KATE

I've lived in New York for a long time now.

BRENDAN

And before that?

KATE

Minnesota.

BRENDAN

That makes you . . . Norwegian.

KATE

Half, my mother. Hey, that's very good, Brendan. How
did you know that?

BRENDAN

Before I started my career as a cleaner I was a student.
American studies for two and a half years . . . Are your
parents still in Minnesota?

                                    KATE

No . . . they're dead.

*She takes a drink. There is an awkward silence.*

                                  BRENDAN

How?

                                    KATE

Cancer. Within six months of each other.

                                  BRENDAN

I'm sorry.

                                    KATE

You know in the States there is a special category of
poverty: the cancer family. It's where one of the family has
a terminal illness. Everyone knows he or she is dying, but
it takes a long time and to pay the hospital fees they sell
everything – the car, the house, everything. We were lucky,
they went quickly.

                                  BRENDAN

When was this?

                                    KATE

About a year and a half ago.

*The pianist begins a new tune, a slow ballad.*

I love this tune.

                              BRENDAN/KATE
                                 (*together*)

'Round about Midnight.'

CUT TO:

*The pianist playing, some couples dancing.*

                                    KATE

Would you like to dance with me, Brendan?

*Brendan and Kate go to the floor and dance. She rests her head on
his shoulder.*

My father had a record of this. It was a 78. It broke when I moved.

*Brendan strokes her hair.*

Are you still watching out, Brendan?

*Brendan has not been watching.*

BRENDAN

Yes.

KATE

Maybe you shouldn't get involved. Perhaps you should leave them to it. None of them are very nice. It's a long time since I danced like this.

BRENDAN

Minnesota?

KATE

Almost.

*The tune finishes. Brendan and Kate return to the bar.*

*A police car pulls up and two policemen come in.*

*The policemen have very short 'crew-cut' hair, open-necked short-sleeved shirts, trousers cut low on the hip, a leather belt with a truncheon dangling. They both chew gum and wear pale sunglasses. They come to the bar.*

*Without being asked the barman pours them each a short drink. They drink and depart without paying.*

*Brendan orders another two drinks. The bar begins to empty. Brendan looks at the Dolci Vita entrance. Some people are beginning to drift out.*

BRENDAN

What did you do in New York?

KATE

I was a waitress, what they call an actress between jobs.

BRENDAN

And here, in between being a waitress?

KATE
(*smiling wryly*)

A sort of actress.

*A newspaper seller comes in with the first edition of the morning paper. The local paper looks not unlike the New York* Daily News. *There is a photo of Cosmo. Kate buys a copy.*

*More people emerge from the Dolci Vita. Brendan sees Finlay and a woman.*

BRENDAN

There he is. I'll be back in a minute.

*The door of the bar is crowded with the sailors who are leaving. Brendan tries to get through. When they see that he is in a hurry they deliberately slow him up. By the time Brendan gets outside Finlay and the woman have vanished. Brendan turns towards the river where lots of cars are parked. He walks along the quay by the car park. He hears a woman's laugh coming from a Mercedes. Brendan approaches the car cautiously. He looks in the side window. From the quick glance it is obvious that Finlay and the woman are about to get down to something. Brendan backs away from the car, ponders and then comes back and politely knocks on the roof. The low moaning stops. She is half undressed. Finlay is looking at her.*

FINLAY
(*muffled*)

Jesus fucking Christ!

*Brendan circles around to the front of the car. The car headlights come on. The electric window comes down.*

BRENDAN

It's Brendan, Mr Finlay.

FINLAY

What the fuck are you doing, Brendan?

BRENDAN

I've got to talk to you, Mr Finlay.

FINLAY

Not now, Brendan. Tomorrow.

BRENDAN

It's very urgent, Mr Finlay.

FINLAY

Tomorrow, Brendan.

BRENDAN

Some men are going to try to hurt you. Something to do with an American.

*There is a pause. Finlay switches off the headlights. He opens the door and gets out.*

FINLAY

Come here.

*Brendan joins him.*

When?

BRENDAN

Tomorrow, in the afternoon.

*Finlay fishes in his pocket and gives Brendan a card.*

FINLAY

Come to my house tomorrow morning, early. I'll give you breakfast. Get a cab, get a receipt. Don't think I don't appreciate this, Brendan, but it's all to do with timing, dynamics.

*Finlay speaks to the woman in the car.*

Say goodnight to Brendan.

WOMAN

Goodnight, Brendan.

> BRENDAN

Goodnight.

*Brendan walks away as Finlay gets back into the car.*

> FINLAY

Breakfast then.

*The window closes.*

EXT. HOPPER'S BAR – NIGHT

*The bar is deserted and now looks very like the* **Nighthawks** *painting. Kate is alone. The barman is washing glasses. Brendan pauses and watches. Kate looks vulnerable. The drummer is packing away his kit; the pianist is playing absentmindedly, going through the changes of some forgotten song. The bass player is talking to a girl.*

*Brendan goes in. Kate looks up and smiles.*

> KATE

Did you find him?

> BRENDAN

Yes, but he was busy.

> KATE

He looked as if he might be.

*They both laugh.*

> BRENDAN

I'll see him tomorrow.

*Suddenly it's time to leave. The barman passes.*

How much do I owe you?

> BARMAN

It's done.

> BRENDAN
> (*to Kate*)

Did you pay?

KATE

Maybe.

*Kate stands. They collect their things.*

BARMAN

Goodnight. See you again.

BRENDAN/KATE

Goodnight.

*As they are about to go out of the door, Kate speaks very quietly without looking at Brendan.*

KATE

Shall I come home with you?

*Brendan pretends not to hear.*

EXT. HOPPERS BAR – NIGHT

*Brendan and Kate coming out of the bar.*

BRENDAN

Will you come home with me?

*A bright yellow London taxi cruises past. Brendan flags it down. They get in. It drives off.*

EXT. BRENDAN'S HOUSE – NIGHT

*Brendan is paying the driver.*

*The sound of the key. Brendan and Kate come in. The room is cold; Kate shivers.*

BRENDAN

It's always cold in these old Victorian houses.

*He strikes a match and lights the gas fire.*

Would you like some coffee?

KATE

No. I'm really tired now. Are you?

> BRENDAN

Yes, I am.

*They look at each other.*

I'll show you the bathroom. Do you want to borrow my toothbrush?

> KATE

Please. Do you have a shirt or something I can wear?

EXT. BRENDAN'S HOUSE – NIGHT

*Bottom window is lit. An upstairs light is turned on. Brendan and Kate are seen. Brendan closes the curtains.*

INT. BRENDAN'S ROOM – NIGHT

*Brendan tidying the bed, laying out a shirt for Kate. Kate comes in. They are now extremely shy of each other.*

INT. BRENDAN'S HOUSE – BATHROOM – NIGHT

*Brendan cleaning his teeth, looking at himself in the mirror.*

EXT. BRENDAN'S HOUSE – NIGHT

*The bathroom light goes off.*

*Brendan turns out the light and undresses to his T-shirt and pants. He gets into bed with Kate. He puts his arm around her.*

> KATE

Is it all right if we just lie together like this?

> BRENDAN

Yes.

> KATE

You don't mind?

> BRENDAN

No.

KATE

It's really nice.
(*she puts an arm around him*)
This shirt needs new buttons.

EXT. BRENDAN'S HOUSE – DAWN

*The early morning bus, bright yellow, fills frame and passes.*

INT. BRENDAN'S ROOM – DAWN

*The sound of the bus recedes. Brendan is awake, Kate is asleep. Brendan turns and looks at her and moves a strand of hair from her face. He looks at his watch, which reads 7.15.*

*He eases out of bed and, taking completely clean clothes, dresses quietly.*

CUT TO:

*Kate. She is awake, watching him. Brendan notices Kate. He sits on the bed. He kisses her on the forehead. Her arm goes around his neck. She is sleepy.*

KATE

Come back to bed.

*Her shirt is open. Brendan kisses her breast lightly.*

BRENDAN

When can I see you today?

KATE

I have to work. I don't know what time I'll finish. If I can, I'll be at the restaurant.

BRENDAN

And if you can't?

KATE

I'll find you.

*Brendan tucks her in like a child and stands.*

                                BRENDAN
I'll see you then . . . Kate.

EXT. CENTRAL HOTEL — DAY

*Establishing shot.*

INT. CENTRAL HOTEL — FOYER — DAY

*Peter Reed, the conference organizer, is examining the decor of the
foyer, which is in its final stages of preparation. Large portraits and
many American and British flags. An assistant approaches him.*

                                ASSISTANT
Telephone for you, Mr Reed.

*Reed walks to the reception desk and picks up the phone.*

                                REED
Hello, yes, speaking . . . Yes, we're expecting them this
morning . . . Oh . . . I'm sorry to hear that . . . absolutely
tragic . . . how awful . . . I hate to say this, but do you have
a replacement . . . I see . . . right . . . Well, thank you for
letting me know.

*He puts the phone down and turns to the receptionist.*

They've crashed on the motorway. We don't have a band
and it's too late to find a replacement. Great.

                                RECEPTIONIST
There's actually a band staying in the hotel. They checked
in yesterday. I'm afraid they're foreign though.

EXT. FINLAY'S HOUSE — DAY

*A taxi is driving off. Brendan is setting off down the path towards a
large suburban house with a beautifully neat garden. At the front
door Brendan rings the bell. The door is opened by Mrs Finlay. Mrs
Finlay is about forty. She is wearing a dressing gown.*

                                BRENDAN
Mr Finlay asked me to come . . .

*Mrs Finlay stands still, watching Brendan. She doesn't speak.*

. . . He said to come at eight. I have some information for him.

*After another silence, Mrs Finlay stands aside to let Brendan into the hallway.*

MRS FINLAY

Wait here.

*She goes upstairs. Brendan hears her talking. She returns.*

He'll be down in a moment. Come and sit down.

*She takes Brendan into the kitchen. It is a long comfortable room. On the kitchen table is the same tabloid newspaper last seen in the Hoppers Bar.*

Coffee?

BRENDAN

Yes, please.

MRS FINLAY

Are you hungry?

BRENDAN

Not really, thank you.

MRS FINLAY

That's very polite of you. Eggs and bacon?

BRENDAN.

Yes, please.

CUT TO:

*Close-up of Mrs Finlay's hand dropping the egg into the frying pan.*

INT. CENTRAL HOTEL — CORRIDOR — DAY

*Reed and a waiter wheeling a trolley down a long hotel corridor.*

INT. CENTRAL HOTEL — ANDREJ'S ROOM — DAY

*Andrej is asleep. There is a knock on the door. Andrej sits up, confused.*

ANDREJ

Come in.

*The door opens and Reed and the waiter come in.*

WAITER

Breakfast, sir.

REED
(*smiling ingratiatingly*)
Mr Slominski, I wonder if I might have a word with you.

INT. FINLAY'S HOUSE — KITCHEN — DAY

*Brendan is eating his breakfast. Mrs Finlay is watching him. He is self-conscious. Footsteps on the stairs. Finlay comes in, unshaven and much the worse for wear. Mrs Finlay exits.*

MRS FINLAY

There's fresh coffee.

*Finlay pours himself a coffee and joins Brendan at the table. He offers Brendan a cigarette. Brendan declines. Finlay lights one.*

FINLAY

OK, Brendan, tell me all about it.

*As Brendan talks the camera goes in tight on Finlay's face. He watches Brendan carefully, evaluating him. He is taking it seriously.*

BRENDAN

Well . . . after I left the club last night, about 8.30, I went to eat at a place just around the corner. It's called Weegees.

FINLAY
(*nods*)
I know it. Go on.

BRENDAN

At the next table there were two men, London accents. I
could hear some of their conversation. They mentioned
the club . . .

(*takes a deep breath*)

. . . They mentioned your name. One of them said . . . it's
tomorrow afternoon . . . and the other one said hurt him
. . . or . . .

FINLAY

What?

BRENDAN

Or kill him. It was a question. Hurt him or kill him?

CUT TO:

INT. HALLWAY

*Mrs Finlay is standing motionless next to the partly open door.*

CUT TO:

INT. BREAKFAST ROOM

FINLAY
(*smiling*)

And what was the answer?

BRENDAN

Hurt him . . . I think. There was a lot of noise, it was difficult to hear.

FINLAY

Last night you said something about an American.

BRENDAN

Yes, that was at the beginning, they called him the Yank.

*Finlay looks very carefully at Brendan.*

FINLAY

That's right. The Yank wants me to sign a bit of paper. So

he sends a pair of London cowboys to hurt me. And you,
Brendan, you just happen to be sitting next to these cow-
boys after being in my employment for a couple of hours.
Are you setting me up, Brendan?

> BRENDAN
> (*confused*)

No, Mr Finlay.

> FINLAY

No . . . I don't think so either . . . Do you like working for
me?

> BRENDAN

Yes.

> FINLAY

You can leave.

*Pause.*

> BRENDAN

No, I don't want to.

> FINLAY

OK. Give me five minutes to shave and we'll go.

INT. CENTRAL HOTEL – ANDREJ'S BEDROOM – DAY

*Reed and his assistant are handing out sheet music to the band, who
are trying on a selection of ill-fitting suits.*

> REED

Well, that's not bad. OK, here is the sheet music. If you
would translate where appropriate, Mr Slominski . . . 'The
Star-Spangled Banner' . . . 'God Save the Queen' . . . I will
cue you when to start each piece.

*Andrej translates. The musicians looking dumbly at the music: none
of them reads music.*

And apart from that, well, some discreet, tasteful cocktail
jazz, which I'm sure will be no problem for your chaps.

*Andrej translates this very seriously. The musicians look very serious and nod their heads. One of them winks at Reed. He laughs nervously, and the musician picks up an alto saxophone and begins to play a very fast passage. This sound continues into the next scene.*

INT. FINLAY'S CAR — DAY

*Finlay is driving fast through a section of multi-lane flyovers. Brendan is in the passenger seat.*

> FINLAY
> Are you sure you'll recognize them?

> BRENDAN
> Yes.

> FINLAY
> By the way, Brendan, the Polish band has been invited to a party tonight by the Polish community. You're to take them. You don't have to stay all night, just make sure they get there. OK?

> BRENDAN
> OK.

INT. CENTRAL HOTEL — BALLROOM — DAY

*The ballroom is ready, empty except for a piano tuner working on the white grand piano. It is the same man as seen in the Quay Club the day before.*

EXT. QUAY CLUB — ENTRANCE — DAY

*Wide-angle, hand-held shot of Finlay and Brendan going up the stairs to Jim's Gym. In the gym four men are training. They are very ugly and tough.*

> FINLAY
> Where's Jim?

> FIRST MAN
> He's on the blower.

                                    FINLAY
Wait here, Brendan.

*Brendan waits. The men ignore him and continue training.*

EXT. CENTRAL HOTEL

*A line of Rolls Royces and Cadillacs disgorging dignitaries.*

INT. CENTRAL HOTEL — BALLROOM

*The band taking position on the stage. The notice still describes them as the Transatlantics.*

INT. CENTRAL HOTEL — BALLROOM

*Waiters showing people to their seats.*

INT. CENTRAL HOTEL — BALLROOM

*Kate arriving. Although not cheerful, she looks stunning in her out-fit. Cosmo, who is near the door, kisses her and shows her to her seat. He catches sight of someone and excuses himself.*

INT. CENTRAL HOTEL — BALLROOM ENTRANCE

*The Lady Mayoress enters. She is a good-looking woman in her early forties. Cosmo greets her.*

*Cosmo catches sight of John Perry, the councillor. He excuses himself from the Lady Mayoress and, after greeting Perry, shows him to his seat next to Kate and himself.*

                                    COSMO
Kate, this is John Perry. John, this is Kate.

*Kate looks up at the two men, unsmiling.*

          CUT TO:

*A close-up of Brendan's face, through glass, looking down. The camera zooms back and we see Finlay and Brendan in the top window of the building housing the Quay Club. Finlay is saying something,*

*but we can't hear him. He leaves Brendan alone, watching the
street.*

INT. CENTRAL HOTEL – BALLROOM

*Peter Reed gives the band a nod. The band strikes up a very discordant 'God Save the Queen'. Everyone stands, then sits. The Lady
Mayoress speaks.*

> LADY MAYORESS
> It is a great honour to be asked to welcome our American
> friends today. It is also a great pleasure. I am confident
> that we are ushering in a new era of transatlantic co-operation and friendship and, last but not least, of prosperity.

*Applause.*

> The qualities that have made America the richest, the
> most powerful and, in my opinion, the most benevolent
> superpower in history, those qualities will, I hope, be
> transmitted to our own British initiative and contribute
> towards a re-emergence of this once great nation.

*Cries of 'Here, here' and applause.*

> I think by now we all know the importance of this project.
> Can I point out that it need not have happened here. Liverpool, Manchester and Glasgow were all considered. We
> wanted it to happen here and, ladies and gentlemen, it's
> going to happen here.

*Cheers.*

> It's going to happen here because we wanted it to, but
> also because of the vision and unremitting labour of one
> man . . .
>> (*points at Cosmo*)
> . . . Francis Cosmo.

*There are loud cheers. Cosmo plays it cool and discreetly looks down.*

*During this speech the camera moves from the Lady Mayoress to the
band. The drummer accidentally knocks over a cymbal.*

*The fat councillor is smiling at Kate, who smiles back blankly.*

*Details of the guests.*

INT. QUAY CLUB

*The camera looking down on to the street over Brendan's shoulder.*

*The red Jaguar drives into shot and parks.*

*A series of acute-angled shots showing Brendan running down the stairs into the club.*

> BRENDAN
> Mr Finlay, they're here.

INT. CENTRAL HOTEL — BALLROOM

*Reed gives the nod and the band strikes up with a bizarre version of 'The Star-Spangled Banner'. Cosmo stands.*

EXT. THE SIDE

*The two London hoods, Patrick and Tony, get out of the Jaguar. They are wearing suits and carrying identical briefcases. On the soundtrack 'The Star-Spangled Banner' continues.*

INT. CENTRAL HOTEL — BALLROOM

*The band finishing. Raucous saxophone cadenza. Reed is looking extremely worried.*

*The fat councillor is patting Kate's leg. She moves her leg away.*

> CUT TO:

*Medium close-up of Cosmo.*

> COSMO
> Ladies and gentlemen, firstly let me thank Margaret for her kind remarks about me. She's certainly the most attractive politician I've seen in a long time . . .

*Laughter.*

... aside from that she's also one of the toughest ...

*Cries of 'Here, here.'*

... which is fine with me ...

EXT. THE SIDE

*Tony and Patrick crossing the street. The camera is low, behind them. The club in the background.*

COSMO (V.O.)
... one of our most misrepresented, or shall I say misunderstood, presidents, once said, 'When the going gets tough, the tough get going ...'

INT. CENTRAL HOTEL — BALLROOM

*Cosmo talking.*

COSMO
... and when I look at England, in particular this area, this once great area, I see that the going is tough ...

CUT TO:

*Medium close-up of a particularly wealthy couple.*

COSMO
... and I see that it's time the tough got going ...

EXT. THE SIDE

*Patrick and Tony going to the club entrance.*

COSMO (V.O.)
... this area requires major surgery. The surgeon's knife may seem crude ...

INT. CENTRAL HOTEL — BALLROOM

*The band watching Reed for their next cue.*

> COSMO
>
> . . . but ask any cancer sufferer that has survived and he will say, 'God bless the surgeon.'

*Applause.*

*Peter Reed nods his head sagely. The band misinterpret it and go into their version of 'The Girl from Ipanema'. Reed immediately stops them, but it takes a few moments before order is restored.*

INT. QUAY CLUB

*Patrick and Tony going downstairs into the club.*

INT. CENTRAL HOTEL – BALLROOM

> COSMO
>
> . . . This is a festive occasion. There are still a few technical details to be straightened out . . .

INT. QUAY CLUB

*Finlay behind his desk on the phone, camera moving in.*

> COSMO (V.O.)
>
> . . . before signatures are put on to the relevant documents.

INT. CENTRAL HOTEL – BALLROOM

*Medium close-up of Cosmo smiling.*

> COSMO
>
> . . . but I know it's going to happen.

*Loud applause.*

*Councillor Perry leans over and says something in Kate's ear. His hand is on her leg.*

INT. QUAY CLUB

*The soundtrack now stays with the Quay Club. The camera is hand-held. Patrick and Tony stand in the empty club. The lights are on. They can hear Finlay talking. Finlay's accent has become thicker, more provincial, slower.*

*Patrick and Tony look at each other and nod. They walk into the office. Finlay looks up at them.*

> PATRICK

Are you Finlay?

> FINLAY
> (*looking worried*)

Yes. Is something wrong?

> PATRICK

That's up to you, Finlay. We've been asked to come and talk to you . . . about this place. You've had a fair offer for it. You turned it down. That's stupid. It was felt that a personal approach . . . would do the trick.

CUT TO:

*Patrick's POV of Finlay. Finlay looks frightened.*

INT. THE CLUB

*Brendan, in the club, is walking to the door of the office. He can see through the half-open door.*

> PATRICK
> (*to Tony*)

Clear the desk.

*Finlay's desk is old and beautiful. On it are his personal things. Photographs, paperweights, cassettes, etc. Using his briefcase, Tony sweeps them all on to the floor, leaving a deep scratch in the surface.*

CUT TO:

*Close-up of Finlay's face. The anger momentarily coming to the surface then vanishing.*

*They ignore him. Patrick opens his briefcase. He takes out a can of hair spray, a hammer, a scalpel, a cigarette lighter and an expensively framed photograph.*

*Close-up of the photograph. It is of Finlay and his wife and two children.*

*Close-up of Finlay looking at the photograph. His eyes narrow.*

*Tension music.*

*Patrick puts on a pair of new white cotton gloves and then arranges the objects on the desk.*

PATRICK
Right you . . . thick . . . fucking . . . northern . . . shithead.
I need a signature. You can sign for me or you can sign . . .
for him.

*The scene has the quality of a sophisticated magic trick. It is the precision which is frightening.*

*Patrick picks up the hammer and smashes it down on the photograph frame. The glass breaks, the wood splinters. He carefully takes out the photograph, wipes it clean and lays it flat on the desk. Picking the scalpel he carefully runs it over the photograph, across the faces. Thick red liquid oozes out of the cut.*

*Patrick uncaps the hair spray, lights the lighter, presses the nozzle and ignites the hair spray. He then uses this improvised flame thrower on the photograph.*

CUT TO:

*Close-up of desk top. The photograph blackens and bubbles, the stage blood sizzles. The varnish on the desk surface bubbles and then catches fire.*

CUT TO:

*Close-up of Finlay's face.*

*The charade vanishes. The anger comes to the surface.*

*Patrick puts down the can.*

FINLAY
You shouldn't have damaged the desk.

*There is something in his voice which reaches Tony and Patrick.*

You shouldn't have damaged the desk.

*The other door in Finlay's office opens and four of the men from the gym come in. In silence the men look at each other.*

*Cut from face to face. Patrick realizes that they have been set up. The photograph is still burning. Patrick smothers the flame with his gloved hand.*

FINLAY

Too late . . . sit down.

*They sit. Finlay looks at them, his rage evident.*

So, you got into your . . . Jaguar . . . and came up to the north . . . where the stupid . . . fucking . . . Geordies live.
        (*does a cockney accent*)
. . . You've got a photograph of my family . . . an image . . . a ghost. The wife, me . . . and the kids . . . and you've cut it . . . red blood comes out . . . and then you've burned it.
        (*pause; quietly*)
How dare you . . . How dare you?

*He looks at Tony.*

And if I didn't sign, you were going to hurt me. That's right, isn't it?

*He opens the second briefcase and looks in.*

Dear me. Don't kill him, but hurt him bad.

*Finlay takes out two wooden blocks. Each has a curved top, one is slightly smaller than the other. Finlay looks at them carefully and then places them on the desk. He rests his wrist on the larger and his elbow on the smaller. He looks up and sees Brendan through the main doorway.*

Come in, Brendan.

*Brendan hesitates.*

Come on.

*Patrick and Tony look at Brendan as he comes in. Brendan is extremely apprehensive and takes a position by the wall.*

*Finlay is deep in thought, looking at the wood blocks. Suddenly he clicks his fingers.*

I've got it. You've lost weight.

*Patrick looks at Tony.*

I know you. You're Tony the pig . . . you were in Durham. You made these in the workshop.

*The camera moves on to Tony. Sweat breaking out.*

Didn't they tell you about me in Durham? Didn't they tell you about me, Tony . . .

*Tony and Patrick are hauled to their feet. Their jackets are pulled off. The contents of their pockets are thrown on to the table. Wallets, rolls of money, the car keys. Finlay picks up the car keys.*

Brendan, you did well.

*Finlay throws the car keys to Brendan, who catches them. Patrick and Tony look at each other.*

Brendan, give the man a pound.

*Brendan meekly does what he is told.*

> (*to Patrick*)
> You just sold him your car. If you ever come here again
> . . . I'll kill you. Have you got that? Have you?

*They nod.*

*Finlay looks at his watch.*

There's a train to London leaves in twenty minutes. Take enough money for two first-class singles, they'll need privacy. Jim, bring the van round to the front.

*Tony and Patrick have relaxed slightly, thinking that this is it. Finlay takes his jacket off and hangs it behind the door.*

(*to Patrick and Tony*)

OK. Let's get this over with.

CUT TO:

*Brendan's face, uncomprehending.*

CUT TO:

*Tony. His arm is laid across the block.*

CUT TO:

*Finlay. He opens the briefcase again and takes out an eighteen-inch length of pipe. One end is heavily bandaged with gaffer tape.*

CUT TO:

*Close-up on Tony's face.*

CUT TO:

*Close-up on Brendan as the penny drops.*

CUT TO:

*A quick shot – eight frames – of Finlay's arm suddenly rising and falling.*

CUT TO:

*Brendan's horror-struck reaction, the sharp crack of the bone snapping.*

CUT TO:

*Finlay, a strange expression on his face.*

FINLAY

Next.

INT. CENTRAL HOTEL

*The Chief Constable has just been made an honorary sheriff. Everyone is laughing at something Cosmo has said. The Chief Constable is slightly embarrassed, the tin star pinned on his dress uniform. Cosmo sticks a big cigar in his mouth. There is renewed laughter.*

INT. QUAY CLUB

*Finlay and his muscle men leave the room.*

FINLAY

Just keep an eye on them for a moment, will you, Brendan?

*The scene takes on a nightmarish quality as Brendan is left alone with Patrick and Tony. Patrick is crying quietly, clutching his arm. Tony is a greenish, whitish colour. The sweat is pouring down his face. He is staring intently at Brendan, his eyes wide open.*

TONY
(*whispers*)
I . . . never . . . forget . . . a face.

INT. CENTRAL HOTEL

*Laughter. Everyone by now has had a lot to drink. The Polish band is playing extremely bizarre cocktail music. The soundtrack is loud with this mix.*

*Councillor Perry slides his hand up Kate's skirt. She smiles at him. Encouraged by this, his hand continues its exploration. Kate, still smiling, slides her hand along his thigh and squeezes his balls extremely hard. His scream is lost in the general sound but noticed by Cosmo. Kate eventually releases the councillor, who doubles up, his head on the table next to an enormous portion of trifle.*

CUT TO:

*Close-up of Cosmo watching Kate leave the ballroom.*

EXT. CENTRAL HOTEL

*Cosmo's stretch Cadillac is parked on a double-yellow line. The chauffeur is in the back, watching a video. Kate appears, takes out a nail file and, as she walks past, puts a long scratch on the side. The camera pulls focus and picks up the Quay Club van as it passes and stops outside the central station. Patrick and Tony are helped out.*

INT. CENTRAL HOTEL — BALLROOM

*The Polish band is out of control and there is an edge of hysteria to the event. Cosmo is now extremely angry. He corners Reed.*

> COSMO
>
> Shut these motherfuckers up.

*Reed begins trying to stop the band, a difficult process as they now have ceased to function as one unit.*

INT. CENTRAL RAILWAY STATION

*The London train is starting to move. Through the window of the first-class compartment we see Tony and Patrick slumped in their seats. On the platform the four men from the gym wave, their faces expressionless.*

INT. CENTRAL HOTEL — FOYER

*The Krakow Jazz Ensemble, coming from the ballroom, is almost hysterical with laughter. Andrej is trying to tell a story in Polish, but every time the phrase 'please stop' occurs he is reduced to helpless laughter. The snooty receptionist is extremely disapproving.*

EXT. RIVER

*A high shot of the London train crossing the river, heading south.*

INT. WEEGEES DINER — DUSK

*Looking out to the street.*

*Brendan, sitting on the wing of the Jaguar outside Weegees Diner.*

*Kate walks down the street. Brendan watches her but doesn't recognize her. She stops.*

EXT. THE SIDE — DUSK

> BRENDAN
>
> Kate.

*They look at each other. They both look drawn.*

> KATE
> My working clothes. Militant hooker.

> BRENDAN
> I think you look . . . fantastic.

> KATE
> Do you, my Brendan? Then give me a kiss.

*Brendan kisses her and she begins to shake. He holds her.*

> BRENDAN
> What's the matter? Don't cry.

EXT. WINDOW – WEEGEES DINER – DUSK

*The manager is watching them.*

> BRENDAN
> Look . . . I've got to take the band to a party . . . it's at a
> Polish club. I want you to come with me. Can you do
> that?

*Kate thinks for a moment, then makes a decision.*

> KATE
> Wait for me, I'll be back in a minute.

*Brendan watches Kate as she goes into the restaurant. She talks to
the manager. He begins wagging his finger and at a certain moment
he points at Brendan. Kate says very little. She pushes his finger
away from her face. He points again. They are standing next to the
bar. Kate picks up a pile of plates and drops them deliberately on the
floor. She repeats the move three times. The manager is frozen to the
spot. Kate exits. She joins Brendan.*

> BRENDAN
> My hero.

> KATE
> I've been a bad, bad girl.

*Brendan grins and opens the door of the Jaguar. Kate is extremely surprised.*

Where did you get this?

                    BRENDAN
I've been a bad, bad boy.

*As the Jaguar drives off, the manager and the catty waitress are both staring out of the restaurant window.*

INT. CABLE CALE HOUSE

*Cosmo's office is quite dark, lit just from the window. Cosmo is standing by the window looking at the development model. Cosmo looks out of the window, then back to the model.*

*The phone rings, breaking the silence. Cosmo lets it ring three times and then walks to the desk and picks it up.*

    CUT TO:

EXT. KING'S CROSS STATION

*Patrick is in a public phone box; Tony is leaning against the railing. In the background the words 'King's Cross' can be clearly seen.*

    CUT TO:

INT. COSMO'S OFFICE

*Cosmo listens to the phone in silence and then replaces the receiver carefully. He flips a switch on the desk.*

                    INTERCOM VOICE
Yes, Mr Cosmo.

                    COSMO
Get Bob.

EXT. HELICOPTER

*Shot of the Jaguar and two taxis driving alongside the River Tyne.*

*Massive cranes and half-built ships dominate the picture. The sky is extremely dramatic as storm clouds gather.*

EXT. POLISH CLUB

*Formerly a Beacon house, the Polish Club is a tall white building standing on a cliff overlooking the Tyne estuary. Behind it there is a harbour and in the distance the river bends and twists, the cranes still visible. The Jaguar and the two taxis pull up in front of the house. The passengers get out. Andrej pays the taxis and they drive off.*

*The door of the house opens and a reception committee comes out to welcome them: white-haired old men with walrus moustaches and wearing brown pinstriped suits; their children and grandchildren who are more anglicized. The old women hang back at first.*

*One of the old men makes a formal welcoming speech in Polish. There is much hugging and then the whole group squeezes into the house.*

INT. POLISH CLUB

*The inside of the house is the Poland of the 1930s. A large book-lined room. Old photographs and maps of pre-war Poland.*

*A large table is set. Through a door a kitchen is visible with lots of activity taking place.*

KATE

(*to Brendan*)

It's so strange, I know this place.

*Brendan doesn't understand what she means.*

*The band sits down. Everyone is given a glass of vodka and toasts are made.*

*The atmosphere is still formal. A young woman comes from the kitchen and is introduced as Christine. Andrej begins to talk to her.*

*Polish dialogue with subtitles:*

POLISH MAN

Christine, these are the famous musicians from Krakow.

CHRISTINE

I'm pleased to meet you. What kind of music do you play?

ANDREJ

Free jazz.

CHRISTINE

Ah, American music.

ANDREJ

No, Polish free jazz.

CHRISTINE
(*disappointed*)

I thought you were rock 'n' roll.

ANDREJ

Tadeusz once played in a rock 'n' roll band but he had a headache all the time and he had to leave.

CHRISTINE

And what do you play?

ANDREJ

I am the manager.

*The local Poles start to fire questions at the band about Solidarity, meat rationing, the Catholic church.*

*Brendan suddenly notices that Kate is not in the room.*

EXT. POLISH CLUB

*Kate is standing alone, looking at the river. Brendan comes out. The sky is overcast.*

BRENDAN

Shall I leave you alone?

KATE

No, come and look.

                          BRENDAN
What's the matter?

                          KATE
I quit my job.

                          BRENDAN
But you wanted to.

                          KATE
Yes . . . but I did it stupidly. I've made trouble. . .
                    (*looks at Brendan*)
. . . Brendan . . . the job . . . it's not very nice . . . I mean
. . . I'm not a nice person to know.

                          BRENDAN
Yes, you are.

                          KATE
But you don't know what you're getting into.

                          BRENDAN
And I don't care. Come on, let's go in.

INT. POLISH CLUB

*Everyone sitting around the large table eating. Christine and Andrej
are together, but Kate and Brendan are slightly separated. Andrej is
telling a modern political joke. The young people laugh; the old people don't get it.*

*Someone asks the band to play. They don't have their instruments.
One of the old men fetches his accordion. The band pass it around
until Tadeusz, the bass player, has it. He starts to play tentatively.
The Poles shout suggestions. He begins to play a sad melody.*

*Polish dialogue with subtitles:*

                          OLD MAN
What's that one? I remember it, I can't remember the
words, come on, someone must know it.

*A woman's voice is heard singing in Polish. Heads turn. It is*

*Kate. Tears stream down her face as she sings. Another voice joins in and then a third with a harmony. When the song finishes there is a short silence and then everyone claps. The old man kisses Kate.*

(in Polish)

Thank you, you are an angel.

KATE
(in Polish)

It was my pleasure.

INT. POLISH CLUB

*The table and chairs have been pushed back, the old man has taken over the accordion, and everyone is dancing. The atmosphere has loosened up. A violin and piano join the accordion.*

*Brendan and Kate stand together holding hands, watching Andrej and Christine dancing.*

BRENDAN

That was pretty good for a Norwegian.

KATE

You see, you're not *so* clever, Brendan. My father was Polish. I spent three summers with my grandparents. They hardly spoke English. I know these photographs, maps, this vodka. It makes me very nostalgic.

*She looks at Brendan. They become mesmerized by each other and kiss very passionately.*

Shall we go soon?

BRENDAN

Let's say goodbye to everyone.

*Brendan walks to Andrej, who is dancing with Christine.*

We're going, Andrej. Say goodnight for us. Just ask them to phone for a taxi when you want to go back.

ANDREJ

I think I might stay here tonight, but I'll see you at the club tomorrow.

*Christine pulls him back on to the dance-floor.*

EXT. POLISH CLUB — NIGHT

*Kate and Brendan come out of the house. There is a flash of lightning followed by a distant roll of thunder. They are both slightly drunk. Brendan opens the passenger door with difficulty. They kiss. Kate gets in the car. Brendan closes her door and gets into the car. He starts the engine.*

BRENDAN

I can't find the switch for the headlights.

*They kiss again. Brendan touches her breasts.*

KATE

Let's go home.

*Brendan tries without success to find the switch.*

*Kate lights her cigarette lighter and opens the glove compartment, as Brendan finds the light switch. She finds the gun that we saw in the very first scene.*

Jesus, look at this.

*She shows Brendan the gun. Brendan drives off.*

*A series of interior and exterior shots as the Jaguar heads back to town. Kate and Brendan are getting turned on by each other. They kiss at traffic lights and touch each other.*

*This sensuality is tempered by the soundtrack music, which is fairly foreboding. It starts to rain. Lightning lights up the sky. The Jaguar joins the multi-lane underpass system. A black American car pulls alongside them. The passenger is smiling and pointing at the front wheel of the Jaguar. He indicates that Brendan should pull over. Kate, her head on Brendan's shoulder, does not see the car. Brendan pulls on to the hard shoulder. The American car pulls over in front at*

*an angle, blocking the way forward. Two men get out. The image is
blurred by rain on the windscreen.*

CUT TO:

*Kate's face.*

> KATE

Why've we stopped?

CUT TO:

*Bob's face becoming recognizable through the windscreen.*

> KATE

Brendan, get away from here quick.

*Brendan revs the engine and struggles with the gear lever.*

> BRENDAN

Where the hell is reverse?

*The gears grind, the two men grab the door handles, and the Jaguar
lurches forward into the American car, smashing the tail light. The
engine stalls. The two men open the doors. Bob on Kate's side, the
second man on Brendan's side.*

> BOB
> (*icy*)

Get out of the car.

*Brendan gets out. Kate gets out. The doors of the American car have
been left open and country-and-western music can be heard coming
from the radio. The thunder is now frequent, the lightning punctuat-
ing each clap. Bob recognizes Kate.*

Kate! Mr Cosmo's going to be really pissed with you.

> BRENDAN
> (*bewildered*)

What do you want?

> SECOND MAN

Where d'ja get this car, shithead?

*Brendan begins to understand.*

BOB

I want you to take a message to your boss for me.

BRENDAN
(*frightened*)

Sure. What is it?

*The second man punches Brendan very hard in the stomach. Kate tries to help him, but Bob slams her against the car. Brendan is on his knees retching.*

BOB

Get up.

SECOND MAN
(*shouts*)

Get up!

KATE
(*shouts*)

Brendan.

*Cars are passing the whole time. Brendan gets up slowly. The second man takes something from his pocket and puts it in his right hand. He suddenly punches Brendan across the side of the head, knocking him on to all fours.*

Leave him alone.

*She tries to move but is again stopped.*

*The second man kicks Brendan in the backside but then lets him get to his feet.*

BOB

Right . . . run, boy . . . run.

*Brendan tries to move away, staggering to the other side of the car. Bob kicks Brendan's legs away. Kate reaches into the car and gets the gun.*

*Bob sees her and, before she can do anything, knocks the gun out of her hand. The gun falls to the ground and skids across to near the unconscious Brendan. Both men turn on Kate.*

You cheap, double-crossing whore.

*The other man begins slapping her.*

CUT TO:

*Bob's POV. Close-up of Brendan's bloodied face. He hears what is happening and makes a huge effort to move. His hand moves painfully slowly towards the gun.*

CUT TO:

*Kate and the men. The other man raises his hand. There is a flash of lightning and a simultaneous clap of thunder and he falls to the ground, a small mark above his eye. Bob turns.*

CUT TO:

*Brendan sitting on the ground aiming the gun at Bob. Brendan's face is twisted with rage. Kate, seeing Brendan's intention, runs to him and takes the gun. Brendan gets to his feet unsteadily and, walking over to Bob, tries to hit him.*

BRENDAN
Don't you hit her, you bastard.

*Brendan has no strength left and only succeeds in knocking Bob down, falling down himself in the process. Kate points the gun at Bob as he gets up.*

KATE
Put your friend in the car and drive off.

*Bob drags the dead man to the car.*

BOB
You're making a big mistake here, Kate. You know this can only go badly. Your boyfriend won't get away with this. Come on, Kate. Come with me. We'll do a deal. I'll tell him it was a mistake.

                            KATE

Get in the car. Drive off.

                            BOB

This is a big mistake.

*Kate aims at Bob's balls. He gets in the car.*

                            KATE

Drive.

*The American car drives off.*

*Brendan is sitting on the ground, leaning on the Jaguar. There is blood on his mouth, one eye is closing and he has a cut on his forehead. Kate's lip is cut. She kneels next to him and hugs him.*

*Brendan is crying. The reality of the situation is starting to sink in.*

                          BRENDAN

Jesus . . . I shot him. Is he . . . dead?

                            KATE

Yes, he is . . . Brendan, we have to go somewhere. Come on, I'll help you.

                          BRENDAN

I saw them hitting you. I wanted to kill them both.

                            KATE

Can you walk?

*She helps him into the passenger seat, and then she gets into the driver's seat and starts the engine.*

                          BRENDAN
                          (*mumbles*)

I love you.

                            KATE
                           (*sad*)

You mustn't say that.

EXT. MOTORWAY

*The Jaguar drives off at speed.*

INT. COSMO'S OFFICE

*Cosmo is behind his desk, illuminated by a small desk lamp. Bob is silhouetted against the window.*

BOB

They've got guns. No one said anything about guns. The bullet took him in the eye. The kid is a pro. If they're going to play it like that we have to tool up as well.

COSMO

Smart thinking, Bob . . . real smart . . .
(*suddenly stands and shouts*)
. . . What do you think this is? Chicago! . . . You meatball. We're legit. One sniff of this gets out and we're blown. A year of talking to these English jerks, their stupid councils, their stupid traditions. All the money we've spent, and you want to go and play Al Capone with some juvenile. He took you, Bob, the kid took you. From now on I handle things.
(*thinks for a while*)
First, lose the body. He never existed. Go to the club . . . say we want a truce. Say I'd like to talk to Finlay. Set up a meeting. Don't fuck up, Bob.

INT. CENTRAL HOTEL — FOYER — NIGHT

*The night porter looks up, startled. Brendan and Kate are looking much the worse for wear. Brendan is wearing dark glasses.*

BRENDAN

Andrej Slominski.

NIGHT PORTER

Room number?

KATE

He's Polish. He doesn't speak any English.

(*the porter looks at Brendan*)
He fell off a bus . . . he's been drinking.

NIGHT PORTER

Musician, is he?

KATE

Yes.

*The porter checks his list.*

NIGHT PORTER

It's 327.

EXT. QUAY CLUB

*The rain is heavy. The black American car draws up, and Bob gets out and goes into the club.*

INT. CENTRAL HOTEL – ANDREJ'S BEDROOM

*The shower is running. Kate undresses Brendan and sits him in the shower. She washes him. The noise of the shower is very loud.*

EXT. QUAY CLUB

*Heavy rain. Bob is coming out of the Quay Club, getting into his car and driving off.*

INT. CENTRAL HOTEL – ANDREJ'S BEDROOM

*The window is open, rain dripping. The noise of the rain is loud with occasional distant thunder.*

*Brendan is lying on the bed; Kate is sitting on him drying him. Brendan touches her bruised mouth.*

*Cut away to the storm, the wet streets.*

CUT BACK TO:

*Brendan and Kate lying together. Kate is cradling Brendan's head. He is asleep.*

*A series of shots showing the storm dying out. Brendan and Kate asleep, covered by a sheet.*

EXT. QUAYSIDE – DAWN

*The river has a light mist on it. The streets are still wet but empty. Close-up of a rat scurrying over cobblestones. A black Cadillac drives along the riverside and stops under the huge iron support for the Tyne Bridge. A white Mercedes comes down the hill and parks a hundred yards from the Cadillac. Finlay and three other men get out. Cosmo and two men get out of the Cadillac.*

*Cut from a long shot of Finlay's group talking to a shot of Cosmo's group talking. Cosmo begins walking to the centre and so does Finlay.*

*Cut to a medium shot of them meeting.*

*Cut from Cosmo to Finlay looking at each other.*

> COSMO
> Thanks for coming, Mr Finlay. I truly appreciate it. I'm sure we can solve this . . . misunderstanding.

> FINLAY
> *(interrupts)*
> Cut the crap. I'm not the council.

CUT TO:

*Close-up of Cosmo looking thoughtfully at Finlay.*

> FINLAY
> I know all about you, Mr Cosmo. The legit business in New York. The other . . . business . . . in Philadelphia. I did my homework, Mr Cosmo, I have American friends. You did not do *your* homework.

*Cosmo and Finlay begin to walk along the quay.*

> COSMO
> You're right, Mr Finlay. That was foolish of me.

> FINLAY
> You obviously thought it wasn't necessary. You had the

suitcase full of dollars and you came in like John Wayne. I
heard all the stories. You worked your act down the street
and I thought to myself, 'Sooner or later the man is going
to make me an offer.' I was prepared, all along, to consider
selling. But you sent an employee. He was insensitive. I
said no. You put more pressure on via the council, the fat
man. I have a photograph of the fat man with a friend that
is more valuable to him than the whole suitcase full of
dollars. You assume too much about the people in this
town, Mr Cosmo. To them you are the American uncle
and they're taking you for the last dollar.

COSMO

I know that, I'm playing them as well. The problem is . . .
I can't do everything myself . . . it's difficult to find the
right . . . partners.

*They walk on in silence for a while.*

Maybe we can discuss some kind of co-operation. I think
we understand each other now.

FINLAY

We're getting there, Mr Cosmo.

COSMO

It's Frank.

FINLAY

I'll stick with Mr Cosmo for now.

COSMO

As you like.

FINLAY

You want the club.
                    (*looks at him*)
Make me an offer.

COSMO

It's market value last month was £75,000. I'll double it.

FINLAY
(*stopping*)

Fuck the market value. The market value was fixed when
this was a run-down area scheduled for nowhere. I'm the
last guy on the block. I'm holding everything up. Everyone
wants the scheme to go ahead. The profit on this deal has
got to be between ten and twenty million pounds . . .
Make me an offer that does not insult my intelligence.

CUT TO:

*Long shot of Cosmo and Finlay. Cosmo's laughter rings out across
the river.*

CUT TO:

*Quick flash of Brendan and Kate asleep in each other's arms.
Cosmo's laughter continues over the shot.*

CUT TO:

*Cosmo and Finlay walking back.*

COSMO

I need this deal to go through quickly. When can we do
the paperwork?

FINLAY

Bring your lawyer to the club tonight. Round about midnight. You know the tune?

COSMO

I'm afraid not . . . Now there is another matter . . . We
have never used guns in England. We're clean here.

*Finlay is clearly puzzled.*

. . . the boy, Brendan. That's an Irish name isn't it?

*Finlay says nothing.*

I'm right, uh. He's a pro. Listen, I sent those boys from
London; the boy pinned them. You hurt them badly. They
understood. They know the code, they accept it. They

bear no grudge. We are even. But your Irish boy takes out
my number two, one shot through the eye. Suddenly we're
talking guns. In England. My boys are very upset.

> FINLAY
> (*incredulous*)

Brendan shot your man?

> COSMO

You didn't know. That's what I thought. The Irish boy's
working solo. A mad dog. We have to balance this thing.
We have to take him out. You understand that. That's how
it is, right?

> FINLAY

He's my responsibility. I'll buy him. Ask them what their
price is.

CUT TO:

*Cosmo's POV of the black Cadillac, the three men standing by it.*

> COSMO (V.O.)

I can't. They want him. He's dead. The girl too. She
knows too much.

CUT TO:

*Wide shot of Finlay and Cosmo talking. It is not clear whether Finlay has given in or not. They part and begin walking back to their cars.*

INT. CENTRAL HOTEL — ANDREJ'S BEDROOM — DAY

*Kate and Brendan sleeping. The room is in semi-darkness apart from a little light from the window. There is a knock at the door. Kate stirs. The knock is repeated. Kate drapes a blanket around her and goes to the door.*

> KATE
> (*quietly*)

Who is it?

> WOMAN (V.O.)

It's room service, madam. Do you want me to clean the room?

> KATE

No, thank you. What time is it?

> WOMAN (V.O.)

It's 1.30, ma'am ...

*The voice recedes, muttering. Kate gets back into bed; Brendan stirs.*

> BRENDAN

What?

> KATE

Go back to sleep.

*Brendan opens his eyes. Kate is looking at him. They kiss in a clumsy way, bruised from the fight. They begin making love. They are very tender with each other.*

*Outside, in the distance, a marching band can be heard playing a Souza march. Brendan winces as Kate embraces him.*

Am I hurting you?

*They both realize the joke and smile.*

CUT TO:

EXT. STREET – DAY

*It is the last day of the American festival and a procession is taking place. Local drum majorettes and bands are proceeding down the street towards the hotel. The lead majorette is giving an impressive display of baton catching. A TV crew is filming the event.*

CUT TO:

INT. WORKSHOP – DAY

*Close-up of a pair of hands stripping a red wire with a pair of wire strippers. A section of work bench can be seen with tools and small*

*electronic components. A tiny black-and-white TV set shows the pro-
cession as filmed by the TV crew. The sound of the band is thin and
tinny.*

    CUT TO:

INT. CENTRAL HOTEL — DAY

*Brendan and Kate making love. There is an element of desperation
and sadness.*

    CUT TO:

EXT. STREET — DAY

*The procession continues. The lead majorette throws her baton high
in the air and . . .*

    CUT TO:

INT. WORKSHOP — DAY

*. . . on the black-and-white TV we see her catch it. The male hands
connect the red wire to a battery terminal. A switch is clicked, a volt-
meter registers full charge.*

    CUT TO:

INT. CENTRAL HOTEL — DAY

*Brendan and Kate making love. The brass band is now very loud as
it passes the hotel.*

                   KATE
                 *(quietly)*
    And I love you.

    CUT TO:

INT. WORKSHOP — DAY

*Close-up of the black-and-white TV. We see details of the procession.
We see the majorette throw the baton higher into the air. The camera*

*pans and the male hands connect a black wire to an electronic timer, pirated from a VHS video recorder.*

    CUT TO:

INT. CENTRAL HOTEL — DAY

*Brendan and Kate locked together.*

    CUT TO:

EXT. THE SIDE — DAY

*Outside the club two workmen are putting up an 'Acquired for re-development' notice. As the procession comes into shot the camera pulls focus and we see the majorette throw her baton high. As it comes down she fumbles the catch and almost drops it.*

    CUT TO:

INT. WORKSHOP — DAY

*Close-up of timing device speeding through the hours of the day and stopping on midnight 24.00 hours.*

    CUT TO:

INT. HOTEL ROOM — DAY

*Brendan and Kate slump apart on the bed.*

    CUT TO:

EXT. THE SIDE — DAY

*As the procession disappears around the corner, Finlay appears and walks up the hill. He sees the workmen putting up the sign.*

                FINLAY
Take that down.

               WORKMAN
I'm sorry, sir, our orders was to put it up.

*Finlay grabs the ladder and begins to shake it.*

All right, all right.

*The workmen bring the notice down.*

INT. CENTRAL HOTEL — ANDREJ'S BEDROOM — DAY

*Kate is standing next to the window. Brendan is in bed. Kate is dressed.*

> BRENDAN
> The man I shot . . . did you know him?

> KATE
> Yes. He works for Cosmo.

> BRENDAN
> Do you?

> KATE
> I did.

> BRENDAN
> What'll happen now?

> KATE
> He will try to have us killed.

*Pause.*

> BRENDAN
> Did you mean what you said?

> KATE
> What did I say?

> BRENDAN
> Oh . . . nothing.

*Kate walks to the bed and kisses Brendan.*

> KATE
> I meant it. Did you?

BRENDAN

You know it.

KATE

Do you have a passport?

BRENDAN

Yes.

KATE

How would you like to come to Minnesota with me?

BRENDAN

I don't have any money.

KATE

I have money. Listen, we're in trouble. You shot someone, this is no dream.

*Kate touches Brendan's bruise. He winces.*

BRENDAN

What do we do?

KATE

They won't try anything here. Stay in this room. Give me your keys and I'll get your things. I'll take the car. I'm safe in daylight. What time does it get dark?

BRENDAN

9.30–10 o'clock.

KATE

Right, I'll meet you at eleven . . .

*Suddenly the door bursts open. It is Andrej and Christine.*

CUT TO:

EXT. QUAY CLUB – FINLAY'S OFFICE – EVENING

*Finlay is sitting behind his desk with his feet up, a glass in his hand and a bottle of scotch on the desk. He is deep in thought, tunelessly whistling 'Round about Midnight'.*

INT. AND EXT. CENTRAL HOTEL — EARLY EVENING

*A series of shots showing Kate leaving Andrej's bedroom, crossing the foyer, getting into the car, driving through town. She turns the radio on and the DJ gives the time as 7.45.*

INT. KATE'S APARTMENT BUILDING

*Kate arrives at her apartment block and drives into the underground car park. She is quite nervous as she locks the car door. She drops the keys.*

*Kate takes the lift to the tenth floor and walks back to the ninth where her flat is. She puts the key in the lock, opens the door and goes into the apartment. She stops dead. The place has been stripped of everything except the bed. There is a suitcase on it. Slowly she begins to walk towards the bed. Kate, already nervous, is shocked when she suddenly notices a seated figure in the darkened part of the room.*

> COSMO
> Kate . . . Kate . . . I don't have to tell you what kind of trouble you're in.

*Cosmo, still talking, gets up and walks towards Kate, who is frightened.*

> You're a clever girl, Kate, you can figure it out for yourself. The fat man is still singing soprano.

*Cosmo begins to laugh.*

*He reaches Kate and puts his hand on her shoulder gently.*

> I kind of enjoyed that. And you've got yourself an Irish stud. Sit down.

*Kate sits on the edge of the bed; Cosmo remains standing.*

> I'd like to think it wasn't personal, Kate, but . . . he killed one of my boys. The others want him dead! What are we going to do, Kate?

INT. BASEMENT CAR PARK — EVENING

*Camera slowly moves towards the Jaguar. Cosmo's voice continues.*

> COSMO (V.O.)
> I don't forget my friends. We were close, Kate, you and
> me.

INT. KATE'S APARTMENT — EVENING

*Close-up of Kate.*

> COSMO
> We were close, weren't we?

> KATE
> (*whispers*)
> Yes.

> COSMO
> That's right. Why, you could have had my child. That's
> why I'm going to help you this one last time. You and the
> boy. But it's the last time, do you understand that?

> KATE
> Yes.

> COSMO
> But in return you must do something for me. Will you do
> that?

> KATE
> Yes.

INT. BASEMENT CAR PARK — EVENING

*The Jaguar is rocking slightly.*

INT. KATE'S APARTMENT — EVENING

> COSMO
> This has got to be personally delivered in New York by
> Monday morning.

*Cosmo takes from his jacket pocket a small package with an address on it.*

> Will you do that for me? No one is to know. Everyone is looking for you both. Leave town tonight, wait until it's dark. Drive to London. Leave the car at Heathrow Airport. Go to the TWA desk. There are two tickets to New York, in your name. The flight is at 11.00 a.m. There will be someone at this address on Sunday night. Do you think you can do it?

*Kate looks at Cosmo for a while and then decides that he is telling the truth.*

                              KATE
>            Yes.

*Cosmo puts the package on the open suitcase and then takes from his pocket two passports. He places them open on either side of the package and from the photographs we see they belong to Brendan and Kate.*

                             COSMO
                          (*fatherly*)
> After that you are on your own.
>                  (*gently strokes Kate's hair*)
> Go back to Minnesota, Kate. I won't see you again. Try to keep the Irish boy out of trouble.

*Kate and Cosmo look at each other and for a moment the physical attraction they have for each other is on the surface. Kate looks away.*

                              KATE
>            Thanks.

INT. QUAY CLUB — NIGHT

*The band is assembled on the stage. The club is half full. Andrej and Christine are holding hands. Finlay comes to the microphone.*

FINLAY

Ladies and gentlemen, will you please give a warm welcome to the Krakow Jazz Ensemble.

*The band goes into a loud aggressive improvisation. The music runs
through the next sequence.*

*The club starts filling up. Some people from the Polish club are there.
Everyone is drinking. Andrej and Christine are looking extremely
unhappy.*

INT. UNDERGROUND CAR PARK — NIGHT

*Kate puts suitcase in the boot, gets in the car, starts the engine, turns
on the lights and drives off.*

EXT. CENTRAL HOTEL — NIGHT

*Brendan, wearing dark glasses and Andrej's coat, comes out of the
entrance and into the metro.*

INT. QUAY CLUB — NIGHT

*Andrej and Christine are necking.*

EXT. DARK COBBLED RIVERSIDE STREET — NIGHT

*The Jaguar driving along the street.*

INT. METRO PLATFORM — NIGHT

*Metro train comes and Brendan gets on.*

*Clock on the platform gives the time as 10.55.*

INT. QUAY CLUB — NIGHT

*Finlay is watching the club scene, a strange expression on his face.*

EXT. REDHEUGH BRIDGE, NEWCASTLE SIDE — NIGHT

*Brendan waiting. A car approaches. We see it is the Jaguar. It stops,
and Brendan gets in.*

*Close-up of the car headlights. They move slightly as Brendan gets in.*

> KATE
> It's going to be OK. I've spoken to Cosmo.

CUT TO:

INT. QUAY CLUB — NIGHT

*The band is playing at full force.*

EXT. REDHEUGH BRIDGE — NIGHT

*The Jaguar is driving over the bridge, heading south. As it reaches Gateshead on the other side, the music of the Polish band fades out.*

EXT. DUAL CARRIAGEWAY — GATESHEAD — NIGHT

*The Jaguar heading south.*

CUT TO:

*Motorway sign:* THE SOUTH AI—MI.

INT. JAGUAR — NIGHT

*Close-up of the radio. Kate's hand switches it on.*

INT. JAGUAR — NIGHT

*Brendan watching Kate drive.*

> BIG WILLIE MICHAELS (V.O.)
> (*on radio*)
> So with the time coming up to 11.35 p.m. there is just twenty-five minutes left of American week. I'm gonna be so sad folks. It's been a thrill for me and when I get on that big Jumbo jet tomorrow . . . (*etc., etc.*)

CUT TO:

*Close-up of Kate's face. She suddenly looks at the radio.*

EXT. DUAL CARRIAGEWAY — NIGHT

*The Jaguar skidding to a halt as it pulls off the road.*

INT. JAGUAR — NIGHT

*Kate turns off the engine and radio.*

> KATE
>
> Oh, God . . . he's setting us up. We're walking into a trap.

> BRENDAN
>
> What?

> KATE
>
> There are no flights to America. I checked a couple of days ago. There's nothing. They're all full.

> BRENDAN
>
> Maybe he's got influence.

> KATE
>
> Maybe . . . I think it's a trap.

EXT. DUAL CARRIAGEWAY — NIGHT

*Kate and Brendan get out of the car. Kate opens the boot, and then opens the suitcase. Very carefully she opens the package. It contains blank papers, nothing else. Kate drops them and they blow around the car. She closes the suitcase without locking it and then slams the boot lid.*

> KATE
>
> The bastard.

> BRENDAN
>
> What are we going to do?

*Kate closes her eyes and shakes her head.*

> KATE
>
> I don't know.

*Kate and Brendan look at each other. They do not move. Cars speed past, blowing the paper around their feet.*

BRENDAN
Listen . . . let's talk to Finlay. He'll help us. He owes me a favour. He'll help . . . he will.

*Kate's face is expressionless. She holds out the keys to Brendan.*

*High-angle shot of the Jaguar doing an illegal 'U' turn and heading back into town.*

EXT. QUAY CLUB ENTRANCE – NIGHT

*Andrej is embracing Christine, who is crying. Cosmo and three men come into the club. José tries to stop them. Finlay intervenes. The band can be heard.*

EXT. TYNE BRIDGE – NIGHT

*The Jaguar at speed.*

INT. FINLAY'S OFFICE – NIGHT

*The lawyers are spreading documents on the desk. The band is heard in the background.*

*Cosmo, Bob and Finlay are seen.*

EXT. THE SIDE – NIGHT

*The Jaguar is parking opposite the Quay Club.*

CUT TO:

*Close-up of Jaguar headlights being turned off.*

CUT TO:

*Close-up of church clock face. We see the minute hand moving to two minutes before twelve.*

CUT TO:

*Brendan and Kate entering the club. In the entrance they meet Andrej and Christine.*

BRENDAN

Andrej! Is Finlay here?

ANDREJ

Yes, he's in the office. Listen, can I ask of you a huge favour?

BRENDAN

Sure, anything.

ANDREJ

I have to take Christine home. Could I borrow your car? I'll be very careful.

BRENDAN

Of course you can.

CUT TO:

*Close-up of clock face. The minute hand moves to twelve.*

CUT TO:

*Low-angle shot of the underside of the Jaguar. There is a loud click followed by a whirring noise and a second click, then silence.*

CUT TO:

*Dream-like wide-angle shot of Kate and Brendan walking through the crowded club.*

EXT. THE SIDE — NIGHT

*Christine and Andrej crossing the street, reaching the car.*

INT. FINLAY'S OFFICE — NIGHT

*The door opens and Brendan and Kate come in. They see Finlay, Cosmo and Bob.*

CUT FROM:

*Finlay's face, to Brendan's face, to Cosmo's face, to Kate's face.*

CUT TO:

*Andrej and Christine in the Jaguar closing the door.*

INT. FINLAY'S OFFICE — NIGHT

*Cosmo looks at his watch.*

> COSMO
> (*whispers*)
> Where's the car, Kate?

CUT TO:

*Close-up of Brendan's face. He suddenly understands.*

> BRENDAN
> (*anguished*)
> Je-sus.

*He suddenly runs out of the room.*

INT. JAGUAR — NIGHT

*Close-up of Andrej's hand putting the key in the ignition.*

INT. QUAY CLUB — NIGHT

*Fast hand-held shot of Brendan running through the club, scattering people.*

INT. JAGUAR — NIGHT

*Andrej turns the ignition, the engine starts, he revs the engine and pulls out from the club.*

EXT. QUAY CLUB — NIGHT

*Brendan running out of the entrance.*

> BRENDAN
> (*desperately shouting*)
> Andrej, Andrej.

INT. JAGUAR — NIGHT

*As they pull away a car approaches them flashing its headlights.*

> CHRISTINE

Lights.

*Andrej flicks a switch, and the wipers come on.*

EXT. THE SIDE — NIGHT

*Brendan running into the street, the Jaguar visible.*

> BRENDAN
> (*shouting*)

Andrej.

INT. JAGUAR — NIGHT

*Extreme close-up of hand on switch.*

> ANDREJ

It must be this one.

EXT. THE SIDE — NIGHT

*A long shot of the Jaguar approaching the camera, Brendan behind. The Jaguar's headlights come on suddenly.*

EXT. THE SIDE — NIGHT

*Plate-glass window reflecting an orange fireball. In slow motion the plate glass implodes.*

EXT. THE SIDE — NIGHT

*Medium close-up of Brendan's face reflecting the bright orange explosion. Half a second later the wind blows the hair back off his face.*

CUT TO:

*Medium shot of Brendan falling backwards.*

*On the soundtrack there is a very loud and long explosion. Afterwards the soundtrack is completely dead.*

CUT TO:

*The Jaguar burning.*

CUT TO:

*Brendan on his knees, his hands over his ears.*

*The soundtrack is now from Brendan's point of view. A high frequency whistling is heard and then slowly the sound of the street starts to come in.*

*The dominant sound is Brendan's own animal like whimpering.*

CUT TO:

*Section of road. Kate's suitcase has been blown out of the car. Clothes, money and their passports lie on the road.*

CUT TO:

*Rear view of Brendan, on his knees, watching the Jaguar burn. Brendan turns and looks past camera.*

CUT TO:

*Brendan's POV.*

*Kate is there. Behind her Cosmo, Bob and Finlay are approaching.*

*Brendan stands. He has the gun in his hand. He walks towards them.*

KATE

No, Brendan, no.

*Bob pulls a gun. Finlay ruthlessly knocks the gun out of his hand and smashes him to the ground. Finlay's face is like a mask. Cosmo looks carefully at him.*

FINLAY
(*to Cosmo*)
No more. No more. Leave them alone.

*Bob is getting up. Cosmo motions him back.*

*Kate is holding Brendan back. She takes the gun away from him. Finlay approaches. Kate gives Finlay the gun.*

*Kate and Brendan start to walk up the hill.*

EXT. QUAYSIDE – NIGHT

*A police car with its lights flashing and siren on is speeding towards The Side.*

    CUT TO:

*Kate and Brendan on the crossroad of The Side and Mosley Street. Kate stops a cab, and they get in. A fire engine passes them and turns on to The Side.*

INT. TAXI – NIGHT

*The taxi is pulling away.*

TAXI DRIVER

Where to?

*Brendan and Kate look at each other. Brendan puts his arm around Kate.*

*High-angle shot of the taxi, traffic building up behind it.*

# Liebestraum

# CAST AND CREW

## MAIN CAST

| | |
|---|---|
| NICK KAMINSKY | Kevin Anderson |
| JANE KESSLER | Pamela Gidley |
| PAUL KESSLER | Bill Pullman |
| LILLIAN ANDERSON | Kim Novak |
| SHERIFF RICKER | Graham Beckel |
| BARNARD RALSTON IV | Zach Grenier |
| DR PARKER | Thomas Kopache |
| MARY PARKER | Catherine Hicks |
| NURSE/WHORE | Anne Lange |
| MIKE | Jack Wallace |

## MAIN CREW

| | |
|---|---|
| *Directed by* | Mike Figgis |
| *Written by* | Mike Figgis |
| *Produced by* | Eric Fellner |
| *Co-producer* | Michael Flynn |
| *Original Music by* | Mike Figgis |
| *Non-original Music by* | Franz Liszt, from *Liebestraum* |
| *Cinematography by* | Juan Ruiz Anchía |
| *Film Editing by* | Martin Hunter |
| *Post-production Supervisor* | Virginia Allan |
| *Production Design by* | Waldemar Kalinowski |
| *Costume Design by* | Sharon Simonaire |

*As the credits appear on black we hear the sound of a violent thunderstorm. The perspective is from inside a building. We hear voices.*

VOICE 1

Goodnight. Have a good weekend, Mr Munsen.

VOICE 2

Thanks. You too. I'll lock up.

FADE UP ON:

INT. MUSIC STORE – NIGHT

*We see a couple of grand pianos in half light. The shadow of a man comes into shot and he turns off lights. The camera starts to move and we see more of the music store. The man comes into shot and turns out the remaining lights by the counter. He walks to the doorway of an office and hesitates for a moment in the light coming from within before going inside.*

*Titles on black. The thunder and rain intensifies.*

INT. OFFICE – NIGHT

*The man's hands come into tight shot. He has a 78 record which he places on to a portable, stainless-steel phonograph. His hands shake as he places the needle on to the record. The music begins. It is* Liebestraum *by Earl Bostic. This is an early 1950s jazz version based on Liszt's melody.*

*The camera tilts up and just before we cut to a new angle we catch a glimpse of a woman in white on the other side of the room.*

ANGLE

*We see the man in shadow looking to camera. The woman in white walks into shot and spins. Tight shot on her feet in high heels as she*

*hesitates and then begins walking deliberately towards the man.*
*Tight shot on her hands as she begins unbuttoning her blouse. Tight*
*shot of their feet as his two-tone shoes go between her high heels.*
*Titles on black. The perspective of the storm changes to exterior.*

EXT. STREET — NIGHT

*An impressive four-storey cast-iron building fills the frame. The rain*
*is very heavy. In the foreground a black period Cadillac comes to a*
*halt.*

TIGHT REVERSE ANGLE *shows the driver to be in his mid-thirties*
*with a moustache and a hat. He looks up at the building.*

INT. OFFICE

*The man and woman are making love against a desk. They tear at*
*each other's clothes and he caresses her breasts.*

EXT. STREET

*The Cadillac drives out of shot and the camera slowly zooms in on*
*the one lit window.*

INT. OFFICE

*The couple making love on the desk. As the camera pulls back we see*
*that they are being reflected in a photograph of the cast-iron build-*
*ing.*

EXT. REAR OF THE BUILDING

*A large truck with the name 'Ralston' is parked. The Cadillac comes*
*around the corner and stops. The headlights are switched off.*

INT. OFFICE

*The camera slowly zooms in on the phonograph, the record spinning.*

*The lovers reflected in the phonograph.*

*Zoom in tighter on the phonograph.*

EXT. REAR OF BUILDING

*The man in the hat walks towards the building through the rain. He opens a door and goes inside.*

INT. BUILDING — FIRE STAIRS

*The man in the hat climbs the stairs wearily and pauses by a large window. Outside a freight train is passing. He looks up and then exits frame. In the distance we can hear the sound of the record finishing. The camera zooms in on the train.*

*In black we hear the sound of lovemaking mixed with the sound of the phonograph-needle trapped in the play out groove of the record. A door opens slowly and we see into the office. On the far side are the lovers.*

> MAN
>
> This is crazy.

> WOMAN
>
> Don't stop. Stay in me . . . come in me . . . tell me you love me . . . say it.

*Close-up on the record spinning.*

> MAN
>
> I love you.

> WOMAN
>
> Then make a baby in me.

*Close-up of the woman's face. She screams. We hear a loud gunshot. Medium shot of the two of them as he takes a bullet hit in his back. A 78 record hits the tiled floor and shatters . . . Very tight shot of the record spinning. We hear the woman screaming . . . a second gunshot. Tight shot of her face as she is hit . . . One of her shoes drops to the tiled floor . . . Tight shot of the record spinning . . . Her hand pushes a pile of records off the desk and she falls across frame . . . The records fall and smash . . . The spinning record slows up and stops. We can read the label.* Liebestraum *by Earl Bostic and his orchestra on the King record label. We hear a third gunshot.*

*Fade to black. Silence for a moment and then the sound of a train in a tunnel.*

TITLE: THIRTY YEARS LATER

INT. CARRIAGE — DAY

*The train comes out of the tunnel and we see a man just waking from a sleep. This is Nick Kaminsky. He is in his early thirties, conservatively dressed in a suit. His tie is loosened. He is a good-looking man, but not in a conventional way. All around him are newspapers and pages of handwritten notes. The paper is the Sunday New York Times. There is an announcement from the Amtrack guard.*

> GUARD (V.O.)
> Ladies and gentlemen, we will shortly be arriving in Elderstown. Next stop will be Elderstown. Passengers for Dearville, Rostock and Bellingham are requested . . .

*Kaminsky begins tidying his papers.*

EXT. HOSPITAL — AFTERNOON

*A yellow cab pulls up in front of a large Gothic building. A sign tells us that this is the Ralston Memorial Hospital. Nick pays the cab driver and picks up his bags.*

INT. HOSPITAL

*Nick steps out of a lift and two nurses in nuns' habits smile at him. The camera tracks with him as he walks to a reception desk. A nurse looks up from her work.*

> NURSE
> Can I help you?

> NICK
> I've come to see Mrs Anderson.

> NURSE
> Visiting time is not for another hour. Are you a relative?

NICK

I'm her son.

INT. WARD — AFTERNOON

*Nick and the nurse come into the ward, which has ten beds. The camera tracks with Nick as he walks from bed to bed, stopping to look at the faces of the women, all of whom are sleeping. After the fourth he turns to the nurse.*

NICK

Which one . . . which one is my mother?

*The nurse points at a bed.*

NURSE

That one . . . I'll be outside. Please don't disturb any of the patients.

CUT TO:

ANGLE

*Nick walks into shot and looks down at his mother. He looks away and then back.*

ANGLE. HIS POV

*Her skin is very delicate, her hair is fine and prematurely grey. She is in her early fifties. She is clearly very ill, but still beautiful.*

INT. DOCTOR'S OFFICE — AFTERNOON

*Dr Parker is seated behind a large desk. A lean man wearing steel-rimmed glasses.*

DR PARKER

Your mother is a very sick woman, Mr Anderson.

NICK

Kaminsky . . . my name is Kaminsky. My mother and I have different names.

*Dr Parker looks at the file in front of him.*

DR PARKER

Ah . . . yes . . . of course.

NICK

I'd like a private room for her.

*Parker is a little uncomfortable.*

DR PARKER

Mr Kaminsky . . . your mother has only the basic insurance. In fact . . . she's over her credit limit . . .

NICK

Just give her a private room, OK? I'll take care of everything.

DR PARKER

All right.

NICK

Does my mother know anyone in Elderstown? Does she
have any friends here?

DR PARKER

Not that I know of.

NICK

Then why was she moved here?

DR PARKER

She was in a very small hospital . . . about 200 miles from
here. Here at Ralston Memorial we can offer the very lat-
est in medical care . . .

NICK

How long?

DR PARKER

We are doing everything we can.

NICK

How long?

*Parker looks very tired suddenly.*

>                    DR PARKER
> I'd say a week . . . more or less.


INT. HOTEL ROOM — EVENING

*On the wall is an old black-and-white photograph which has been torn in half. A young woman is smiling at the camera. A man's arm around her shoulder.*

ANGLE

*Nick walks in from the shower naked, toweling his hair. He looks pretty good, his body's in good shape. He walks to the window and looks out at the view. The camera moves in behind him and we see the cast-iron building featured in the opening sequence. Now the building is semi-derelict, the windows boarded up. On the roof of the building are huge metal letters spelling out R-A-L-S-T-O-N.*


EXT. MAIN STREET — NIGHT

*The street is deserted as Nick walks out of Schmidt's Diner. He stops for a moment and looks at something off-camera.*

ANGLE

*The Ralston Building at night. Nick walks into the shot and approaches the boarded-up entrance of the building. He taps the façade, which gives off a hollow, metallic sound.*

>                    NICK
> Cast iron!


INT. LOBBY — RALSTON BUILDING — NIGHT

*We see Nick peering into the dark interior of the lobby. The camera pans into the darkness and we just make out the face of a mannequin.*


INT. LOBBY OF THE HOTEL — NIGHT

*The camera moves in with Nick as he approaches the desk. The desk clerk is attending to a man and woman. Nick waits and his attention is caught by the couple's two children. They in turn stare at*

*Nick. The girl is about fourteen. Her skin is very white, her hair red and long. The boy is younger but also very pale. The desk clerk gives Nick his key.*

DREAM: *A dead tree against a night sky. White mist moves slowly. The camera tilts down and we see the girl and the boy from the lobby. The boy faces the camera but the girl is looking away. A tyre on a rope is attached to one of the branches and it swings slowly. A white picket fence defines this long and narrow garden which stops just short of a railway track. A freight train passes from left to right and the girl turns to face camera. She has her hands behind her back. As she begins to walk towards camera we begin to track back. We hear Nick's voice very closely mic'd. (We do not hear the train.)*

> NICK (V.O.)
> Give it back to me.

> GIRL
> Give it back to me.

> BOY
> Give it back to me.

> NICK
> Give it back to me . . . please.

*She continues to mimic him as she walks towards camera. The train continues to pass but we don't hear the sound of the train in any realistic way. The train is back-lit and shafts of light come through the gaps in the freight containers illuminating the girl's face as she gets closer. Nick's voice now has an edge of panic in it.*

> Give it to me or I'll tell my mom and dad.

IMAGE: *A close-up of the torn photograph that we saw earlier. It holds for a very short time. When we return to the garden image we see an older man and woman in shadow, close to the camera.*

> GIRL
> They're not your mom and dad . . .

IMAGE: *We see Nick's mother as she is now but in the same pose as in the photograph, a man's arm around her shoulder.*

... your mother's a crazy woman, everyone knows that.

*On the soundtrack the phrase 'crazy woman' repeats over and over and is mixed with a banging noise and laboured breathing that becomes sexual...*

INT. HOTEL ROOM – NIGHT

*Nick fights his way out of the dream, and as he opens his eyes we realize that it is the sound of a couple making love in the next room; the bed head is banging against the partition wall. The woman is making a lot of noise, the man is silent apart from the odd low grunt. The passion increases and Nick gets out of bed and switches on the TV, turning up the volume to drown the noise. He flicks through the stations until he finds an old black-and-white film –* Invasion of the Bodysnatchers. *Nick watches as the hero discovers that his girl has fallen asleep and become one of the bodysnatchers.*

> WOMAN
>
> I went to sleep, Miles, and it happened.

> MAN
>
> Oh, Becky.

> WOMAN
>
> They were right.

> MAN
>
> I should never have left you.

> WOMAN
>
> Stop acting like a fool, Miles, and accept us.

*Nick looks out of the window at the building and the camera begins a slow zoom towards the second-floor window where the murders took place. On TV the voices continue...*

> MAN
>
> No... never...

> WOMAN
> (*shouting*)
>
> He's in here... he's in here... get him.

*The camera ends its zoom tight on the window and we fade to black.*

TITLE: MONDAY

EXT. STREET — DAY

*Workmen are busy on the Ralston Building. We see tools being hauled up in a bucket on a pulley and a man in a hard hat leaning out to haul them in on the roof. As he does so he supports himself on the metal letters. We get a sense of danger from a combination of the height and the almost casual way that the workman behaves.*

ANGLE. WIDE SHOT OF THE BUILDING

*The empty bucket is coming down for more tools. A man steps into the foreground of the shot and looks around. He is in his early to mid-thirties. He is wearing a suit. There is a tough but likeable quality about him. This is Paul Kessler.*

PAUL

Where's Buddy . . . Hey . . . Buddy.

ANGLE

*Nick looking at the activity. Something takes his eye and he walks until he is standing next to Paul, who is talking to his foreman Buddy. Buddy walks away and Nick continues to stare at Paul. He smiles as Paul looks at him.*

NICK

Hello, Paul!

PAUL

Kaminsky . . . Kaminsky . . . Nick fucking Kaminsky!

NICK

How are you, man?

PAUL

What the fuck are you doing here?

NICK

Just what I was going to ask you. I thought you were in Chicago.

PAUL

I was, I was . . . but then I came down here . . . got an offer I couldn't refuse . . . so here I am. In Elderstown. But what about you? Jesus Christ . . . the last thing . . . you were teaching some architectural . . . post-doctoral . . . pre-sexual type thing in upstate New York . . . right?

NICK

I am.

*Paul suddenly becomes very cautious.*

PAUL

You're not here to check this out, are you?

*Nick looks suitably puzzled.*

NICK

Check what out? I'm here to see my mother, she's in hospital.

*Paul looks highly relieved.*

PAUL

That's too bad . . .

*A large truck causes them to move off the street and on to the sidewalk.*

ANGLE

*Another bucket of tools is seen going up on the pulley. The workman leaning out to guide the ropes.*

ANGLE. NICK AND PAUL

PAUL

Hey . . . I read your books . . . well, I didn't exactly read 'em. But I bought 'em . . . my wife read 'em. Says she enjoyed 'em . . .

(*laughs*)
. . . but you never can believe a woman . . .

ANGLE. THEIR POV OF THE BUILDING

PAUL (V.O.)
So what do you think of this?

NICK
Jesus, it's beautiful, isn't it? How long is it going to take?

PAUL
Four days . . . a week at the most. This is a great crew.

NICK
A week? To do what?

PAUL
Demolish it!

ANGLE

*Camera, long lens, follows a black stretch limo as it approaches the building.*

NICK (V.O.)
Oh, come on . . . You're joking.

PAUL
This fucker's coming down.

*Paul excuses himself and goes off to talk to Buddy, while Nick looks dazed and stares up at the building. The limo comes to a halt and the tinted window opens to reveal a strange-looking man with a mournful face. He is in his mid-thirties. He stares intently at the activity. This is Barnett Ralston.*

ANGLE. TOP OF THE BUILDING

*We see the workman's boots as he leans over . . .*

ANGLE

*Barnett Ralston looks up at the top of the building.*

ANGLE

*Paul and Buddy suddenly notice Ralston.*

> PAUL
>
> What the fuck is he doing here?

ANGLE

*The workman's POV as he leans out from the building.*

ANGLE

*Extreme close-up of a section of rusted metal frame. A bolt sheers off under the pressure of the workman leaning on it.*

ANGLE

*Nick watching Paul and Buddy.*

ANGLE

*Barnett Ralston looking up at . . .*

LOW ANGLE *of the building . . . The letter 'N' is falling from the top of the building.*

ANGLE

*Nick looks up and sees the letter. He runs towards Paul and Buddy.*

> NICK
>
> Watch it . . .

*He pushes them to the ground as the letter crashes through the scaffolding and smashes into the sidewalk in a cloud of dust.*

ANGLE

*Barnett Ralston caresses his face with a piece of white cloth the way a small child comforts himself with a blanket-edge. Nick helps Paul to his feet. The workman is pulled to safety by his mate on the roof. The black limo cruises away. Paul hugs Nick.*

> PAUL
>
> I owe you one.

> NICK
>
> It's lucky that I looked up.

> PAUL
No . . . I owe you one.

> NICK
Well . . . don't worry about it.

> PAUL
What are you doing tonight?

> NICK
Nothing . . . but you don't have to . . .

> PAUL
I'm having a party . . . it's my wife's birthday . . . you gotta
come.

CUT TO:

INT. HOSPITAL — PRIVATE ROOM — DAY

*A door opens and a nurse comes in carrying red roses.*

> NURSE
These are beautiful, Mr Kaminsky.

*She puts them on a bedside table and we see Nick sitting in a chair,
a book on his knee.*

That's the call button, just press it if you need anything.

*She leaves. Nick stares at his mother, who is asleep in the half-light
from the window. Nick looks down at his book.*

ANGLE

*We see that it is a textbook on cast-iron architecture. The page he is
looking at has a photograph of the Ralston Building. Nick settles in
his chair and closes his eyes.*

CUT TO:

EXT. HOSPITAL — AFTERNOON

*The black limo pulls up outside the hospital. A chauffeur gets out
and opens the passenger door.*

INT. MOTHER'S ROOM — AFTERNOON

*Nick has been sleeping. His eyes open and it takes him a moment or two to remember where he is. He glances over to where his mother is and his face registers surprise.*

*His POV: She is awake and is staring at him, has been for some time. It is a long time before she speaks.*

> MOTHER

You're Nick?

> NICK

Yes.

*She begins to turn away from him, her face twisted with emotion. She starts to cry and covers her face with her hands, her whole body shaking. Nick is alarmed and doesn't know what to do. He shouts for the nurse.*

CUT TO:

INT. TAXI — NIGHT

*Nick is sitting in the back of the taxi in the dark. The only light is from passing cars and streetlights. We only ever see the driver in the rear mirror. The scene has a strange quality. Nick is holding a bunch of red roses. He holds them close to his face to smell them.*

> TAXI DRIVER

You OK?

> NICK

I'm fine . . . going to a party.

> TAXI DRIVER

Look like you already went.
> (*pause*)
Mind if I ask you a personal question? Are you in show-biz? I mean . . . I feel like I know you . . . You in TV or what?

*Nick looks at him.*

> NICK

What?

> CUT TO:

EXT. ELDERSTOWN SUBURB — NIGHT

*The taxi drives off, leaving Nick alone in the dark. Paul's house is large and there are no other houses near it. It's many miles out of town. Nick stands still and listens to the sounds of a swinging party that come from the brightly lit windows.*

> CUT TO:

INT. PAUL'S HOUSE — NIGHT

*Nick walks into a room full of party people. He is carrying the roses. He looks around the room but there is no sign of Paul. We see Nick drinking, watching the guests who are mainly his age. Two men stare at him, and Nick finishes his drink and goes off in search of Paul. He is looking a little the worse for wear.*

INT. CORRIDOR — NIGHT

*As Nick comes to the end of the corridor he sees a waiter coming out of the kitchen.*

> WAITER

Si . . . si, Mrs Kessler.

*The waiter walks past Nick with a tray of food, and Nick walks to the kitchen door and looks in. A woman is checking something in the oven. She is wearing a simple black dress cut low over her breasts. She has very short hair, like a boy. She is very beautiful. She is unaware that Nick is watching her. He finds her extremely attractive from this first moment. She moves out of his sight.*

> NICK

Hello.

*She looks around the corner and sees Nick. The following exchange has a very intense quality. Nick is quite aggressive.*

WOMAN

Hello.

NICK

You're Paul's wife?

WOMAN

Yes . . . I am.

NICK

What's your name?

WOMAN

Jane.

NICK

Happy birthday, Jane.

JANE

Thanks . . .

*She moves out a little further to get a better look at Nick.*

I recognize you . . . from that photograph in your book . . . yeah, you're Nick.

NICK

Yeah . . . Where's Paul?

JANE

He's around.

NICK

These are for you.

*He hands her the roses.*

JANE

That's very kind of you.

*She takes the roses and smells them, stares at Nick.*

NICK

They're looking a bit sad. I hope it's not too late.

                               JANE
I don't think so. I can fix sad roses.

*She hears a door opening and looks away as . . .*

ANGLE

*Paul comes into the room.*

                               PAUL
Honey . . . you about ready because . . .

*He becomes aware of Nick. Jane gives Nick a deep look before turning away.*

   Nick Kaminsky has arrived. Great . . . great. You won't
   regret it . . . it's going to be a great party. You met my
   wife?

*Jane turns from the sink where she is putting the roses in a vase.*

                               JANE
Yes.

CUT TO:

INT. STAIRS

*Nick and Paul climb the stairs. Paul is telling how cheap house
prices are in Elderstown. They pass a drunk who is giving a girl the
eye. This is Sheriff Ricker.*

INT. MAIN PARTY ROOM

*Nick and Paul watch the action from the entrance to the loft, which
is being used as the main party room.*

                               NICK
Can I ask you a favour?

                               PAUL
Sure, anything, you saved my life.

                               NICK
That building you're going to pull down.

PAUL

The Ralston Building?

NICK

I'd like to have a closer look, maybe write something while
I'm in town. Is that possible?

PAUL

You aren't gonna say something snotty about me destroy-
ing the cultural heritage of Elderstown or anything like
that, are you?

NICK
(*laughing*)

No . . . no . . . Paul, it's just that it's a beautiful building
. . . I'd like to write something.

PAUL

You aren't gonna inflict any guilt for this?

NICK

I promise.

PAUL

OK, we're going in there at eight o'clock. You're welcome
to join us.

NICK

Why was it closed in the first place?

*A hand falls on Nick's shoulder. He turns and sees Dr Parker from
the hospital.*

DR PARKER

Young man . . . we meet again! I didn't realize you knew
our distinguished host.

NICK

Paul and I went to college together . . .

PAUL

. . . ten years ago . . . and this fucker shows up on Main
Street!

DR PARKER
Quite a coincidence . . . may I introduce my wife . . . ?

*A sexy blonde turns around. She seems a little stoned and is swaying to the music. She is a lot younger than her husband. She looks bored with the party.*

Mary . . . Mr . . . unh?

NICK
Kaminsky.

DR PARKER
Mr Kaminsky's mother is in our care at the hospital.

MARY
Good luck!

*There is an awkward silence while Paul tries to make it a joke.*

NICK
Are you in the same profession as your husband, Mrs Parker?

MARY
It's kind of connected. I work at the hospital.

*She begins to laugh and Nick laughs with her.*

NICK
Are you a doctor?

*Dr Parker comes in on their conversation.*

DR PARKER
Mary works in the pathology department, down in the morgue. Fascinating world.

MARY
It has its moments.
                    (*slides up to Paul*)
Paul . . . are you going to dance with me?

*It is clear that there is some private drama being played out here.*

ANGLE

*Jane coming up the stairs. She looks over at them ...*

> PAUL (V.O.)
> I've got some hosting to catch up on ... but Nick here
> used to be quite the mover.

ANGLE

*Mary Parker stares right back at Jane. Nick tries to get out of danc-
ing.*

> DR PARKER
> You'd be doing me a big favour.

*Mary Parker walks off without even bothering to check if Nick is
following. He finishes his drink and joins her near to where Jane is
talking to Sheriff Ricker. Nick is a little unsteady on his feet. She
slowly spins around in a stoned way.*

> NICK
> You're a really good dancer.

*She looks at him for the first time.*

> MARY
> I'm an even better fuck.

*The camera moves to Jane. She and Mary Parker stare at each
other.*

> CUT TO:

INT. BATHROOM

*Nick splashes cold water on to his face and leers at himself in the
mirror. Someone is knocking on the door.*

INT. MAIN PARTY ROOM

*Sheriff Ricker pulls a reluctant Jane on to the dance-floor.*

LANDING — OUTSIDE BATHROOM

*Nick comes out of the bathroom and is reluctant to go back to the party. He sees a partly open door and goes to take a look.*

MAIN PARTY

*On the dance-floor Paul and Mary Parker are deep in conversation.*

LANDING

*Nick walks into a dark room where something has taken his attention.*

DANCE-FLOOR

*Sheriff Ricker spins Jane around a little too enthusiastically and she almost loses her balance. She looks a little angry but continues dancing.*

INT. ROOM

*We see that the room Nick is walking into is a photographic dark-room. Lots of photographs are pinned up on the wall and Nick looks at them. The camera goes in tight on one of them. It is a window of the Ralston Building.*

DANCE-FLOOR

*Ricker is holding Jane tight and she is trying to get away from him as another dancer lurches into him and the drink that he is holding goes over Jane. Paul sees what is happening and leaves Mary to help Jane. He arrives as Ricker is trying to dab a napkin on Jane's breast.*

PAUL
I'll take it from here . . . you OK?

JANE
I'm fine, how are you? Are you having fun?

*Jane looks over to where Mary is standing.*

PAUL

Yeah . . . a great time.

JANE

Exactly.

*Jane storms off down the stairs. Paul looks a little whipped.*

INT. DARKROOM

*Nick is looking at the photographs. He hears something and as the camera moves around we see that the darkroom is connected to the bedroom. Jane crosses the doorway, taking off her dress. She walks towards the darkroom in her underwear and high heels. Nick tries to hide but there is nowhere.*

JANE

Stupid fucking bastard.

*She gets to the sink and turns on the light. She suddenly becomes aware of Nick and turns, clutching the dress to her bosom. She is really angry now.*

What the hell're you doing in my room?

NICK

I was looking at the photographs. I didn't mean to frighten you . . . They're really very good.

*They stare at each other. She is a little less angry. He is very confused.*

Who took them?

JANE

I did!

NICK

They're excellent.

*Nick looks down but makes no effort to leave.*

JANE

Are you all right?

NICK

My head . . . spinning. There's a lot of people up there . . .
had to escape. Excuse me.

*Jane looks at him a little more sympathetically. He heads for the
door but takes one last look at the photographs.*

Ralston Building . . . right?

JANE

Yes.

NICK

It's beautiful.

JANE

Yes, it is.

*Nick looks at her and smiles.*

NICK

Cast iron.

JANE

Mmm.

NICK

I'd better get back down.

*He reaches the door and then comes back.*

I'm really very . . . very sorry.

*Jane smiles at last.*

JANE

It's OK.

NICK

Goodnight.

JANE

Goodnight.

CUT TO:

MAIN ENTRANCE AREA

*The Parkers are leaving.*

> DR PARKER
>
> Say goodnight to Jane for me. I couldn't find her any-
> where.

> PAUL
>
> Yeah . . . I don't know where she went. Thanks for com-
> ing, thanks for the present. Mary . . . goodnight.

*Nick steps in to say goodbye to Paul.*

> NICK
>
> Quite a party.

> PAUL
>
> Yeah. Been a while, unh?

> NICK
>
> Yeah . . . I'd better get some sleep. Can I phone for a cab?

> PAUL
>
> No . . . absolutely not necessary. Pete?

*Sheriff Ricker is just passing.*

> Can you give Nick a ride back into town?

> RICKER
>
> Yeah . . . yeah, yeah, yeah. Ready to go?

*Ricker hops from foot to foot.*

> NICK
>
> Well . . . thanks again.

> PAUL
>
> Thank you . . . for saving my life.

> NICK
>
> Oh, fuck you.

> PAUL
>
> No . . . see you tomorrow, eight o'clock, sleep well.

CUT TO:

EXT. THE HOUSE — NIGHT

*Ricker unzips his fly as he and Nick walk to his squad car. He stands next to the driver's door and begins to piss. A couple walk past on the way to their car.*

> RICKER
>
> Nice party, unh?

*They do not answer.*

> Republicans!

*Nick waits by the passenger door while Ricker carries on pissing. He looks at Nick.*

> Get in. It's unlocked.

*Nick does so. Ricker carries on.*

> I love a good piss.

*After some considerable time Ricker finishes and gets into the squad car.*

> You can't beat that.

*He starts up the car, guns the engine and drives off at great speed, putting the car into a spin as he goes around the first corner.*

INT. SQUAD CAR — NIGHT

*This is an instant nightmare. Ricker drives very fast, very badly, using both sides of the road. Nick fastens his safety belt. Ricker gives him a look of contempt.*

> RICKER
>
> You an old friend of the Kesslers?

> NICK
>
> I was at college with Paul, this is the first time I've met his wife.

> RICKER

She's some hot little bitch, unh? If I was Kessler I'd keep her under lock and key.

> NICK

They seem like a happy couple to me.

*Ricker looks at Nick, opens his mouth and roars with laughter. The car starts to veer across the road . . . Nick flinches and at the last possible moment Ricker straightens out.*

> RICKER

I like the way you said that. They seem like a happy couple. That's great.

> NICK

I think we should slow down here.

> RICKER

You like pussy?

*The car heads straight for another car. Nick covers his eyes.*

You like it . . . or you don't like it?

*At the last moment before collision Ricker steers the car out of trouble.*

> NICK

I like it.

> RICKER

You LIKE it . . . I LOVE IT!

EXT. ROAD HOUSE — NIGHT

*The squad car, with all of its emergency lights on, drives into the parking lot and skids to a halt inches from the entrance to the bar.*

CUT TO:

INT. ROAD HOUSE — BROTHEL

*A blind girl is playing the 'Moonlight Sonata'. The camera pans up and we see Cindy, the madam of the brothel, sitting on the bar. The door opens and Ricker comes in, his arm around Nick. He staggers up to Cindy and kisses her.*

> CINDY
> Hi there, Mr Ricker. The usual? And what would your friend like?

> RICKER
> He'll have the same.

*Ricker hugs Nick as Cindy pours the drinks.*

> His name is Nick. Where's Maxine?

> CINDY
> Out on a date . . . Betty's here, though.

> RICKER
> She'll do just fine.

> CINDY
> Betty . . . room nine.

ANGLE

*We see Betty getting up from a table. Behind her there are another two girls sitting together on a sofa. Betty smiles a little apprehensively as Ricker turns to leer at her.*

> RICKER
> They're all clean . . . I have 'em checked out once a month . . . take your pick, Nick. It's on me.

*Ricker slaps Betty hard on the bottom.*

> BETTY
> Don't do that, it makes a bruise on my butt.

*Ricker puts his hand to his mouth in mock surprise and then follows Betty out. Cindy gets down off the bar and looks at Nick for a moment before going to the table where Betty was sitting. She pours herself a drink.*

CINDY

Come and sit with us, Nicky.

*He struggles to clear his head. He finishes his drink and walks over to the table and sits down opposite Cindy. The pianist is working towards the climax of the piece and the music is getting louder. Suddenly Cindy turns on her and screams.*

Annie . . . you are depressing the fuck out of everyone.

*Annie stops playing. Michele, one of the girls on the sofa, looks at Cindy.*

MICHELE

Take it easy, Cindy.

*Annie picks up her glass and smashes it on the floor. Cindy slowly turns to face Nick again.*

CINDY

Anything you'd like to do, Nicky? Michele . . . stand up. Let Nick see you.

*Michele gets up and walks over to Cindy. She is wearing a black transparent nightgown. She leans down so that her face is level with Cindy's.*

Michele's reputation is built around her mouth. It's big . . . it's perfect.

*The women look at each other. Michele sticks out her tongue and Cindy dips her finger into her drink and then strokes the tongue. Michele stands up and flicks her fingers open over her breasts. Her nails are very long and bright red.*

Sit down, Michele. Barbara . . . come here.

*Barbara stays put on the sofa and stares insolently back at Cindy.*

BARBARA

No.

*Cindy looks very angry as she gets up and walks over to the sofa.*

CINDY

Get up!

*Barbara slowly gets up and walks over to the table.*

What are you, Barbara?

*Barbara leans over and leans on the table.*

BARBARA

I'm a bad girl, ma'am.

CINDY

She can be so unpleasant . . . but, Nicky . . . You don't have to put up with any fucking nonsense from this whore . . .

*Cindy walks over to the table.*

You just put her across your knee . . .

*She slaps her hard on the bottom and Barbara smiles at Nick. Cindy sits down and they both stare at Nick. Annie has started to play again. It is the last slow section of* Liebestraum.

She has fine qualities as well. Do you like to eat?

NICK

Yes.

CINDY

Let him try some, Barbara.

*Barbara stands, hands her cigarette to Cindy and then pulls up her dress and puts her hand between her legs for a moment. She then offers the hand to Nick.*

Try some.

*Barbara advances on Nick and touches his lips with her fingers.*

Come on, Nicky . . . try some.

*Nick looks up at Barbara and then takes the fingers in his mouth and sucks them. The hand is withdrawn as the music concludes. Nick has his eyes closed. He opens them.*

FADE TO BLACK.

INT. RALSTON BUILDING — DAY

*A series of shots show the dusty interior of the building in a gloomy half-light. In the distance we can hear the sounds of activity as Paul's crew begin to break in.*

TITLE: TUESDAY

EXT. RALSTON BUILDING

*A close-up of an oxy-acetylene torch cutting through the metal bars on the main doors of the building. Through the sparks we see Jane taking photographs of the action. Nick walks into shot and watches also. Jane becomes aware of him.*

>                    JANE
> Good morning.

>                    NICK
> Morning.

*Jane takes another photograph.*

>                    JANE
> So what's so special about this building? For you, I mean.

>                    NICK
> It's cast-iron. A building like this . . . it's the missing link in American architecture.

*Jane starts to move away to get a better angle to photograph.*

>                    JANE
> What do you mean?

*Nick follows her.*

>                    NICK
> Well . . . before the cast-iron building came along . . . the height of a given structure was governed by the thickness of the outer, load-bearing walls. The higher the building

. . . the thicker the walls had to be. Eight floors was about as high as you could go.

*Jane moves again and he follows her, both looking at the building.*

These buildings were very popular with the new Barons . . . like Ralston because you could choose a style . . . Roman . . . Greek . . . this one's Victorian . . . from a catalogue.

                         JANE
Unh huh.

                         NICK
Instant European culture in Elderstown.

*Nick laughs, warming to the subject as Jane takes another picture. He touches her.*

Come here . . . I'll show you something.

ANGLE

*The torch is cutting through the metal.*

ANGLE

*Paul looks at his watch, worried, and then looks up and sees Nick and Jane talking. He looks sad.*

ANGLE

*Nick brings Jane to the façade of the building.*

You see . . . the whole of this front . . . is in sections . . . it's just bolted together and fixed on to the building.

*Jane looks at him attentively.*

But all this metal . . . it's very heavy and it has to be supported. So someone came up with the bright idea of a metal frame . . . for the entire building, instead of the traditional bricks and mortar.

                         JANE
Unh huh.

NICK

With a steel frame . . . all of the stress is shifted away from
the outer walls . . . to the horizontal . . . so that the support comes from the centre. You can go as high as you
like.

*Jane smiles at him.*

JANE

Hence the sky-scraper.

*Nick goes a bit quiet and then looks at her.*

NICK

You know all this, don't you?

JANE

I read your book on cast iron. I just wanted to know if you
were as passionate about it as you seemed.

NICK

I'm passionate about it.

JANE

Good . . . it must be nice to be one of your students.

*Jane walks away, leaving Nick alone.*

ANGLE

*The torch cuts through the last section of metal and it falls away.*

INT. RALSTON BUILDING

*We see a silhouette against the dirty glass of the main doors and
then the doors open, knocking down a mannequin and raising some
dust. Paul and Nick and Jane come in holding flashlights, followed
by Buddy and the crew. The camera slowly cranes down from a high
position.*

PAUL

Jesus . . . I don't believe this.

JANE

I do.

NICK

This is fantastic . . . did you know all of this stuff was in here?

PAUL

No . . . Buddy. Look at this fucking mess. What are we going to do?

BUDDY

It's not going to be a problem. I'll bring some dealers in.

*Nick and Jane proceed further into the building.*

PAUL

Jane, Jane. Where are you going?

JANE

I'm right here.

PAUL

Be careful. I don't know about the floorboards.

ANGLE

*A hand wipes away the dust from a store directory.*

PAUL (V.O.)

OK . . . let's bring some power in here.

EXT. STREET — DAY

*A workman starts up a generator.*

INT. STORE

*One by one the interior lights come on and we see a whole department of the store lit up.*

CUT TO:

INT. SCHMIDT'S DINER – LUNCHTIME

*The place is jumping with the lunchtime crowd. Nick, Paul and Jane are having a sandwich and a coffee at one of the tables. Nick is quite worked up.*

NICK

Paul . . . that's a cast-iron building over there. It's fucking crazy to knock it down. What do these townspeople think?

PAUL

They don't give a shit, they hate the place, it's a bad memory for most of them . . . they'll probably give me a medal.

*Jane has been listening quietly.*

JANE

If they don't, the Glendale Development Corporation certainly will.

*Paul glares at her and there is a flash of something between them. He smashes his fist on to the table and shouts . . .*

PAUL

The fucking place is coming down. No more crap . . .

*His bleeper goes off and he reaches for it.*

. . . everything is done. We have dates, we have contracts. In six months' time there will be a busy, successful shopping mall, the Ralston Centre . . .

*He stands and turns his attention to Nick.*

. . . and one more thing . . . Nick, remember you promised me last night . . . you are not going to fuck the whole thing up with this article . . . right? I'm not the bad guy.

*Paul goes off to make his call leaving Nick and Jane together. They are both a little shell-shocked.*

JANE

I'm sorry.

ANGLE. SCHMIDT'S PHONE BOOTH

*We see Paul on the phone in a booth. He is having a very heated conversation. We can see from this and the previous scene that he is under a lot of pressure.*

ANGLE. NICK AND JANE

*The outburst has created a kind of intimacy for them. Jane looks at Nick.*

> JANE
>
> So . . . are you going to write something about the building?

> NICK
>
> I'd like to. I've never seen anything like that before.

> JANE
>
> I know.

> NICK
>
> How about you? Are you going to photograph that?

*Jane smiles.*

> JANE
>
> You bet.

ANGLE. TELEPHONE BOOTH

*Paul slams the phone down and looks at Nick and Jane talking for a moment before setting off.*

ANGLE. TABLE

*The waitress is serving coffee as Paul arrives. He sits down and looks a little dejected. He reaches out and touches Jane.*

> PAUL
>
> I'm sorry.

> JANE
> (*cool*)
>
> It's OK . . . what's up?

PAUL

Oh . . . the architect's fucked up again. I've got to go to
Chicago tomorrow.

JANE

For how long?

PAUL

Oh . . . a day . . . maybe two.

*Nick is very uncomfortable.*

NICK

I should get to the hospital.

*Paul turns to him.*

PAUL

Nick . . . I was thinking. Are you going to need any photographs for that article? . . . because Jane's work is very
good.

*Nick doesn't quite know how to react. Nor does Jane.*

CUT TO:

INT. HOSPITAL ROOM — AFTERNOON

*A screen is removed from around Nick's mother's bed. She looks
very drawn and ill. The nurses exit and one of them speaks to Nick,
who is standing by the door watching.*

NURSE

She's been in a lot of pain today. We've just given her
some morphine. It'll make her sleepy, I'm afraid.

*The nurse exits. Nick's mother is not yet aware that he is in the
room. There is a TV at the foot of the bed and she is watching an
afternoon 'soap' with the sound down low. She gives off a high nervous energy and her hands tremble and play with the sheets. She
looks from the TV to the window, the two sources of light in the
room. Nick waits for a while before speaking.*

NICK

Hello, Mother.

*She still doesn't look at him. Nick goes to the bed and sits next to her. She looks up at him.*

MOTHER

Jesus . . .
          (*laughs and shakes her head*)
I think you're even prettier than that son of a bitch was. Yes, I think so.

*Nick smiles.*

Do you have a cigarette?

NICK

No, I don't.

MOTHER

You don't smoke?

NICK

Sometimes.

MOTHER

He smoked two packs a day. They won't let me smoke here, they say it's bad for my health. Bring me a pack next time you come.

*A pain spasm hits her and her whole body tenses and then relaxes as it passes.*

That's better. Sometimes the pain is like a knife. It's my punishment, you know.

NICK

No . . . stop that . . . you mustn't say that.

*She rests for a while. Her eyes are closed.*

MOTHER

Nick . . . I asked them to contact you. It must be very upsetting. I'm sorry.

NICK

Don't be. I'm glad you did.

MOTHER

Really?

NICK

Really. How did you find me?

MOTHER

Couple of years ago . . . I was in a bookshop and I saw your picture. I got a real shock. I knew it was you before I saw the name. I have all your books, over there in the drawer. Are you writing another?

NICK

Yes, I am. I'm going to dedicate it to you.

MOTHER

I'd be so proud, Nick.

*She takes his hand and there is a very strong feeling between the two of them. She looks up at him, tears in her eyes.*

He was so handsome . . .

*She hesitates for a moment and then decides to carry on.*

One night . . . he came in very late. I was carrying you, I was awake. He came in real quiet so's not to disturb me, so I didn't let on. He slipped into bed . . . was asleep in minutes . . . His hand was there on the pillow between us . . . I gently took it and began to kiss the fingers, one by one . . .

*She looks at Nick, a desperate expression on her face.*

. . . and I could smell the cunt on them.

*She closes her eyes and Nick looks away . . . lost.*

CUT TO:

INT. RALSTON BUILDING — LATE AFTERNOON

*At first the screen is black and then a camera move reveals a section of the store. Jane is walking around looking at things to photograph. She sees Nick, silhouetted against a window. She hesitates.*

JANE

Nick?

*He turns and Jane sees that he is upset.*

Is your mother OK?

NICK

She's . . .

*He can't get anything out. He covers his face with his hands and cries.*

JANE

Are you all right? .

*He shakes his head and turns into the wall. She puts her bag down and goes to him, placing herself between him and the wall. She holds his head as he cries.*

Hey . . . it's all right.

*She kisses him gently. They look at each other for a moment and then he kisses her hard and she responds. They part and he looks away.*

CUT TO:

EXT. SCHMIDT'S DINER — NIGHT

*A car drives by.*

INT. SCHMIDT'S

*Paul and Nick are sitting at the bar, drinking. Paul seems quite drunk. They clink glasses and drink. A customer eyes Paul cautiously.*

PAUL

Jane used to have really long hair . . . it was beautiful . . .
she could sit on it. And then she cut it all off . . .

*Paul stares into space. He seems quite dangerous.*

She found a pair of black lace panties in the back of my
pick-up . . .

*He stares at Nick and Nick keeps quiet, wondering where all this is
leading. Paul signals to the barmaid.*

Diane . . . just one more . . . for the road. And then I have
to go home . . . I have to pack . . . did I say that already?

NICK

No.

*Paul's expression changes, his mood becomes ugly as he turns on
Nick.*

PAUL

I have said that already . . . you fuck.

*Nick takes a drink. Paul slams his glass down on the counter.*

This cast-iron building . . . you can come and go as you
please . . . just don't come in Jane.

*Nick starts to protest, looks baffled. Paul puts his arm around Nick's
shoulders and then pulls him towards him, gently at first and then
increasing the pressure around his neck using both hands. He is very
strong.*

NICK

Paul, what are you doing, Paul?

PAUL

I'm fucking serious, Nick.

*Paul holds him tight for a moment and then lets him go, awkwardly.*

Hey . . . I gotta have one . . . for the road, and then I gotta
pack. I . . . already said that once . . . didn't I?

INT. HOTEL ROOM – NIGHT

*Nick falls on to the bed and closes his eyes. The camera moves off the bed into the dark . . .*

IMAGE: *Jane wearing the black dress from the party, spinning around. The camera move takes it to the window and it begins to zoom into the Ralston Building.*

MIX TO: IMAGE: *Jane stops spinning and undoes the strap to her dress. She lowers the top of the dress and cups her breast which is now exposed.*

IMAGE: *Nick's mother, her face contorted with rage, moves her head from side to side.*

IMAGE: *Jane looks directly into the camera whilst caressing her breast.*

MIX TO: IMAGE: *The camera slowly moves over a figure covered in a white sheet. There is some sensual movement under the sheet. The move continues and then reveals Jane in bed. Her hand is inside her nightdress, touching her breast and she is just waking from a dream. The camera moves back and we see Paul beside her in bed. His hand is between her legs. She is very aroused. His hand moves up her body and she turns away from him and curls her body up. He rolls on to his back and stares at the ceiling.*

FADE TO BLACK.

TITLE: WEDNESDAY

EXT. RALSTON STORE ENTRANCE – MORNING

*Nick opens the main doors and walks into the deserted building.*

INT. RALSTON BUILDING

*Nick walks into one of the rooms and looks around. He sees something and walks towards camera. The camera moves with him and reveals Jane, who is preparing her cameras. She looks sad. She turns as he approaches.*

NICK

Morning.

JANE

Good morning.

NICK

You're early.

JANE

I . . . wanted to get my equipment set up. I was a little nervous.

*There is a long silence. Nick stands behind her, looking at her.*

There's a coffee there for you.

NICK

Thanks.

*As he picks up the coffee she turns to look at him and then turns away again.*

JANE

You look a little better than Paul did this morning.

NICK

This is a hard-drinking town, I don't know how long I'd survive.

*He moves right behind Jane.*

What are you nervous about?

JANE

We haven't talked or anything . . . I don't know what you want.

NICK

I don't know either . . . I'd just like to capture everything . . . just the way it is right now.

MONTAGE: *Shots of the building – Jane taking photographs – Nick watching her work. The music here is a sad piano blues which we will come to associate with Nick and Jane.*

ANGLE

*Jane taking a photograph. She is holding a shutter-release cable and counting before releasing it.*

> JANE
>
> My . . . father . . . was a photographer, weddings, that kind of thing, so I've known how to use a camera since I was very small. I used to help him print . . . I gave it all up when I went to college.

*Nick walks into the shot, looking at what she is photographing.*

> NICK
>
> What made you take it up again?

*Jane looks down at her viewfinder.*

> JANE
>
> Paul.

EXT. RALSTON ENTRANCE – DAY

*Workmen are carrying out things from the store. Dealers are looking at carpets and furniture and there is a lot of activity as Nick and Jane walk out of the building. Jane points at a beaten-up, red pick-up truck.*

> JANE
>
> Here.

> NICK
>
> A pick-up?

> JANE
>
> What did you expect?

> NICK
>
> I dunno . . . a Volvo.

*They both get in the pick-up, laughing, and Jane starts up the engine and drives off. This is all watched with great interest by Buddy, who is talking to a dealer.*

EXT. RALSTON MEMORIAL HOSPITAL — DAY

*The red pick-up pulls up outside the hospital entrance.*

> JANE
> This must be very difficult for you. Are you very close?

> NICK
> It's strange . . . I never met my mother before this week.
> My father was killed in a car accident . . . just before I was
> born. She went . . . kind of went crazy for a while.

*He looks at Jane.*

> I was adopted.

*Jane looks very startled and turns her head away.*

> What?

> JANE
> I was adopted.

*She changes the subject quickly.*

> Is that why you don't drive . . . because of your father?

*Nick starts to get out of the car.*

> NICK
> Kind of. I just like being driven around by beautiful
> women. Thanks for the ride.

*He smiles at her, she at him, closes the door and walks away.*

> CUT TO:

INT. HOSPITAL ROOM

*From the doorway we see Nick's mother in bed. She is very still. We
hear footsteps and then Nick comes in.*

> MOTHER
> Hello, Nick. How are you?

> NICK
>
> I'm good, how about you?

> MOTHER
>
> Just great, much better. Come and sit over here, by me.

*Nick sits by the bed.*

> I want to talk to you. I'm not crazy you know . . .

*Nick starts to protest. The camera begins a slow move in on her face.*

> I know what's happening inside of me.

> NICK
>
> This is a good hospital . . . the best . . .

> MOTHER
>
> Don't bullshit me, Nick. It's true, isn't it?

*Nick's head drops and he nods. She smiles.*

> Did you bring the smokes?

*Nick fishes in his pocket and brings out a bottle of Scotch.*

> NICK
>
> Let's have a drink.

> MOTHER
>
> Better close the door.

CUT TO:

INT. RALSTON BUILDING — DAY

*High angle looking down. Some dealers are just leaving as Jane comes in. It seems very dark in the building and the music which has been playing through the previous scene takes on a slightly menacing quality. Jane begins photographing and has her back to the camera as it begins to crane down from its high position to just behind her. She turns, as if aware of something, and the camera cranes up, back to its high position. In the following cross-cut sequence the music does much of the linking.*

INT. HOSPITAL ROOM

*Nick's mother is holding a cigarette. The ash is long and she never actually smokes it. In her other hand is a small glass of whiskey.*

MOTHER
Have you ever had morphine?

NICK
No. What's it like?

MOTHER
Well . . . you have no idea of time. Sometimes I'm a little girl . . . I see my father . . . my mother . . . I talk with them. Sometimes I think I'm dead already. The first day you came was like that . . . when I was still in the other room. You came in with the nurse . . .

INT. RALSTON BUILDING

*At first the screen is black but then a camera move reveals Jane from a high angle through some banisters at the top of the stairs. Nick's mother's voice continues over this scene.*

MOTHER (V.O.)
. . . you didn't recognize me of course . . . but I knew it was you . . .

*Jane moves to the foot of the stairs and begins to climb.*

. . . she pointed at my body.

INT. HOSPITAL

*Nick stares intently at his mother.*

MOTHER
. . . sometimes I'm with your father.

*She drinks the Scotch.*

NICK
What was my father like?

*There is a knock at the door. Nick hastily finishes his drink as the nurse comes in.*

                              NURSE
     Mrs Anderson . . .

*She notices the drink and cigarettes.*

     I think Dr Parker will have something to say about this.

INT. RALSTON BUILDING

*A bright red glass vase, bathed in light, dominates the screen. Behind it, in the gloom, we see Jane walking towards camera. Suddenly she hits light . . .*

EXT. HOSPITAL

*Nick runs down the steps to the taxi rank. A man stands next to a taxi reading a German newspaper.*

                              NICK
     Can I get a ride back into town?

*The man lowers his paper and nods at Nick.*

     Are you the driver?

*The man thinks carefully before speaking.*

                              MAN
     I . . . don't . . . speak English.

                              NICK
     All right . . . forget it . . . thanks.

                              MAN
     Goodbye.

INT. RALSTON BUILDING — MUSIC ROOM

*Through a half-open door we see the silver metal phonograph that was in the opening sequence. It is on the desk. Jane crosses frame from right to left. She looks down at the floor.*

ANGLE

*On the floor we see broken pieces of 78 records.*

ANGLE

*She walks to the desk and picks up a record sleeve, blows the dust off it. The dust hangs in the air like a ghost. On the record sleeve is written 'Ralston'. She puts down the sleeve and opens the lid of the phonograph. There is a record on the turntable, covered in a fine layer of dust. Jane wipes it off the label to read the title. It is upside down so she turns the record to read it. The needle is on the record and the movement of the record causes the turntable to start spinning. As it does so we see . . .*

FLASH IMAGE: *The two lovers from the opening sequence lying on the floor covered in blood. The record gets up to speed and we hear that it is the music from the opening sequence.* Liebestraum *by Earl Bostic.*

ANGLE. *Jane.*

*She closes her eyes and listens to the music. Tears run down her cheeks. The camera begins a slow move in on her.*

FLASH IMAGE: *The lovers.*

ANGLE. *The record spinning.*

ANGLE. *Jane.*

*From the darkness behind her a hand comes on to her shoulder. She opens her eyes but is not frightened. She turns and we see that it is Nick. After a moment she takes the needle off the record.*

> NICK
> I was looking for you . . . are you all right?

*Jane looks at him.*

> JANE
> Let's get back downstairs.

CUT TO:

INT. RALSTON BUILDING — MAIN SPACE

MONTAGE OF DESTRUCTION: *Nick and Jane, both wearing face masks, photograph the destruction of the store. The noise is deafening. Workmen with sledgehammers smash the fittings whilst others carry out objects. The air is filled with dust. Sequence ends with a close-up of Nick watching the carnage.*

EXT. RALSTON BUILDING

*The black stretch Cadillac drives off, revealing a group of old people watching the building.*

INT. RALSTON BUILDING — LATE AFTERNOON

*Everything is quiet now. Nick and Jane sit by the window where they kissed the day before. She is cleaning her cameras with an air spray.*

> NICK
> What are you going to do now?

> JANE
> Go home and develop these films.

> NICK
> Will you have a drink with me . . . first?

*Jane concentrates hard on cleaning a lens and then looks up at him.*

> JANE
> I don't think that's such a good idea.

> NICK
> Why?

> JANE
> We both know why . . .

*She carries on cleaning the cameras.*

> . . . I should go home . . . take a shower . . .

NICK
Use mine.

*Jane concentrates hard on what she is doing and speaks very softly.*

JANE
All right.

*She looks at him for a long time.*

CUT TO:

INT. HOTEL LOBBY

*The desk clerk stares at Nick and Jane, who are waiting for the lift. Both of them look very dirty. Behind them an electrician is working on some exposed wiring. The lift arrives and they get in.*

INT. BEDROOM

*We see the torn photograph on the wall. Jane walks around to look at it. The bathroom door opens and Nick comes out, a towel around his neck, his hair wet.*

JANE
Is that your mother?

NICK
Yeah.

JANE
She was very beautiful.

NICK
Yes . . . she was.

JANE
Who's the man?

NICK
I dunno . . . my father, I guess.

*Jane goes into the bathroom and Nick stares at the photograph.*

ANGLE

*Jane in the shower.*

ANGLE

*Nick lying on the bed. The phone rings and he looks at his watch, not expecting a call.*

ANGLE

*Jane towelling her hair by the mirror. She reacts to the sound of the phone.*

ANGLE

*Nick picks up the phone.*

> NICK

Hello . . .

ANGLE. *Jane by the mirror.*

. . . hey, Paul . . .

ANGLE. *Nick.*

. . . she left about twenty minutes ago. She said she had to pick up some dry cleaning or something so she should be on her way home . . . bye.

*Nick puts the phone down and curses. He gets off the bed.*

ANGLE. *Jane listens. Through the door.*

Jane?

> JANE

Yes.

> NICK

I left something in the building. I'll see you down there, OK?

> JANE

OK . . . I'll meet you there.

*She looks at herself in the mirror.*

INT. RALSTON BUILDING LOBBY

*Nick slams his keys down on to a glass counter and swears. He walks up to a group of mannequins and shoves them hard, knocking them over.*

> NICK
> Shit . . . fuck.

INT. RESTAURANT — NIGHT

*Nick and Jane face each other in a booth. The place is quite full and noisy. They are both drinking beer. Jane is smoking.*

> NICK
> This isn't right. I pushed it. I'm sorry.

> JANE
> Don't be sorry . . . so what are we going to do?

> NICK
> Nothing I guess. It's just that I . . .

*He touches her hand.*

> JANE
> I really like you too.

*They hold hands.*

> NICK
> OK.

> JANE
> Let's go. I want to show you something.

INT. HOSPITAL — NIGHT

*A needle is pushed into an arm. We see the night nurse.*

> NIGHT NURSE
> There. That should make you feel better, Mrs Anderson.

ANGLE. *Nick's mother.*

                    MOTHER
Stay with me a while.

                 NIGHT NURSE
What's the matter?

                    MOTHER
I'm frightened.

*It is now possible to see that the same actress who played Cindy in the whorehouse is also playing night nurse. The same is true of the other whores: they are also the other nurses.*

EXT. STREET — NIGHT

*Jane's pick-up pulls up outside a large Victorian mansion which is floodlit.*

                     JANE
I thought this might interest you. It was built by the same architect who designed the store.

                     NICK
I like the store better. Who lives there?

                     JANE
The last surviving Ralston. Barnett Ralston the . . . fourth.

*Someone comes out of the house. The black stretch limo is parked by the door, the chauffeur waiting.*

That's him.

*She turns off the engine and the headlights. Ralston stops to light a cigarette before getting into his car.*

                     NICK
What happened to the rest of the family?

                     JANE
You don't know . . . about the murders? That's why the store was closed down. His mother was having an affair with an employee. They used to meet at the store, very late at night . . . and his father found out.

*The limo drives out of the entrance and exits.*

> . . . and he caught them one night . . . and he shot them
> . . . and then he killed himself. The next day, when the
> police found the bodies, they discovered that she was still
> alive. She'd been shot in the head. She was brain dead, but
> still alive.

*Nick strokes the back of Jane's head.*

> The Ralston Memorial Hospital was opened the following
> year.

NICK

She must be dead by now.

JANE

Yes, she must be.

*Jane closes her eyes as Nick continues stroking her.*

NICK

Jane . . .

*She turns to him and they kiss.*

CUT TO:

INT. HOSPITAL — NIGHT

*Nick's mother is almost asleep but her lips move feverishly. She is
very disturbed.*

MOTHER

I wouldn't have hurt him . . . please don't . . . don't take
him away from me . . .

NIGHT NURSE

No one is going to take him away . . . shhh.

*The nurse strokes her hand gently.*

CUT TO:

EXT. HOTEL — NIGHT

*The pick-up drives off and Nick walks over to the hotel entrance.
The door is locked and the night porter is asleep, his leg in a cast.
Nick curses as he remembers leaving his keys in the Ralston Build-
ing.*

INT. RALSTON BUILDING

*At first it is black and then we hear the door opening and a shaft of
light reveals the keys on the glass counter where Nick left them. Nick
picks them up and the camera moves up to his face just as he hears
something. It is the sound of a woman.*

ANGLE

*Nick on the stairs, listening. He begins to climb.*

ANGLE

*Nick in the Music Department. He shines a flashlight around. We
hear the sound of piano strings and he shines his flashlight on to one
of the grand pianos. Nick walks towards the piano and takes a step
up on to a little stage. He looks into the open lid of the piano and
there is a tremendous noise as a cat jumps out leaving a dead rat
behind. Nick gets a huge fright.*

ANGLE

*Nick comes down the foot of the stairs into a group of mannequins.*

                              NICK
        Fucking cat . . . scared the living shit out of me.

*He walks through the mannequins and again he hears something.
He looks around but everything is still. He carries on, but frightened
now. Suddenly we see a figure move quickly behind a mannequin.
Nick looks at the space and slowly Barnett Ralston appears.*

                            RALSTON
        Munsen?

*He begins to walk towards Nick, who runs through the mannequins,
knocking them over. He trips and falls, striking his head against the*

*edge of a counter. Ralston's face fills the screen as he looks down at
Nick.*

Munsen . . . you're dead.

DISSOLVE TO:

INT. JANE'S DARKROOM

*In the red safety light we see Jane in her bra and pants working on
her photographs. She pulls a print out of a tray and holds it up to
inspect it. We see that it is a photograph of Nick.*

DISSOLVE TO:

INT. RALSTON BUILDING — DAWN

*Nick lying in a pool of blood in the grey dawn light coming from the
open door. The camera is above him and moves down as he wakes
and touches his head.*

CUT TO:

BLACK.

TITLE: THURSDAY

*In black we hear very loud noises of destruction and then as the pic-
ture fades in we see the feet of workmen as they go about the business
of demolition in the building. We see a pair of high-heeled shoes and
the camera pans up to reveal Jane as she comes into the building
looking for Nick. She covers her ears to block out the din and walks
carefully over splintered wood and debris. She looks up the stairs
and sees Nick as he comes down. He has a band-aid on his forehead. They stand close together at the foot of the stairs.*

JANE

Hi.

NICK

Hi.

                          JANE
    I'm late . . . sorry.

                          NICK
    It's all right.

*She sees the cut on his head.*

                          JANE
    What happened to you?

                          NICK
    I fell.

                          JANE
    It looks pretty dirty . . .

                          NICK
    Can we get out of here?

    CUT TO:

EXT. PAUL AND JANE'S HOUSE – DAY

*Jane's pick-up pulls up outside her house.*

INT. HOUSE

*A maid is cleaning the hall as Nick and Jane come in. Jane is surprised.*

                          MAID
    Hi, Mrs Kessler.

                          JANE
    Maria . . . what are you doing here?

                          MAID
    I always come on Thursdays, Mrs Kessler.

                          JANE
    Oh . . . right . . . OK.

*Nick and Jane exit.*

INT. DARKROOM — DAY

*Nick looks at the photograph of himself that Jane has pinned up on the wall along with the pictures of the building. He is very serious. He is hardly recognizable as the same person from three days earlier. Jane is cleaning the cut on his head.*

> NICK
>
> The guy that was killed in the building, not Ralston, the other guy, what was his name?

> JANE
>
> His name was Munsen.

*Nick looks up at her. She has her hands on his head. He slides her skirt up and touches her. She drops the cotton swab that she was holding and holds her skirt as he puts his hand between her legs. She moves back to the wall where the pictures are.*

> Don't do that.

*Nick stands and walks to her. He touches her breasts and she covers his hands with hers. As they kiss . . .*

ANGLE

*The maid passes the open door and sees them. She turns away. Jane moves away from Nick.*

> MAID
>
> Shall I do the bathroom now, Mrs Kessler?

CUT TO:

INT. HOSPITAL ROOM — DAY

*Nick's mother is bright and cheerful as a young nurse fusses around her bed straightening the sheets.*

> MOTHER
>
> What's the time, nurse?

> NURSE
>
> Your son will be here soon, Mrs Anderson.

EXT. HOSPITAL

*Jane's pick-up comes around the corner.*

INT. HOSPITAL

> NURSE
> Here . . . I've brought you a newspaper to read.

*The nurse gives Nick's mother a local paper to look at.*

EXT. HOSPITAL

*Nick kissing Jane passionately through the window of the pick-up.*

INT. HOSPITAL

*We see a blurred image that comes into focus as the Ralston Building. It is the front page of the newspaper.*

> MOTHER
> Nurse, what town are we in? What's the name of this town?

*The nurse is worried by the tone of her voice and answers cautiously.*

> NURSE
> Why, surely you know, Mrs Anderson, we're in Elders-town, of course.

ANGLE

*Mother makes a huge effort to get out of bed, finding reserves of strength that should have been long exhausted.*

> Oh . . . don't get out of bed, Mrs Anderson.

*She tries to stop her but cannot. She shouts.*

> Sister!

INT. HOSPITAL CORRIDOR

*As Nick steps out of the lift he hears a frail scream. He stops and listens . . .*

ANGLE

*The door opens and the sister runs in to help the nurse. Nick's mother is out of control, screaming and crying as she tries to escape from the bed. Nick comes into the room and sees all this. He is very upset. The sister eases him out of the room.*

SISTER

I think it would be better if you waited outside, Mr Kaminsky.

CUT TO:

INT. DR PARKER'S OFFICE

*Nick, alone in the office waiting for Dr Parker. He sees his mother's file on the desk and he picks it up and begins looking through it.*

TEXT: *Widespread cancer . . . further surgery not advisable . . . fourth term in mental institute . . . treatment for depression . . .*

*Nick skips lots of pages and arrives near the front of the file.*

TEXT: *Patient wishes to revert to maiden name of Anderson.*

ANGLE. *Nick's face.*

*Nick is very puzzled by this. He slowly turns the page one nearer to the front of the file.*

CLOSE UP ON THE PAGE

*On the top of the page is his mother's married name.*

TEXT: *MUNSEN, LILLIAN (MRS)*

*Extreme close-up of Nick's eyes as he absorbs this information.*

CUT TO:

INT. POLICE STATION – FILE ROOM

*Sheriff Ricker leads Nick around the room. Shelves are stuffed with old files. Ahead of them is a clerk.*

>                          RICKER
> If anybody can find this, Matt can.

>                          MATT
> Ralston . . . Ralston . . . Ralston . . . it's around here some
> place.

*Matt climbs a ladder and we see his face in close-up framed by files
as he looks for it.*

> I remember the case well. I was just a rookie at the time. I
> was the first cop on the scene . . . lotta blood, whole lotta
> blood. Guys pecker was still up like a pole . . . good-looking
> broad . . . what a waste, took the lab boys for ever to get
> there . . . and I was staring at her and . . . noticed this little
> vein in her neck was still kind of . . . throbbing . . .

ANGLE

*Nick lost in thought below as Ricker leers at him.*

> Ah . . . here it is.

*He hands the file down to Ricker, who hesitates before handing it
over to Nick. Nick walks away with the file.*

>                          RICKER
> Nick . . .

*Nick turns.*

> They seem like a real happy couple.

> CUT TO:

EXT. MAIN STREET – LATE AFTERNOON

*Nick is walking quickly down the street. He is very agitated and
breaks into a run. He is carrying the file.*

> CUT TO:

INT. HOTEL ROOM

*The door opens and Nick comes in but then stops short.*

*Nick's POV.*

*The room has been gutted. All his things have gone. The furniture has gone. The floorboards have been ripped up. Bared cable can be seen. We hear the sound of the desk clerk approaching.*

                          CLERK
Ah . . . Mr Kaminsky . . . The electricians had a change of plan, Mr Kaminsky, and they needed to get to the wiring in your room. We've moved all your things into the adjoining room. It's exactly the same size.

                          NICK
The room where the couple were staying?

*The clerk looks puzzled.*

                          CLERK
There's nobody else on this floor, Mr Kaminsky, just you . . . all week. This way please.

*The clerk walks off, leaving Nick in a state of complete confusion. On the soundtrack we hear the slow piano blues which plays through the next sequence.*

    CUT TO:

NEW HOTEL ROOM

*The door closes and Nick looks around. The room is a mirror image of the other room. Everything is in the opposite position to before. Everything has been carefully laid out in its opposite position. Even the photograph of his mother has been pinned on to the wall.*

ANGLE

*Nick sits on the bed and puts the box file next to him. He opens his filofax and looks up a number which he then dials. It takes a while to connect and he opens the file and starts to take out the contents one by one. We hear the ringing tone through the receiver.*

ANGLE

*We see ballistics reports, autopsy reports, coroner's reports. The ring-*

*ing stops and we hear the characteristic sound of a recorded mes-
sage. It is Jane's voice. As he listens, Nick pulls out a brown photographic envelope. He opens the flap and takes out a pile of ten by
eight photographs.*

> JANE (V.O.)
> Hi, neither Paul nor Jane Kessler is in right now, but if
> you leave your name and number we'll get back to you as
> soon as we can. Thanks for calling . . . please speak after
> you hear the tone.

*The pictures show the office in the Ralston Building as it was after
the murder. The three bodies are on the floor. Barnett is slumped
near the door. His wife is near the desk, her white dress up past her
waist. Munsen is near her.*

ANGLE

*We hear the tone on the phone but Nick doesn't leave a message, he
just stares at the picture.*

CLOSE-UP OF THE PICTURE

*We zoom in slowly on the black-and-white photograph, homing in
on the face of Peter Munsen. It is Nick. Munsen and Nick are so
alike it is like looking at the same person. Nick covers his face with
his hands.*

> DISSOLVE TO:

INT. HOTEL ROOM — MIDDLE OF THE NIGHT

*High angle shot of Nick asleep on top of the bed. He is still fully
clothed. All around the bed are the contents of the police file. The
photographs.*

> DISSOLVE TO:

EXT. RALSTON MANSION — MORNING

*Nick gets out of a yellow cab.*

ANGLE

*Nick walks up the steps of the mansion and the front door opens as he gets there. The chauffeur asks him in. Nick is wearing a dark suit, white shirt and tie and seems to have pulled himself together again.*

INT. MANSION

*Looking down the stairs we see Nick and the chauffeur come into the hallway.*

> CHAUFFEUR
> Mr Ralston would like to know the name of the newspaper that you work for.

> NICK
> It's not a newspaper . . . it's a quarterly magazine . . . on architecture. Here's my card.

*The chauffeur takes the card and goes upstairs, looking at it.*

> CHAUFFEUR
> He'll be down shortly.

ANGLE

*Nick walks down the hallway and looks into a red room. Very faintly on the soundtrack we hear* Liebestraum. *Nick listens and then walks on.*

ANGLE

*Nick opens a mirrored door which reveals a dark passageway. The music is louder. He walks into the passage and another set of doors opens in front of him.*

ANGLE

*Nick looks at a ballroom. Strong white light coming in from the many-curtained windows. On the far side of the room is Jane, who is sitting in a chair next to a small table. She is crying, her head in her hands. On the table is the metal phonograph from which the music is coming. Nick walks towards her.*

NICK

What's the matter, Jane?

ANGLE

*In another part of the room an empty wheelchair spins around.*

ANGLE

*Jane looks up at Nick. She has blood on her hands and a wound on her forehead.*

JANE

Help me . . . please . . .

IMAGE: *Nick running through the mannequins.*

INT. HOTEL ROOM — NIGHT

*Nick sits up in bed screaming. The phone is ringing by the bed but then it stops. He is drenched with sweat. He puts his hands to his head. His cut is bleeding.*

CUT TO BLACK.

TITLE: FRIDAY

INT. DR PARKER'S OFFICE — DAY

*Dr Parker is seated behind his desk, talking to Nick.*

DR PARKER

What do you want us to do, Nick? Your mother is slipping away from us. Now . . . we can keep her alive for quite a long time. It's an expensive process. I'd like you to think about it.

NICK

May I see her?

DR PARKER

As soon as she regains consciousness, we'll call you.

CUT TO:

INT. RALSTON BUILDING — DAY

*Buddy and two of his workmen are blocking the entrance as Nick comes in. They seem quite sinister.*

>                         NICK
> Hi.

>                         BUDDY
> Hey . . . how're you doing? Say . . . you about finished in here now? It's going to be getting dangerous . . . I'd appreciate it if you'd keep away now.

>                         NICK
> Paul told me that if I . . .

>                         BUDDY
> I just spoken with Mr Kessler. I have his OK on this.

*The men stare at each other for some moments.*

> CUT TO:

INT. BEDROOM — HOTEL — AFTERNOON

*Nick is sitting on the bed, looking out of the window. On the sound-track we hear the slow piano blues with some clarinet. There is a gentle knock on the door. Nick gets up and opens the door. It is Jane. They are shy with each other.*

>                         JANE
> Hello . . .

>                         NICK
> Hi.

*Jane smiles nervously. Nick gently pulls her into the room.*

MONTAGE: *They lie down on the bed and begin to make love, undressing each other.*

FLASH IMAGE: *Nick's mother writhing around, her face contorted with anguish.*

ANGLE

*Jane takes Nick's hand and puts it between her legs. He begins to arouse her. The camera begins to track along them towards the wall.*

> JANE
>
> Fuck me.

*The camera reaches the wall and starts to go into a black area. As it does so the phone begins to ring. The camera goes through the wall and into the wrecked room where Nick was before. We hear them through the wall . . .*

> NICK
>
> I've got to get it . . . it could be the hospital . . . Hello . . . this is Mr Kaminsky . . .

*The camera comes back through the wall and into the bedroom. Nick is sitting up on the bed talking on the phone. Jane is twined around him, still making love to him.*

> Un huh . . . I'll be there as soon as I can, Dr Parker.

*He puts the phone down. Jane kisses his back and tries to pull him down on the bed.*

> CUT TO:

INT. PICK-UP – AFTERNOON

*Jane drives. Nick watches her. They are both still very aroused.*

> NICK
>
> Will you come in with me?

> JANE
>
> If you want me to.

*Nick plays with her hair and touches her breast.*

> I'll crash if you do that.

> CUT TO:

INT. HOSPITAL CORRIDOR

*Nick and Jane come out of the lift and Nick walks ahead towards*

*his mother's door. He stops and as Jane catches up he kisses her pas-*
*sionately. A nurse passes and goes into a room. They part.*

JANE

Go on.

*Nick walks reluctantly to his mother's room, opens the door and goes*
*in. Jane looks around the deserted corridor and sits down opposite*
*the lift. There is the sound of a distant storm. Thunder rumbling.*

INT. MOTHER'S ROOM

*High camera angle looking down. Nick's mother is in bed, very still.*
*Seated by the bed is a young nurse reading a magazine. Nick is*
*standing at the foot of the bed.*

NURSE

Mrs Anderson . . . your son is here.

*Nick sits down in the other chair by the bed.*

INT. CORRIDOR

*Close-up of Jane sitting, leaning against the wall. Her eyes are*
*closed. She is humming quietly to herself. The camera angle widens,*
*revealing the corridor behind her. Two orderlies are pushing a wheel-*
*chair down the corridor towards Jane. It is not possible to see*
*whether the figure in the wheelchair is a man or a woman. One of*
*the wheels gives off a squeak as it rubs against something. The score*
*starts to increase the tension. The thunder is a little closer. The order-*
*lies arrive at the lift with the wheelchair. One of them presses the*
*button but the light does not come on.*

FIRST ORDERLY

Shit . . . someone left that door open again. Wait here, I'll
go and fix it.

*Jane watches, amused, as he goes off leaving the other orderly alone*
*with the figure in the wheelchair. The corridor is very gloomy and it*
*is not possible to make out anything but a silhouette.*

INT. MOTHER'S ROOM

*Nick's mother tries to speak but has great difficulty. The nurse reads her magazine.*

EXT. CORRIDOR

*The remaining orderly waits. Down the corridor a door opens and the sister appears. She sees the orderly.*

                              SISTER
Ben . . . would you come here for a moment?

                              ORDERLY
I'm waiting for Jack . . . this elevator's stuck . . .

                              SISTER
This will only take a moment.

                              ORDERLY
I'm supposed to wait here with her, you know.

                              SISTER
Ben!

                              ORDERLY
OK.

*The sister goes back in and the orderly leans down to talk to the woman in the wheelchair.*

        Ma'am . . . I'll just be a sec . . . OK?

*He goes off leaving Jane alone with the woman.*

INT. MOTHER'S ROOM

*Nick's mother tries to speak again and succeeds in making a small but unintelligible sound. The nurse turns a page of her magazine.*

INT. CORRIDOR

*The lift doors open just in front of the wheelchair.*

INT. MOTHER'S ROOM

CLOSE ANGLE *on Nick's face. His mother's hand comes slowly up into frame. She opens her hand, inviting him to hold it.*

INT. CORRIDOR

*Jane looks worriedly at the woman in the wheelchair. She looks down the corridor but it is empty.*

ANGLE

*Close-up of the wheel of the wheelchair. A lifeless hand falls into frame. It twitches.*

INT. MOTHER'S ROOM

*Nick stares at his mother's hand. He hesitates and then brings his hand to hers. She grasps it. Nick is very nervous.*

INT. CORRIDOR

*The hand tries to push the wheelchair towards the open lift. Jane watches, worried.*

> JANE

Ma'am?

*Jane gets up and goes to help the woman.*

Ma'am . . . I think you should wait for the nurse . . . ma'am?

ANGLE. *Jane's POV.*

*The woman slowly brings her head up and we see that she has a large indentation on her forehead, a bullet-wound scar. Jane is very frightened. She backs off in horror as the sightless eyes of the woman look from left to right.*

ANGLE

*Jane backs towards Nick's mother's room.*

INT. MOTHER'S ROOM

*Nick's hand is slowly brought towards his mother's face.*

INT. CORRIDOR

*Jane edges backwards, away from the woman in the wheelchair, towards Nick's mother's room.*

INT. MOTHER'S ROOM

*Nick's mother kisses his hand.*

INT. CORRIDOR

*Jane opens the door and goes in as . . .*

INT. MOTHER'S ROOM

*Nick's mother looks at him strangely.*

                          MOTHER
        I can smell her on you.

*The door closes and they both look at Jane as she comes in, horrified by what she has already seen.*

                          NICK
        Jane? What's the matter?

ANGLE

*Nick's mother makes a huge effort and tries to climb out of bed to get at Jane. She is like an animal. In slow motion we see the nurses trying to restrain her and the orderlies coming into the room to help. Jane is in shock and edges out of the door as Nick's mother is dragged back into the bed.*

INT. CORRIDOR

*The next sequence is hand-held and all in one take.*

*Jane runs out of the room and is again confronted by the woman in the wheelchair. The lift doors close. Jane stops and looks at her. There*

*is pathos in this moment. The camera wheels around her in a half
circle, momentarily revealing two men walking down the corridor
towards her. Jane hesitates for a moment. She is crying. Then she
walks down the corridor passing the two men, who are Dr Parker
and Barnett Ralston. As she passes them, Dr Parker recognizes her.*

                         DR PARKER
Jane . . . why how very nice . . .

*Jane walks down the corridor and out of sight as Ralston goes to the
woman in the wheelchair and kneels by her. In the background we
see Nick running out of his mother's room.*

                           NICK
Jane . . .

*He stops short when he sees Ralston, who looks at him for a moment
before turning back to the woman in the wheelchair. He holds her
hands.*

                         RALSTON
Hello, Mother.

CUT TO:

EXT. STREET — NIGHT

*Rain is falling heavily on the street. Thunder is heard. A jeep drives
into shot and Buddy goes to the window of the car, which winds
down and reveals Paul.*

                           PAUL
Hey, Buddy . . . How's it going?

                          BUDDY
We're a little behind, but we'll make it. I wasn't expecting
you till tonight.

                           PAUL
I got the early flight. You seen Jane?

                          BUDDY
Not since this morning.

                                    PAUL
    OK . . . I'll check back with you later.

*The jeep drives out of shot.*

    CUT TO:

INT. HOSPITAL − NIGHT

*Nick's mother is in a coma, watched by the night nurse. A drip-feed
can be seen in the background.*

    CUT TO:

INT. HOTEL ROOM

*Nick sits in the window watching the rain. He is smoking a cigarette.*

ANGLE

*The photograph of his mother on the wall.*

ANGLE

*Closer shot of Nick. He notices something on the street below.*

EXT. STREET

*The rain is torrential as Nick crosses the street. He is not wearing a
coat. A young man with his girlfriend stops Nick and says something to him. It's as if he knows Nick. Nick walks on towards the
Ralston Building.*

ANGLE

*Close shot of the first-floor window of the music-room office.*

    CUT TO:

INT. MUSIC ROOM

*Nick walks into the wrecked and empty music department and
stops. In the following sequence the use of colour indicates present
time, the use of black and white indicates a flashback to the time of
the opening scene.*

ANGLE

*In the office we see Jane in silhouette. She is waiting for Nick, who walks into the shot and goes to her. She is leaning against the desk. He takes her coat off. She stands and kisses him then pulls up her dress and takes off her pants. He pulls her down to the floor.*

IMAGE. BLACK AND WHITE: *High-heeled shoes spinning. We saw this in the opening sequence of the film.*

EXT. BUILDING

*Paul's jeep pulls up in the rain and he gets out and walks towards the building.*

IMAGE. BLACK AND WHITE: *The woman in white, spinning.*

INT. OFFICE

*Nick and Jane making love on the floor. She is sitting on him.*

IMAGE. BLACK AND WHITE: *The man in the hat coming into the rear entrance of the building. In the background is the period Cadillac. It is raining.*

INT. HOSPITAL

*Nick's mother. She is agitated. Her head moves from side to side. She is upside down in the frame.*

INT. OFFICE

*Nick and Jane making love. They are both very aroused.*

INT. HOSPITAL

*Nick's mother agitated. Her eyes open and look straight into the camera.*

IMAGE. BLACK AND WHITE: *The man in the hat walking up the stairs.*

INT. MUSIC DEPARTMENT

*We see a hand holding a gun. The camera tilts up to the face and we see it is Paul. He looks into the office. We can hear the sound of the lovers.*

INT. OFFICE

*Nick and Jane making love.*

> JANE
>
> Oh . . . come in me.

> NICK
>
> Tell me that you love me. Say it . . . say it . . .

> JANE
>
> I love you.

INT. HOSPITAL

*Nick's mother's body arches up, her head goes back and her mouth opens as she tries to scream.*

SEQUENCE. BLACK AND WHITE: *The door to the office opens and we see the lovers from the opening sequence making love against the desk . . . The screen is black but then we see the rounded stomach of a pregnant woman crossing frame from left to right . . . We see the lovers reflected in the glass that covers the photograph of the Ralston Building . . . In close-up we see a woman's face as she comes out of the shadows. Her cheeks are wet with tears. The sound of the lovers is very strong. It is the woman in Nick's photograph – his mother as a young woman . . . We see the lovers clearly and although they are in the period clothes of the 1950s we see that it is Nick and Jane . . . The young mother points a gun . . . The lovers are like animals with each other . . . The young mother fires the gun . . . All of the sound goes from the soundtrack . . . The woman in white mouths a scream as her lover is hit.*

INT. HOSPITAL – COLOUR – PRESENT TIME

*Nick's mother mouths a silent scream.*

BLACK-AND-WHITE SEQUENCE (*cont'd*): *Fast zoom in on the woman in white as . . . the young mother fires again.*

INT. HOSPITAL — COLOUR — PRESENT TIME

*Nick's mother reacts again.*

BLACK-AND-WHITE SEQUENCE (*cont'd*): *The young mother fires again and . . . the man in the hat clutches his stomach as he is shot.*

INT. OFFICE — COLOUR — PRESENT DAY

*Jane's head goes back as she and Nick climax.*

INT. HOSPITAL — PRESENT TIME

*Nick's mother, her body still arched, starts to slip back down.*

INT. OFFICE — PRESENT TIME

*Jane slowly brings her head down to Nick. She passes through bars of light and it seems as if she is falling.*

INT. HOSPITAL — PRESENT TIME

*Nick's mother's head comes to rest on the pillow and the tension goes out of her body. The nurse stares at her for a moment and then reaches over and closes her eyes and then makes the sign of the cross. As she does so the sound fades back in and we hear the thunder which is abating.*

INT. MUSIC DEPARTMENT — PRESENT TIME

*Paul stares into the office. He is crying. There is no sound of the lovers.*

INT. OFFICE — PRESENT TIME

*High angle of Nick and Jane. They are lying together on the floor, completely still, their arms and legs wrapped around each other. On the soundtrack we hear the opening to the piano version of* Liebestraum.

INT. MUSIC DEPARTMENT — PRESENT TIME

*Paul turns and walks into the shadow.*

IMAGE: *A young girl sits at a piano and is playing the music that we can hear. It is the girl with the red hair that we saw in Nick's first dream. She is positioned to the left of frame and the rest of the frame is black. In this black space the end credits begin to roll and continue to do so until the end of the piece of music.*

# Leaving Las Vegas

# CAST AND CREW

## MAIN CAST

| | |
|---|---|
| BEN SANDERSON | Nicolas Cage |
| SERA | Elisabeth Shue |
| YURI | Julian Sands |
| PETER | Richard Lewis |
| MARC NUSSBAUM | Steven Weber |
| SIMPSON | Thomas Kopache |
| TERI | Valeria Golino |
| BANK TELLER | Carey Lowell |
| MOBSTER 1 | Mike Figgis |
| MOBSTER 2 | Waldemar Kalinowski |
| MOBSTER 3 | Ed Lauter |
| CONVENTIONEER | R. Lee Ermey |
| LANDLADY | Laurie Metcalf |

## MAIN CREW

| | |
|---|---|
| *Directed by* | Mike Figgis |
| *Based on the Novel by* | John O'Brien |
| *Screenplay by* | Mike Figgis |
| *Produced by* | Lila Cazès and Annie Stewart |
| *Line Producer* | Marc S. Fischer |
| *Executive Producer* | Paige Simpson and Stuart Regen |
| *Original Music by* | Mike Figgis |
| *Cinematography by* | Declan Quinn |
| *Film Editing by* | John Smith |
| *Production Design by* | Waldemar Kalinowski |
| *Costume Design by* | Laura Goldsmith |

TITLE ON BLACK: 'IO P.M. — LOS ANGELES'

DISSOLVE TO:

I INT. SMART BAR IN BEVERLY HILLS — NIGHT

*It is the kind of bar where the well-to-do folks of LA go to pick up –
or be picked up. Lesser-known actors, agents and executives of all
ages. Into this bar comes Ben.*

*Ben is in his thirties. He is wearing an Armani suit that could use a
visit to the dry-cleaner's. He hasn't shaved in the last twenty-four
hours (but neither has any of the actors in the bar). He is a good-
looking man but is clearly in trouble of some kind. Although still in
control of his faculties, it becomes clear in the following scene that he
is much the worse for wear with drink. He looks around the room
until he sees someone he recognizes and then walks over to a table
where two couples are seated. The men are young execs, the girls,
both blonde and busty, have very white teeth and smile all of the
time. The camera follows Ben over to the table. One of the execs
looks up as Ben gets close. He recognizes him but delays his recogni-
tion until the last moment in the hope that Ben is not looking at
him.*

                              BEN
Peter!

                             PETER
Ben . . . how are you, man?

*They shake hands. Ben is not invited to take a seat, and Peter waits
for a while before being forced to introduce him to the table.*

Ben Sanderson, Marc Nussbaum, Sheila, Debbie.

                             MARC
Nice to meet you. I think I spoke to you on the phone a

couple of years ago. Weren't you both at MGM with Lad-
die?

BEN

That's right. Are you still at ICM?

MARC

No, I'm at Tri-Star now.

BEN

That's great. Say hello to Mike for me. That's a beautiful
dress, Debbie, and those are fabulous earrings, Sheila.

*There is an awkward silence. Ben does not make a move and is not
invited to join them. The girls smile.*

MARC

I gotta tell you, I'm a big fan of your writing. I loved *Bay
of Pigs*.

BEN

Thanks a lot. I didn't actually write it, I just got the credit.
I was fired.
                    (*to Peter*)
Can I talk to you for a moment?

*Peter gets up and he and Ben walk to the door together. Peter speaks
very quietly.*

PETER

Listen, Ben, I can't help you any more. Do you understand?

BEN

This is the last time. Promise. I just need some cash
tonight. I lost my credit cards. The money'll be on your
desk first thing tomorrow morning, Scout's honour.
How's the new one coming along? I hear you got Richard
Gere.

*The two men look at each other for a while. Peter's friends are look-
ing at them, as are other people in the room. Peter takes out his wallet and extracts some notes.*

PETER

This is all I have in cash. Please don't drink it here.

BEN

Yes, that's fine. I'll messenger it over to you tomorrow.

PETER

I don't want it. Ben . . . I think it would be best if you
didn't contact me again.

*And he turns and walks away, back to his table.*

CUT TO BLACK.

TITLE: 'LAS VEGAS — 1.20 A.M.'

FADE UP ON:

2 EXT. HELICOPTER SHOT — DAY

*Las Vegas. A blaze of colour in the middle of a desert.*

*Credit sequence begins.*

CUT TO:

3 INT. LOBBY OF EXPENSIVE HOTEL — NIGHT

*A mixture of businessmen and gamblers creates a sense of activity
and superficial excitement. Music wafts across the soundtrack,
almost drowned by the dense texture of thousands of slot machines,
creating an insane New Age symphony.*

*Credit sequence ends.*

*Into the lobby from the street comes Sera.*

*It's hard to tell how old Sera is — somewhere between twenty-five
and thirty-five. She is a beautiful American girl. Her face has the
freshness of a model in a Sears catalogue. She is dressed simply in a
short black skirt and matching jacket. High heels complete the picture. Heads turn as she passes a group of businessmen and it's clear
they find her very sexy. She acknowledges their glance with a half-
smile and steps into the elevator. She could be a secretary, or a P.A.*

*to one of the many execs here in Las Vegas at a convention. The*
*body language is a bit different, though.*

4 INT. PENTHOUSE SUITE OF HOTEL — NIGHT

*A view of night-time Las Vegas through a window. Traffic up and*
*down The Strip; bright, gaudy neon flashing and winking. We hear*
*the sound of men laughing and the camera pulls focus and we see*
*reflected in the glass . . .*

*. . . a group of people.*

*On the table are bowls of potato chips and dip and sandwiches. The*
*TV is on at a sports channel and two boxers pound the shit out of*
*each other.*

    CUT TO:

5 INT. ELEVATOR — NIGHT

*Sera looks at herself in the gold-tinted mirror in the elevator. She*
*takes out a lipstick and freshens her lips. Some people get out and*
*the elevator climbs higher. We see from the indicator that she has*
*punched the Penthouse button. Camera moves in tighter and we see*
*that she is nervous but concealing it well. The elevator stops, the*
*doors open, and she steps right into the Penthouse.*

6 INT. PENTHOUSE — NIGHT

*A bottle of Scotch is almost empty. The man talking is Yuri. He is*
*Russian, in his early forties, a little overweight, a big man wearing a*
*blue silk suit. His thick black hair is greased and combed back. He*
*wears a lot of jewellery, all gold. Rings, a bracelet and a Rolex. Two*
*men in business suits and a weird stoned woman in her late thirties*
*listen to him.*

            YURI
    . . . but please, my friends, call me Yuri. It is my American
    name . . . I picked it myself.

*The three people laugh. There is a hint of contempt in the way that*
*they speak to Yuri.*

FIRST BUSINESSMAN

Where are you from, Yuri? I mean, you sure don't talk like you're from this neck of the woods.

*Yuri smiles at them.*

YURI
(*silky voice*)

No . . . you are right, my friend. How very observant you are. I am from Latvia.

WEIRD WOMAN

Tough place.

YURI

Yes, I hear this too. But I am not a tough man. I am a simple man who is here to learn from my new American friends.

*The door opens and Sera comes in. Everyone stares at her.*

WEIRD WOMAN
(*turned on*)

Is this your friend, Yuri?

YURI

Ah, yes . . . Sera.

*The second businessman takes out a manila envelope from his inside pocket.*

Sera is my gift to you, my friends from New York City. You may do with her as you wish in this beautiful room, which is also my gift for the night to my friends. You will find her a very willing girl, for all of you . . . just as we arranged.

*Yuri smiles again as the second businessman hands him the envelope. The rest of them just stare at Sera, aroused by the idea of her.*

SECOND BUSINESSMAN

Of course, Yuri. I think you'll find this just as we discussed.

*Yuri gets up.*

> YURI

So, my friends . . . I have other business to attend. Enjoy.

*He heads for the door, passing Sera. She holds his arm as he passes.*

> SERA
> (*whispering*)

Yuri . . . please! Can I talk to you for a moment?

*Still smiling, he takes Sera's arm and leads her into the bedroom.*

> YURI

My friends . . . excuse us for just one moment.

7 INT. BEDROOM — NIGHT

*Mirrors reflect mirrors.*

> SERA

I don't want this. Yuri, please. I really don't want this. You know I don't like to do groups.

> YURI
> (*playful*)

I want this, Sera. I need this!

> SERA

Please, Yuri.

*He holds out his arms. Sera goes to him. He hugs her with one arm. He pulls up her skirt so that her panties are exposed.*

> YURI
> (*seductive*)

These are pretty.

*Sera watches in the mirror as he pulls her panties to reveal her buttocks. He strokes her there gently with his other hand. We see that there are two fine scars there. He speaks gently, like a father to a daughter.*

Is this how you would repay me for coming all this way to find you again? Driving through the desert to protect my little Sera.

CUT TO:

FLASHBACK – SILENT – GRAINY BLACK AND WHITE

8 INT. ROOM – NIGHT

*Yuri and Sera – different time, different place. Sera looking fright-*
*ened, backing away from Yuri, who pulls a switchblade from his*
*jacket and opens it.*

CUT BACK TO:

9 INT. PENTHOUSE – NIGHT

*Yuri enters from the bedroom. The weird woman is doing a line of*
*coke.*

> YURI
> (*cheerful*)
> Sera wanted me to ask if she might undress at once for
> you. She has a very beautiful undergarment which she
> would like you to see.

ANGLE ON BEDROOM DOOR

*Sera comes into the room. She smiles and begins unbuttoning her*
*jacket.*

*She takes it off and drops it on the floor, and then unzips her skirt*
*and steps out of it. Sera is now in control and playing the room. In*
*the background, Yuri leaves the room.*

> WEIRD WOMAN
> (*strange voice*)
> Come here.

*Sera walks over and something strange takes place between them.*

> CUT TO:

10 INT. BEN'S BAR – LA – MORNING

*The bar is dark but through a small window we see that it is a very bright sunny day outside. The bartender reads the* Los Angeles Times. *The bar surface is red vinyl. There are five customers, all single men. One of them is Ben and he is sitting at the bar watching TV. A game show is in progress and the TV sound is loud. Ben finishes his drink and grimaces before indicating to the barman that he'd like a repeat. Barman pours him a whiskey – Cranberry – and the camera moves in closer to Ben, ending up in a close-up. Ben takes a big hit from the drink and concentrates on the TV. We hear from the TV sound that it is a word game with a big prize. Ben smiles to himself.*

BEN'S POV OF TV

*The talk-show hostess, an American TV beauty, is showing the audience the prizes available in today's game show.*

ANGLE ON BEN

*As he finishes that drink and asks for another. The camera moves in close on his eyes.*

BEN'S POV OF TV

*She turns from the prizes and looks straight into the TV camera, which starts zooming into her. At first, what she is saying makes complete sense, but then things change . . .*

                              HOSTESS
                        (*smoky, sexy voice*)
Just look at this studio, Ben, filled with glamorous merchandise, including an extra special prize chosen just for you! A big, bad, BMW motorcycle, complete with saddle bags stuffed with thousands of US dollars.

*There are 'oohs' from the audience.*

So, Ben . . .
                        (*tosses her hair*)
. . . let's find a bar, get drunk and go for a ride.

*The studio lights dim.*

Then we can get a suite somewhere and order up a case of champagne while we fuck ourselves silly.

*Close-up on males in audience doing the grunt.*

> This is it, just for you, Ben.

*She unbuttons her top, licks her fingers and makes her nipples hard.*

> Because you've been so patient, and because I want to fuck you, take care of you, and because there's nothing else in the world worth doing.

*Section of the audience clapping – some women dabbing their eyes.*

> Tell you what, Ben, let's go to Vegas. The bars stay open twenty-four hours night and day. Just you, just me, Ben, think about it, all right?

ANGLE ON BEN

*Lost in this fantasy.*

BEN

> I'll think about it.

*He looks back at the screen, but the show has returned to what is known as 'normal'. He finishes his drink and then an attack of nausea hits him. He takes a deep breath and rolls his neck and his head. The barman puts down a fresh drink. Ben looks at his own hands . . . which are steady.*

BARMAN

> You should go on that show.

CUT TO:

11 INT. SMART BUSINESS SPACE – MORNING

*Ben sitting at a desk with a phone wedged on his ear, a cup of black coffee on the desk. The walls are covered with framed film posters and one complete wall has shelves jammed with scripts. He nods from time to time and sometimes says 'yes' or 'OK', but it becomes clear that there is no one on the other end. He drinks from the coffee cup. A woman comes up to his desk, a business colleague. She puts a wad of messages down on the desk.*

                              BEN
Yeah, but what's the back end like? By the time we're
through with P and A, the above-the-line is going to take
it to about fifteen and with something like this . . . I don't
know if Disney will go for it . . . can I call you back on
this? OK . . . chow for now.
                        (*to the woman*)
Good morning.

                              WOMAN
                          (*cautious*)
Ben . . . Mr Simpson was looking for you. I said that you
had a doctor's appointment. He said for you to go in as
soon as . . . are you OK?

                              BEN
                    (*pulling himself together*)
I'm fantastic, but I gotta go out now . . . very important
meeting, could make a coupla million for the company.

*Ben gets up and as he passes her he grabs her and dances a few
steps. It is clear that she likes Ben, but when his face gets close to hers
she smells the alcohol on his breath and she turns away. Ben stops
dancing and smiles sadly.*

                              WOMAN
                          (*tender*)
Ben?

                              BEN
What?

                              WOMAN
You should go now.

*She leaves the room and Ben goes through some routine at the desk.
He opens a drawer of a filing cabinet and puts in his whole arm,
looking for something at the very back. He pulls out a small vodka
bottle and opens it and then pours the contents into his coffee cup.
With cup in hand he leaves the room.*

CUT TO:

12 INT. SMART OFFICE — DAY

*Ben is sitting opposite his boss, Mr Simpson, who is very upset. He hands Ben an envelope. Ben opens it and pulls out a cheque. He looks at the amount.*

> BEN
> (*genuinely moved*)
> This is too generous, Peter.

> SIMPSON
> (*close to tears*)
> Well . . . we liked having you around, Ben, but you know how it is.

> BEN
> (*ashamed*)
> Sure thing . . . and I'm sorry.

*Ben takes a swig from his coffee cup.*

> SIMPSON
> (*trying to cheer things along*)
> Well . . . what are you going to do now?

> BEN
> I thought I might move out to Las Vegas.

*Simpson looks puzzled.*

> The bars never close.

CUT TO:

13 INT. BEN'S BMW — DAY

*Ben drives through Beverly Hills. He pours the contents of a small bottle of vodka into an empty Coke can, puts the empty bottle under the seat and then drinks from the can.*

*He slips a tape into the player and we hear 'Lonely Teardrops' by Michael McDonald, one of Ben's favourite songs. At a traffic light a cop on a bike pulls up next to him and Ben takes a pull from the Coke can and smiles, mouths the word 'hot'. The cop nods back at him, the light changes, and they both pull away.*

CUT TO:

14 EXT. SANTA MONICA STREET — DAY

*Ben carries a brown paper bag which clinks. Camera follows him as he walks down the street. He looks at . . .*

BEN'S POV

*A girl walking ahead of him in the same direction. She is walking her dog. She is attractive from behind. We hear Ben's thoughts.*

> BEN (V.O.)
> Beautiful. Not just the shape, which is nice, but the whole walk, the feeling, the movement. This girl is pleased with herself. Maybe this is the only art I can appreciate . . . I don't know if this is good or bad, but right now she is really beautiful. When I was a boy it would have been really important that she have a very pretty face, to go with this body, I mean. I still would like to see her face, but her beauty is not dependent on her face.

*The dog gets interested in something on the sidewalk and she bends down to pull at its collar.*

> I wonder what kind of panties she's wearing. Shit, that's too specific, but . . . on the other hand, you can never be too specific . . . but then, the infinitesimal must be, by definition, as infinite as the infinite.

*Suddenly the girl stops. Ben catches up with her and cannot resist looking into her face.*

> God, she's so young.

*The girl sees Ben and smiles an innocent smile.*

> GIRL
> Hi!

> BEN
> Hi . . .

CUT TO:

15 EXT. BEN'S HOUSE IN SANTA MONICA – DAY

*Ben walks up to his house still carrying the paper bag. A young boy of about thirteen years of age is fixing a beat-up bike. Ben greets him.*

> BEN
>
> Hey, Brad . . . how's it going?

> BRAD
>
> Hey, Ben. There were a couple of guys looking for you.

> BEN
>
> What did they look like?

> BRAD
>
> Suits. I didn't tell them anything. You know anything about gears?

*Ben takes a look. The gear mechanism is all bent out of shape. He bends down to have a look. It is clear from the way he deals with this mechanical problem that he is good with his hands. He doesn't try to force anything but he moves the chain and the gear mechanism to get to the problem.*

> BEN
>
> How'd this happen?

> BRAD
>
> I was going real fast down on the beach and something slipped and everything got all jammed up.

> BEN
>
> The news is not good, kid. This bit here . . . see there . . . it's broken. You need a new one.

> BRAD
> (*upset*)
> How much, do you think?

BEN

I don't know. I'll find out though.

*Ben gets up, picks up his bottles and heads for his house. He looks back and Brad is sitting still by the bike, looking totally dejected. This really seems to upset Ben.*

CUT TO:

16 INT. BEN'S HOUSE – AFTERNOON

*Ben is naked and the shower can be heard in the background. The house is austere, only the minimum of furnishing. He pours a large tumbler of vodka and takes a gulp, then tops up the glass. He turns on the stereo, selects a record – Miles Davis,* Kind of Blue *– and puts it on the turntable. He turns on the cassette recorder and inserts a new blank tape. He puts the machine into the record mode. He kneels down next to the deck and with complete precision puts the needle on the second track without any problem. The music starts and continues through the next sequence.*

17 INT. SHOWER – DAY

*Ben in the shower with the glass in his hand.*

18 INT. BATHROOM – DAY

*Ben shaving with the glass in his hand. He does the area around his mouth first so that he can drink while he does the rest.*

19 INT. LIVING SPACE – DAY

*Showered and shaved and wearing a smart dark suit, Ben looks handsome and normal. He selects another record and again sets up the cassette machine to record. He turns the stereo up full and dances by himself while watching MTV silent. He tries a turn which is a bit ambitious and loses his balance. In slow motion we see him fall. Ben lies still on the floor. He smiles to himself and decides to stay there for a while . . .*

FADE OUT.

FADE IN:

20 INT. SERA'S BEDROOM — LAS VEGAS — DAY

*Sera wakes up in bed next to Yuri. (The camera is high above the bed looking down.) She is completely drenched in sweat. A thin shaft of light comes from the crack in the drapes and falls across their bodies. Other than that, the room is in darkness. To get out of bed she would have to climb over him. She lies still. Yuri speaks without opening his eyes . . .*

> YURI
>
> I missed you, Sera. You have been lonely?

*Sera blinks and turns her head towards him.*

> SERA
>
> I'm older now, Yuri.

*He puts his hand between her legs, over the sheets and grasps her there.*

> YURI
>
> You have been lonely?

> SERA
> *(tensing a little)*
>
> I've been all right.

> YURI
>
> I will keep you safe. We are both older.

*He climbs on to her and mounts her. Familiarity.*

> You have been lonely?

> SERA
> *(flat voice)*
>
> I am lonely, Yuri.

*He begins thrusting into her.*

> YURI
>
> Yes . . . so am I.

*Camera moves slowly into a tight portrait of Sera.*

> SERA (V.O.)
> I had a new dress . . . we were at the fair, Daddy bought
> me an ice-cream and I spilt it on my dress . . .

CUT TO:

21 INT. DOCTOR'S OFFICE – DAY

*Sera is sitting on a sofa talking to an unseen person. (Although it is
not entirely clear when this is taking place, the sense of it is that we
are in the present, i. e. all the events in the film are in the past
tense.)*

> SERA
> . . . Mom was with Helen, and Dad looked around first to
> see if she was watching and then he scraped it all off and
> threw it on to the grass and then he kissed me and hugged
> me and told me it was all right . . .

22 INT. SERA'S KITCHEN – LATER THAT DAY

*Yuri is tucking into a hearty breakfast. Sera plays with her food.*

> YURI
> (*planning his day*)
> This is such a small apartment, Sera. I cannot stay here.
> We will find a big apartment. You know how much money
> I can bring you. I belong in . . .
> (*laughs*)
> . . . wealth and luxury.

*He suddenly looks up from his food and smiles at her.*

> Why did you run away from me in Los Angeles?

*Sera says nothing.*

> Because you are sly. Mmm? You knew all along that there
> was more money in Las Vegas. Didn't you?

*Sera nervously plays with her food.*

You have nothing to fear from me. You know why?
Because we belong together, Sera. Don't we?

*Sera forces a smile.*

> SERA
> (*quietly*)
>
> Yes.

QUICK CUT TO:

FLASHBACK:

23 INT. ROOM – NIGHT

*Grainy black-and-white image. Sera on a bed, pinned down by Yuri, who has a knife.*

> CUT BACK TO:

24 INT. SERA'S HOUSE – DAY

> YURI
> I'm pleased with you, Sera . . . how you have moved up in the world. I showed you a glamorous world when I took you off the streets . . .
> (*shaking his head*)
> . . . and how you repay me.

> SERA
> Where have you been staying?

> YURI
> With an old friend.

*He drops his fork.*

> But that is none of your affair. You will call this morning and book me into a hotel suite where I will make new contacts for us.

*The mood has changed and Sera does her best to move out of these dangerous waters.*

SERA

You'll need some money, then.

*Yuri nods. Sera rises, goes to a kitchen drawer and finds money.*

YURI
(*becoming angry*)

It is, after all, Sera, my money.

SERA
(*calmly*)

Yes, of course. How much do you need?

YURI
(*shaking his head*)

All of it. I need to buy many things . . . all of it!

*Yuri is very angry and as Sera hands him the money, he hits her, hard, knocking her back into the refrigerator. His ring cuts her cheek.*

(*shouting*)

Don't look at me like that.

*And then his anger goes and he becomes quite tender with her. He takes her face in his hands to look at the cut.*

It's not so bad. It is nothing.
(*whispers*)

I need money, Sera. I need it fast. You must go on the street tonight. For me.

*He sits down with shaking hands. He suddenly seems more vulnerable than she is. He goes to the window and looks out, left and then right, as if he expects to see something.*

I need money fast, Sera. I want you back on the street. Tonight.

FADE OUT.

FADE IN SLOWLY — SOUND FIRST:

25 INT. BEN'S HOUSE — NIGHT

*Ben opens his eyes. The only light comes from the TV. The Miles
Davis record has got caught on a scratch and is repeating the same
phrase over and over again. He looks at his gold Rolex and then fingers the wedding band on his finger.*

CUT TO:

26 INT. BEN'S BAR — LA — NIGHT

*Ben is sitting at the bar. He drinks a large glass of something very
quickly and then immediately orders another.*

*He drinks this a little slower but still way too quick, finishes it and
then orders another. He looks around the bar and sees a woman sitting by herself, thirtyish, pretty and receptive. She looks and sees
Ben, and he smiles at her. She smiles right back. Ben talks across the
bar.*

> BEN
> (*charming*)

Good evening.

> PRETTY WOMAN
> (*pleased*)

Hi.

> BEN

I'm Benjamin . . . Ben.

> PRETTY WOMAN

I'm Teri.

*Ben walks over to where she is.*

*She is pleased that this good-looking man has come over to make a
play. She makes a noise with her straw to indicate that her glass is
empty.*

> BEN

I'll get you another one . . . and me too. Mind if I join
you?

*She watches him walk to the bar.*

*He gets the drinks and walks back to her. He sets the drinks down on the table and sits down. As he does so, his face gets close to hers and she smells the booze on him.*

> PRETTY WOMAN
> Wow . . . been drinking all day?

> BEN
> But of course.

*She looks at him, a disappointed expression on her face. She is no longer interested in being seduced by this man and this much is clear to Ben.*

> Why don't we finish these and go to my apartment on the beach?

*She doesn't respond.*

> We can watch a movie and I'll mix you up a gooey blender drink.

*Ben winces at his own words. He shakes his head.*

> PRETTY WOMAN
> I have to get up pretty early tomorrow. I'll just finish this and go. Thanks anyway.

*They drink in silence for a while. Ben takes a deep breath.*

> BEN
> (*pathetic*)
> I really wish that you'd come home with me. You're so cute and I'm really good in bed . . . believe me . . . you smell good too . . .

*He stops and frowns as he stares into his empty glass.*

> No, OK.

*Ben tries to stand and has to pull himself up by holding the bar. It's a strange thing with drunks like Ben . . . when they're up they have balance and timing, but when they're down it all falls apart. She starts to speak but then doesn't. A look of great sadness comes over her.*

> PRETTY WOMAN
> I have to go now. Thanks anyway.

*She stands to go.*

> Maybe you shouldn't drink so much.

*She walks to the door and Ben turns to the bar, watched by the barman, who is a little concerned.*

> BEN
> (*to himself*)
> Maybe I shouldn't breathe so much, Teri. Ha . . . ha.

> BARMAN
> (*severe voice*)
> Time to go, buddy . . . We're closing up.

*Ben gets out his wallet but his hands are shaking so much that he cannot extract any bills. He is very embarrassed and tries again, but to no avail.*

> BEN
> Would you . . .?

*The barman shakes his head in disgust as he goes into the wallet and takes some money.*

CUT TO:

27 EXT. LA STREETS — NIGHT

*Ben is cruising in his car, listening to music on his stereo.*

CUT TO:

28 INT. STRIP CLUB — NIGHT

*Ben comes into the club and sits down next to the stage, where a dancer is doing her thing accompanied by a live blues trio. A swim-suited waitress comes to the table.*

WAITRESS

There's a one-drink minimum per show, I hope you saw
the sign when you came in. Anyway, they're supposed to
tell you.

BEN

Yes, I heard, and it's not a problem.

WAITRESS

What do you want?

BEN

What are my choices?

WAITRESS

Everything's ten dollars, and there's no alcohol.

BEN

No alcohol?

WAITRESS

No alcohol. You gotta get something else. Everything's ten
dollars. What do you want?

BEN

What do you think I should get?

WAITRESS

Non-alcoholic malt beverage?

BEN

. . . Noooo.

WAITRESS

Orange soda?

BEN

No.

WAITRESS

Coffee?

BEN

No.

                    WAITRESS
Sparkling apple cider?

                      BEN
No.

                    WAITRESS
Water?

                      BEN
Water?

                    WAITRESS
One drink minimum per show. Everything's ten dollars.
Now . . . tell me what you want or I'll eighty-six you.

                      BEN
                   (*decides*)
Water.

*She writes down W-A-T-E-R and walks away. Ben calls her back.*

Just how much would it cost for you to eighty-six me?

ANGLE ON THE STAGE

*A tough black girl dances in a world of her own, impervious to the
men who stare at her. The trio grinds out a dirty blues. A man opposite Ben places a dollar bill on the stage and as the dancer squats
down to pick it up he stares between her legs and winks. The waitress
puts down a styrofoam cup and a bottle of water in front of Ben but
refuses to look at him.*

                    WAITRESS
                   (*hostile*)
Three-fifty.

*Ben puts down a hundred on to her tray.*

                      BEN
                    (*polite*)
Could I have fives please? Keep one for yourself.

*This throws the waitress for a loop.*

CUT TO:

29 INT. BATHROOM OF STRIP CLUB — NIGHT

*Ben drinks all of a fifth of bourbon. Other guys come and go, pissing against the urinal.*

*Ben offers one of the guys a drink, the pianist from the trio. He takes a shot.*

CUT TO:

30 INT. STRIP CLUB — NIGHT

*Ben sits next to another man watching the show. On stage a tall blonde dances with her own reflection in a mirror. Ben turns to his neighbour.*

> BEN
> To me there is nothing more beautiful than the relation-ship between the reflection of a woman and the woman who has created it.

> NEIGHBOUR
> (*completely uninterested*)
> No shit!

30A EXT. LA STREETS — NIGHT

*Ben drives in his car.*

CUT TO:

31 EXT. SUNSET BOULEVARD — LATER THAT NIGHT

*Ben is cruising in his car, listening to 'Lonely Teardrops' again. He's looking for a prostitute. He sees a girl, but when he slows down she ducks into a doorway.*

*He looks in his rear-view mirror and sees a cop car coming up fast. Ben panics for a second. There is a bottle between his legs. The cop car draws level and cruises alongside him for a while, but then puts its lights and siren on and speeds off, doing a U-turn.*

*Ben continues and then sees an Hispanic girl and stops. He winds down the window. He is by now almost incoherent.*

> BEN

Good evening.

32 EXT. KERBSIDE — NIGHT

*The girl looks up and down the street and then walks over to the car and bends down to the window.*

> HISPANIC GIRL

You wanna date? You wanna date me?

*The girl's eyes shift constantly from Ben to the street and then back again.*

> BEN
> (*cut to the chase*)

I'll give you a hundred dollars for a straight forty-five minutes. You get the room.

*Ben shows her the money.*

> HISPANIC GIRL
> (*trying to take him*)

The room is twenty. You pay for it.

*Ben laughs.*

> BEN

OK . . . but only because I think that the concept of surrender fits in with the big picture right now. How about over there?

*He gives her a twenty and indicates a motel across the street. She sets off and he gets out of the car. As he does, a wave of nausea hits him. He shakes his head violently and then lurches across the street, causing two cars to hit their brakes. The camera follows him into the dark parking lot of the motel, where the Hispanic girl is waiting.*

(*slurring badly*)
I canrember . . . if mywifeleffme . . . or Ileff her . . .
bufuckittanyway . . .

*The girl laughs at Ben and says something in Spanish.*

*Slowly the picture gets darker, until all that can be seen are the headlights from the passing cars on Sunset . . . and then . . .*

CUT TO:

33 INT. BEN'S HOUSE – DAWN

*Ben wakes up on the kitchen floor. The fridge door is open and its light is what lights Ben. Inside the fridge are one green pepper and four bottles of vodka. Without too much effort Ben feels for his wallet and sees that it is still there, as are his car keys. He closes the fridge door and in the grey light from the window he lies still. The first birds start singing. (The birdsong continues through the following sequence, which does not have sync sound.)*

CUT TO:

FLASHBACK:

34 EXT. SUNSET BOULEVARD MOTEL – PARKING-LOT DUMP-STERS – NIGHT

*At the rear of the motel. Next to some garbage hoppers, the Hispanic girl hugging him and kissing his neck. He tries to kiss her on the mouth, but she turns her face away.*

CUT TO:

35 INT. BEN'S HOUSE – DAWN

*Ben lying on the floor, thinking.*

CUT TO:

FLASHBACK:

36 EXT. SUNSET BOULEVARD MOTEL — PARKING-LOT DUMP-
STERS — NIGHT

*The Hispanic girl kneeling before him, unzipping his trousers.*
*Through a gap in the fence, we see traffic going up and down Sunset.*

    CUT TO:

37 INT. BEN'S HOUSE — DAWN

*Ben lying on the floor, thinking . . .*

    CUT TO:

    FLASHBACK:

38 EXT. SUNSET BOULEVARD MOTEL — PARKING-LOT DUMP-
STERS — NIGHT

*The girl takes his hand and kisses it. She begins sucking the fingers,*
*taking the whole hand into her mouth.*

    CUT TO:

39 INT. BEN'S HOUSE — DAWN

*Ben suddenly sits up and looks at his hand. His wedding ring has*
*gone. He thinks about this for a long while.*

    CUT TO:

40 INT. BANK — MORNING

*Ben waiting in line to cash a cheque. He looks unwell and is having*
*difficulty standing straight. At last it is his turn. He goes to the*
*counter and hands over a cheque to the girl.*

                  BANK GIRL
    OK . . . \$4,600 . . . one moment, sir . . .

*She looks at her computer read-out.*

    . . . that'll leave five dollars in your account. Would you
    sign the back of the cheque, please?

BEN
(*surprised*)
You couldn't cash it just like it is?

BANK GIRL
(*puzzled*)
I'm sorry, sir. Is there a problem?

*Ben picks up a pen and tries to sign, but his hands are shaking so much that he cannot do it.*

BEN
(*embarrassed*)

Well . . . to tell you the truth, I'm a little shaky right now. I just had brain surgery . . . Why don't I come back after lunch, when I'm feeling a little better? We can take care of it then.

*He picks up the cheque with some difficulty and exits.*

CUT TO:

41 INT. BEN'S BAR — LA — MORNING

*Ben seated at the bar, a pile of bills in front of him. The barman sets down a vodka, picks up the empty glass and takes some bills, shaking his head in disapproval. The TV is on, same game show as before, and Ben watches carefully, looking for a sign from the girl, but the show proceeds in its 'normal' fashion. The only difference is that the hostess is played by the girl in the bank. Ben grabs the barman's attention.*

BEN

I think, when I'm done with this, I'll have gin and tonic . . . Bombay gin and tonic.

*The barman loses it.*

BARMAN
(*angry*)

You should be having coffee. Do you know what time it is? You're a young man.

(*calmer*)

It's none of my business, but if you could see what I see, you wouldn't do this to yourself.

*Ben is taken aback by the emotion in his voice. In his mind, cynicism and the desire to cry fight it out. He holds the emotion back, and looks down at the bar.*

BEN

I understand what you're saying . . . I appreciate your concern. It's not my intention to make you uncomfortable. Please . . . serve me today and I will never come in here again.

(*cheerful*)

If I do, you can eighty-six me.

BARMAN

Sure, sure, I can eighty-six you now if I want to. Stop fucking with me. I don't give a fuck what you do.

*He picks up a bottle of gin, fills a glass, slams it on the counter in front of Ben and knocks twice with his knuckles on the bar.*

On the house, son.

*Ben looks at the TV for a sign. None is forthcoming.*

CUT TO:

42 INT. BANK – DAY

*Ben waiting in line again. The same bank girl is there and she is dealing with her customers in the same inanely cheerful way that the game-show hostess dealt with her prize-winners. She notices Ben waiting and an irritated look flashes across her face. Ben studies her. She is pretty in an ordinary kind of way. We hear Ben's thoughts as voice-over (or maybe he says them out loud to himself).*

BEN (V.O.)

Are you desirable? Are you irresistible? Maybe if you drank bourbon with me, it would help. Maybe if you kissed me and I could taste the sting in your mouth, it would help.

*Close-up on the bank girl as she does her thing, efficiently counting money, smiling, perfect teeth framed by a Cupid mouth. She is wearing a white blouse through which frilly lingerie can just be made out.*

If you drank bourbon with me naked . . . if you smelled of bourbon as you fucked me, it would help . . . it would increase my esteem for you. If you poured bourbon on to your naked body and said to me . . . drink this . . .

*Camera moves in tighter on her face as she chats with a customer about the weather.*

. . . if you spread your legs and had bourbon dripping from your breasts and your vagina and said drink here . . . then I could fall in love with you, because then I would have a purpose, to clean you up, and that would prove that I'm worth something. I'd lick you clean so that you could go away and fuck someone else.

                              BANK GIRL
Next!

*Ben takes a moment to come out of his reverie. He smiles and comes to the counter, completely in control of himself.*

                              BEN
I'm back, I've got my cheque . . . and, baby . . . I'm ready to sign.

*He flips the cheque over, makes sure she is watching and signs with a flourish.*

There . . . Steady as a fucking rock, excuse my French.
                            (*serious*)
Wanna have dinner with me?

*She counts the money out and glares at him as she hands it over.*

                              BANK GIRL
I'm glad you're feeling better. Do you need validation?

*Ben looks at her and smiles.*

CUT TO:

43 INT. SUPERMARKET — DAY

*Ben throws items into a trolley. Garbage bags, firelighters and char-coal lighter fluid.*

    CUT TO:

44 INT. BEN'S KITCHEN — DAY

*Ben putting all the kitchen utensils into a large garbage bag. Three other bags are already filled and the kitchen is looking empty.*

    CUT TO:

45 INT. BEN'S BEDROOM — DAY

*Ben is stuffing all the bedding into a garbage bag. Next he opens a drawer on the dresser and begins taking out clothes and stuffing them into another bag. He pauses for a moment to take a drink from a tall glass.*

    CUT TO:

46 INT. BEN'S LIVING ROOM — DAY

*All the books from the bookcase go into another bag. Then all the records. But he selects certain favourites and as this sequence pro-gresses we see that Ben is making tapes of these tracks. As soon as he is done with the recording, he throws the album into a garbage bag.*

    CUT TO:

47 EXT. BEN'S YARD — NIGHT

*Ben pours lighter fluid on to a pile of photographs and then throws a match on to it. It bursts into flames. He throws more stuff on and the fire blazes. A curious neighbour watches from a safe distance, not wanting to get involved.*

ANGLE ON THE FIRE

*A watercolour, a poem to his wife, a photograph of him and his wife, a Polaroid of a naked woman, his medical records, his birth and marriage certificates, divorce papers, strips of photographs from booths, postcards from Hawaii. Two small children (his?).*

ANGLE ON BEN

*Now the flames are high and Ben has to stand back as he throws things on to the fire . . . his camera, an engraved box, his wife's 'left behind' clothing, a clock . . .*

    CUT TO:

48 EXT. BEN'S HOUSE – DAWN

*Fifteen neatly tied garbage bags and Ben's furniture are stacked up on the sidewalk. Ben comes out of his front door carrying a racing bike. He walks to the neighbours' house and places the bike on the porch. We see a label saying 'To Brad from Ben.' He walks to his black car with a small suitcase, gets in and drives off.*

    CUT TO:

49 EXT. DESERT LANDSCAPE WITH ROAD – DAY

*A high wide shot shows a small black car making its way across the frame.*

    DISSOLVE TO:

50 INT. CAR – DAY

*Through the window we see a dead straight road stretching to infinity.*

*The sunlight is painfully bright. On the soundtrack we hear one of Ben's chosen tapes, which continues through into the next shot.*

    DISSOLVE TO:

51 EXT. GAS STATION IN THE DESERT – DAY

*Ben is filling his car. A towncar drives in and stops next to the BMW. Three men get out. They look like Russian Mobsters. Ben nods at them and they nod back.*

    CUT TO:

52 INT. CAR — NIGHT

*Same angle through the window but this time we see Las Vegas at night as Ben drives down the main drag. An overdose of neon.*

52A EXT. LAS VEGAS STRIP — NIGHT

*Ahead we see the light changing, but Ben doesn't notice until it's almost too late. The car stops and we see Sera crossing in front of the car. She gives Ben a look of real attitude because he is over the line and she has to change course to cross in front.*

CUT TO:

53 EXT. HOTEL FORECOURT — NIGHT

*Sera is talking to Yuri. A middle-aged man gets out of a cab and Yuri shakes him by the hand and introduces him to Sera. He hands Yuri an envelope and then Sera and he go into the hotel together. Yuri looks around thoughtfully before getting into a cab and driving off.*

54 INT. DOCTOR'S OFFICE — DAY

*Improvised scene.* \*

55 INT. MOTEL RECEPTION — NIGHT

*Ben waits to check in while the manager explains the house rules to a family of large white people from the Midwest.*

MANAGER

All rooms to be paid a week in advance, maid service is optional, use of the pool is at your own risk, there is no lifeguard on duty.

*Above the manager's head is the name of the motel,* The Whole Year Inn. *Ben stares at it and then smiles.*

BEN'S POV

*The sign has changed to* The Hole You're In.

*Dialogue for this scene appears in the Afterword.

CUT TO:

56 INT. LIQUOR STORE — NIGHT

*Ben has almost filled a trolley with bottles of various brands. He is whistling and seems happy.*

57 INT. DOCTOR'S OFFICE — DAY

*Improvised scene.* *

CUT TO:

58 EXT. THE STRIP — NIGHT

*Ben driving. He sees Sera and follows her, then drives up on the sidewalk. She sees him.*

> BEN

Hello!

> SERA

Hello.

> BEN

Are you working?

> SERA
> (*tough*)

Working? What do you mean, working? I'm walking.

*And she walks a few steps to prove it, stopping on the passenger side of his car. They pause for a moment and Ben is confused. He is quite taken with her beauty, but this is not going according to plan. He reaches into the car quickly and picks an open can of beer, draining it before tossing the empty back on to the rear seat.*

Isn't it illegal to drink and drive?

> BEN
> (*laughs*)

That's funny.

*Dialogue for this scene appears in the Afterword.

> (*seriously*)
I wonder if you'll take $250 to fuck me?

*Sera doesn't say anything.*

> That is, if you'll come to my room for an hour, I will give
> you $500.

SERA

Maybe you shouldn't stand in the road like that. You're
pretty drunk.

*He bites his lips as he waits for her to respond.*

> (*softer*)
You're pretty drunk.

BEN
(*factual*)

Not really. My room's not far. The Whole Year Inn. You
can drive with me if you want . . .

*She makes no response.*

> . . . or we can walk . . . or I'll give you cab fare.

*Takes out his money.*

> Whatever you want.

*She touches the door handle.*

SERA

Why don't you give me the money when I'm in the car,
and I'll drive with you.

*It takes Ben a moment or two to register that she is saying yes. He
comes around the car to open the door for her.*

BEN

I'm Ben.

*They shake hands.*

SERA

I'm Sera.

*She gets in. Ben gets in.*

    CUT TO:

59 INT. CAR – NIGHT

*Ben hands her the money.*

BEN

Sarah – with an H?

SERA

No – S-E-R-A.

*They grin at each other.*

    You wanna start the engine?

*They drive off.*

60 EXT. MOTEL PARKING LOT – NIGHT

*They sit in the car for a while before speaking.*

SERA

I'm sort of curious . . . if you're willing to pay me two-fifty
. . . not that I mind . . . I mean, I'm OK with that – why
aren't you staying in a real hotel?

BEN

We can go to one if you'd prefer.

SERA

No, this is fine. I was just wondering.

*Ben switches off the engine but makes no move to get out of the car.*

BEN

Well . . . I'm here because I'm a drunk who tends to pass
out at odd hours for unpredictable stretches. I'm going to
a hotel soon. A room with balcony to pass out on . . . or
off.

*He falls silent.*

SERA

Umm. We can stay in the car for an hour if you want. But I really have to go then. It's your time.

BEN

Right, I'll get your door. I tend to fade in and out lately.

SERA

I guess I do too.

BEN

You what?

SERA

I sometimes fade out.

BEN

Oh . . . well, maybe we better synchronize our spells . . . or stagger them.

SERA
(gently)
You were going to get my door.

*He gets out and she waits for him to open her door. She gets out and he offers her his arm. She takes it and they walk into the motel.*

CUT TO:

61 INT. BEN'S ROOM – NIGHT

*As Ben closes the door, Sera surveys the room.*

SERA
(amused)
What this room needs . . . is more booze.

SERA'S POV

*There are bottles everywhere. Ben has gone to a lot of trouble to lay them out in a pleasing way.*

BEN

Do you think so?

*She turns and looks at him, appraising him. Suddenly she's all business, in control, and Ben likes it.*

> SERA
>
> Mind if I use the bathroom?

> BEN
>
> Of course.

*She goes into the bathroom.*

> Want a drink? I'm having one.

> SERA (O.S.)
> A shot of tequila, if you can spare it.

> BEN
>
> Of course.

*Ben smiles, happier than we've ever seen him. He gets her order ready and then he takes a big swig from a bourbon bottle. He sits on the edge of the bed.*

*The bathroom door opens and Sera comes in wearing a black bra and panties. She's acting the hooker now, tough and sexy.*

> SERA
> For two-fifty we can do pretty much what you want.
> You've been drinking, so it might be better if I got on top,
> but the other way's fine too. I have some jelly in case you
> want to fuck my ass, that's up to you. If you want to come
> on my face, that's OK too, just try to keep it out of my
> hair, I just washed it . . . and my eyes, it stings.

*She walks to the table and downs her tequila in one. Then comes to the bed, where Ben is sitting. She kneels, unzips his fly and begins sucking him. Ben watches her, looks at her reflection in the closet mirror, reaches for the bottle and drinks some, being careful not to disturb Sera. After a while Sera comes up.*

> Do you want to fuck now?

> BEN
> (*confused*)
>
> Maybe another drink first. More tequila?

> SERA
>
> OK . . . whatever.

*She takes the bottle and drinks. She goes down again. Ben stops her.*

> What's the story? Are you too drunk to come?

> BEN
> (*sincere*)
>
> I don't care about that. There's time left. You can have
> more money. You can drink all you want. You can talk or
> listen. Just stay, that's all I want.

*She looks at him, confused. She sees a strange look on his face. It throws her.*

*This is a turning point. Both of them are momentarily exposed.*

*Ben lifts the sheet and moves to one side, indicating that she should come into the bed. She's as confused as he is. She gets in with him and he hands her the bottle.*

> CUT TO:

62 INT. CASINO – NIGHT

*Yuri is losing at one of the tables. He continues to bet though, putting half of what he has left on one number. He loses again. He mops his face with a red silk handkerchief and places another bet.*

63 INT. SOMEWHERE IN THE CASINO – NIGHT

*The three Russian Mobsters we saw in the desert are walking through the casino, looking for someone.*

> CUT TO:

64 INT. BEN'S ROOM – NIGHT

*They are both in bed, drinking.*

> SERA

So, Ben, what brings you to Las Vegas? Business convention?

*They both laugh and Ben hands her the bottle.*

> BEN

No, I came here to drink . . . myself . . . you know . . .

> SERA

To death?

> BEN

Yes, that's right.

*He looks at her, she at him, not sure whether to believe him or not.*

I cashed in all of my money, paid my AmEx card, gonna sell the car tomorrow.

> SERA

How long's it gonna take, for you to drink yourself to death?

> BEN

I think about four weeks, and I've got enough for about 250 to 300 dollars a day.

> SERA

Yes . . . that should do it. What am I? A luxury?

> BEN

Yeah. And your meter just ran out.

*Ben looks at his watch.*

> SERA

It's OK . . . nice watch. Go on. Talk some more.

*Ben yawns, suddenly deeply tired.*

> BEN

In LA I kept running out of booze and the store would be closed because I'd forget to look at my watch . . . so I decided to move here because nothing ever closes and because I got tired of getting funny looks when I would walk into a bar at six o'clock . . . even the bartenders started preaching.

> (*yawns again*)

Here, everyone's from out of town so no one cares, no one is overtly fucking up.

CUT TO:

*Later.*

SIDE ANGLE

*Sera is in focus, Ben is asleep.*

> SERA (V.O.)
> I guess I was intrigued by him . . . There was a lot of stuff that I wanted to ask him about but didn't because I didn't want to sound too interested in a trick. But I felt as if a relationship was being forged very quickly.

65 INT. DOCTOR'S OFFICE — DAY

*Improvised scene.*[*]

CUT TO:

65A EXT. SERA'S APARTMENT COMPLEX — DAWN

*Sera gets out of a cab and makes her way towards her apartment, changing out of her high heels as she walks.*

66 INT. SERA'S HOUSE — DAWN

*Sera lets herself in. Yuri is standing in the shadows. She gets a fright when she sees him.*

> YURI
> Where have you been?

> SERA
> It was a slow night. I went to a hotel for a few drinks.

[*]Dialogue for this scene appears in the Afterword.

*Yuri holds out his hand for her bag. She gives it to him. He finds the money and counts it.*

> YURI
>
> A full night on the street and this is all?

> SERA
>
> Like I said . . . it was a slow night . . . I'm sorry. It was hard to score.

*Yuri slaps her.*

> Don't hit me.

> YURI
>
> What do you think . . . you are sixteen years old on Hollywood Boulevard?

*Yuri talks in Russian, becoming angrier, and slaps her again. He spits on the floor.*

*Sera falls against the kitchen table and picks up a lethal-looking knife. Yuri stops.*

> SERA
>
> Maybe nobody wants to fuck a chick with a cut on her cheek.

*She throws the knife to Yuri, who catches it. She bends over the table and pulls up her skirt.*

> There, go ahead!

*She mimics him.*

*A shower of Russian comes out of Yuri, but he doesn't touch her. He tries to regain his dignity by putting on a coat.*

> YURI
>
> I could kill you. You know that.

*He goes to the door.*

> Work, tonight, bring me money, no matter the hour.

*And he exits. Sera is still on the table.*

> SERA

I will, Yuri. I will.

CUT TO:

67 INT. PAWN SHOP — DAY

*The proprietor is handing over some cash to Yuri, whose jewellery is on the counter. He pockets it and, as he turns to leave, Ben comes in. They pass without taking much notice of each other. Ben removes his Rolex and shows it to the man.*

CUT TO:

68 EXT. STREET — LAS VEGAS — DAY

*Yuri is walking in the hot sun, sweating. We see him through long-lens heat haze. The camera wanders into the traffic and we see the black towncar crawling along behind him, the three men inside.*

CUT TO:

69 INT. DOCTOR'S OFFICE — DAY

*Improvised scene.* *

CUT TO:

70 INT. MAIN BAR — HOTEL — NIGHT

*A lounge singer belts out a fair rendition of a Tony Orlando number. Sera sits at the bar, an empty seat on either side of her. She watches a younger hooker in the final moments of pulling a dangerous-looking man. The girl is aware of Sera without even looking at her. The guy she is with looks around and sees Sera. The girl shoots her an icy look. A man sits next to Sera: a conventioneer.*

> CONVENTIONEER

About ready for another drink?

---

*Dialogue for this scene appears in the Afterword.

> SERA

Yes, that would be great. Are you here for the convention?

> CONVENTIONEER

Do I look that obvious? My name's Paul.

*They shake hands.*

> SERA

No, of course not, just a wild guess. I'm Sera and that's a Margarita.

*The barman is already pouring. The young hooker leaves with her dangerous guy. She pauses long enough to give Sera a nasty smile. The conventioneer pays for the drink and is a little lost for words. Sera tries to help.*

So . . . are you alone, or are you just using me to make someone else jealous?

> CONVENTIONEER
> (*laughs nervously*)

Alone. Alone. I'm here alone.

> SERA
> (*friendly*)

Where are you staying?

> CONVENTIONEER
> (*suspicious*)

Right here in the hotel. Why?

> SERA
> (*moving a little closer*)

Well . . . I thought you might be looking for a date.

> CONVENTIONEER
> (*shocked*)

A date. What, are you a hooker?
> (*voice getting louder*)

What do you mean a date?

(*and louder*)
I've got a wife back home. I just came over to talk for a
few minutes.

> SERA
> (*quietly*)
> I'm sorry, I guess I misunderstood.

*She looks around.*

> Please don't raise your voice. I won't bother you about it
> again.

> CONVENTIONEER
> (*calmer*)
> Sorry. Look . . . you seem like a nice girl. I'm just sick of
> everyone in this town trying to get my money.

*He gets up.*

> Here, have another drink. I gotta go.

*He leaves. Sera is uncomfortable. People watch her, aware that
something has been going on. The barman comes over to where Sera
is sitting. He speaks quietly, not unfriendly.*

> BARMAN
> Maybe you should give it a miss for this evening.

*He walks away. Sera finishes her drink and leaves.*

> CUT TO:

71 EXT. THE STRIP – NIGHT

*Sera at work is looking more carefully than usual, hoping to see
Ben.*

*A huge silver limo pulls up and, after some negotiation, she gets in.*

> CUT TO:

72 EXT. THE STRIP – NIGHT

*Long-lens shot of Ben, very drunk on the street. He falls and lies still for quite a long time before getting up. He falls into the road and tries to hail a cab, but none stops. A cop car cruises to a halt and Ben more or less imitates a normal person as he walks out of shot.*

73 EXT. THE POOL — MOTEL — DAY

*Ben dives in and swims a length under water. He pulls himself out and sits next to the large Midwestern family. The father says hello and introduces his family to Ben. They are all very friendly. It's a nice atmosphere around this pool and for a moment Ben even looks healthy.*

CUT TO:

74 EXT. THE STRIP — NIGHT

*A limo pulls up and Sera gets out. She sees something.*

SERA'S POV

*Ben sitting at a bus stop, drinking out of a cocktail glass. When he sees her he gets up, a little unsteadily.*

BEN
I couldn't remember what happened last time. I was afraid that I might have been rude, or mean to you.

*He looks at her.*

If I was, I'm sorry.

SERA
No, just drunk . . . but that's OK. Where's your car?

BEN
I sold it this morning. I'm going to take cabs from now on in.

*Sera looks up and down the strip.*

Don't run away.

> SERA
> (*defensive*)

Why should I? I know you're not a cop, so what is it tonight? Another two-fifty to watch you sleep?

*Ben sits back down, a little hurt.*

> What's up?

> BEN

I was looking for you tonight. I don't know if you have a boyfriend . . .

*He thinks.*

> . . . or a girlfriend, but if you have some free time . . . maybe we could . . . have dinner.

> SERA
> (*tough again, but pleased*)

Are you serious?

> BEN
> (*deadly serious*)

I think you know I'm serious. I'll pay you if you like . . . but I'd like to see you.

> SERA

No, I can't have dinner with you.

*And she hails a taxi, which stops immediately, and she gets in.*

> The Mojave Hotel, please.

*Ben watches the cab drive off.*

> CUT TO:

75 INT. CORRIDOR OF HOTEL – NIGHT

*Sera walks along, checking numbers on doors. She finds the right one and knocks firmly.*

> YURI (V.O.)

Yes? What?

>                         SERA

It's me, Yuri.

*The door opens a crack and Yuri peers out.*

>                         YURI

Sera! It's . . .

*He looks around for a clock.*

>     . . . it's late.

76 INT. YURI'S ROOM – NIGHT

*Sera comes into the room, takes her purse out and counts out $700.*

>                         SERA

Sorry, Yuri . . . good night . . . lots of tricks . . . I think
things are picking up.

*Yuri sits on the bed. He looks unwell and disoriented. His face is
covered with a thin film of sweat. He seems to be listening for something, because he stops her talking by putting his fingers to his lips.
He looks at her and then beckons her to the bed. Sera is nervous. As
she walks to the bed, she begins unbuttoning her blouse. Yuri stops
her with a wave of his hand. Sera is puzzled and frightened now.
Yuri seems to be deranged.*

>                         YURI

Have you told anyone that I'm here?

>                         SERA

No.

*Yuri suddenly hears something. He grabs Sera's hand and takes her
to the wall. He presses her head to the wall.*

>                         YURI

Do you hear that?

*He looks at her.*

>     They're talking about me.

*He pulls himself together.*

Go, Sera.
> (*whispers*)

Go. Stay at home. I will call you tomorrow.

SERA

Yuri . . . are you . . .

YURI
> (*patiently*)

Sera . . . please go.

*He indicates the wall.*

This is very important . . . and I must listen. Now go.

*They face each other for a moment and then Yuri does an almost comic gesture to tell her to go. He hustles her to the door and shoves her out as she is still buttoning up her blouse. He slams the door.*

> (*through the door*)

Goodbye, Sera. Don't come back here. I will not see you again.

*Sera stands there for a while, almost in shock, and then she begins to walk. The camera follows her as she makes her way down the endless corridor of doors. Ahead of her, three men are walking towards her, checking the door numbers as they make their way. Sera doesn't take them in. They pass and turn a corner. We recognize them as the men from the black towncar.*

ANGLE

*The men have stopped outside Yuri's room. The camera pans and we see Sera down the other corridor getting into the elevator.*

FADE OUT.

77 INT. BEN'S ROOM AT THE MOTEL — NIGHT

*Ben is lying on the bed watching a game show, drinking.*

*A coughing fit hits him. He is very short of breath. We see how ill he really is.*

*There is a tap at the door.*

> BEN

No thanks . . . I'm fine.

*The tapping persists and eventually Ben gets off the bed and unlocks it, but keeps the chain on. It is Sera.*

> SERA

Still want to have dinner?

*Ben stares at her for a while.*

> BEN

Yes.

> SERA

I have to change and take a shower first. If you want to come home and wait.

*Ben opens the door.*

We should pick up a bottle of tequila on the way. I owe you one.

> BEN

You do?

CUT TO:

78 INT. SERA'S HOUSE – NIGHT

*Sera is finishing in the shower and Ben is sitting at the kitchen table. He gets up and walks around the house, trying to get a sense of her. The furniture is very plain and there is a spartan quality about the house. He looks with interest at the bookshelf, which has a good selection of literature.*

> BEN
> (*to himself*)

This is the home of an angel.

> SERA (O.S.)

You OK out there?

                                    BEN
Yes. Take your time. I'm fine.

*He pours himself another drink.*

                                    SERA (O.S.)
Pour yourself another drink.

*He sits down and she comes in, towelling her hair.*

You OK?

                                    BEN
Of course. Wow . . . you look extremely beautiful.

                                    SERA
Thank you. What time is it?

                                    BEN
Don't know. My watch went the way of the car.

*He holds up his empty wrist for her to see. Then looks up and sees
her watching him.*

I'm rambling. I really like you. You make me want to talk
. . . I don't know what time it is.

                                    SERA
I like hearing you talk.
                              (*businesslike*)
If you feel up to a short walk, there's a place to eat around
the corner. All the food in Vegas is terrible so the place
doesn't really matter. How does that sound to you?

                                    BEN
Do they have drinks?

CUT TO:

79 EXT. THE STRIP – NIGHT

*Ben and Sera walk and talk.*

80 INT. RESTAURANT — NIGHT

*Ben and Sera are eating. He plays with his food, eating very little of it. Finally he pushes it away and orders another drink.*

> SERA
>
> I'm from the East. I went to college, did an arts course. I now live in Vegas. I think of it as home. I came here deliberately to carve out a life. I was in LA before, but I'll come back to that later.
>
> (*pause*)
>
> The tough times are behind me now. I can deal with the bad things that happen. There will always be dark characters. But my life is good. It is as I would want it to be. So, why are you drunk?

> BEN
>
> Is that really what you want to ask me?

> SERA
>
> Yes.

> BEN
>
> (*worried*)
>
> Well, then I guess this is our first date . . . or our last. Until now, I wasn't sure it was either.

> SERA
>
> Very clever.

*Sera thinks for a while and decides to give in to him on this.*

> First. It's our first. I'm just concerned. So . . . why are you killing yourself?

> BEN
>
> Interesting choice of words. I don't remember. I just know that I want to.

> SERA
>
> Want to what? Kill yourself? Are you saying that you're drinking as a way to kill yourself?

*And she leans across the table to be close to him, listening intently.
Ben becomes uncomfortable and tries to joke it off.*

BEN

Or killing myself as a way to drink.

*Sera continues to stare at him, wanting to know the real answer. He
takes a slug from his drink. She sits back.*

We'll talk about it some other time maybe. OK?

*Sera relaxes and continues with her food. We hear her thoughts for a
moment.*

SERA (V.O.)

It wasn't so important to me. I mean, he never asked me
why I was a hooker, and that was impressive. I really liked
him. So I decided to just play my part. I mean . . . it's
good to help someone once in a while, it's a bonus to
being alive, and that was my plan . . . to stay alive. I suddenly came to a decision.

BEN

What are you thinking? Are you angry with me?

SERA
*(decides something)*

Ben, why don't you stay at my place tonight? I mean . . .
look, you're so drunk. I like you. I trust you.

BEN

That's astonishing. Sera, look . . .

SERA

I hate to think of you in that cheesy motel. I mean . . .

*And she folds her arms and grins at him.*

Let's face it, what the fuck are you doing in Las Vegas?

BEN
*(overwhelmed by her)*

I'm going to move to a smart hotel, tomorrow if it'll make
you feel better.

(*looks at her*)
Let's talk about tomorrow. Wanna do something?

SERA
(*warmly*)
Sure . . . tonight. Then please stay at my place.

BEN
Sera . . . you know I'm not much good in the sack.

SERA
It's not about sex, Ben. I'll make you up a bed on the sofa.
Do it for me. We can talk till late and then sleep till late.
As you know, I am my own boss.

*Ben laughs loud, the most animated we've seen him, and his laugh
is infectious, and Sera joins in. Other diners turn to stare at them.
They seem like a couple.*

CUT TO:

81 EXT. THE STRIP – NIGHT

*Ben and Sera walk and talk, holding hands.*

82 EXT. DESERT – DAY

*A wide shot. The black towncar makes its way across frame. Left to
right.*

CUT TO:

83 INT. SERA'S HOUSE – DAY

*Ben is asleep on the sofa. As he wakes up, he becomes aware that
Sera is watching him from across the room. They smile at each other.*

BEN
How long have I been here?

SERA
Three nights, two days. When is your rent coming up at
the motel?

BEN

I don't know.

(*sits up*)

I'll go and sort it out today. Why don't you come? . . .
We'll find a real room for me. You can pick it out, a tower
on the strip.

SERA

There's no reason to blow all your money on a hotel
room.

BEN

What do you mean?

SERA

What I mean is that you should bring your stuff over here.
We're spending all this time together . . . what the fuck!

BEN

Sera . . .

SERA

Let's face it, Ben, we're having fun here. I've never done
so much talking in my life.

BEN

Me neither.

SERA

So! Let's dispense with the formalities. I want you here
. . . now!

BEN

Sera . . . you are crazy.

SERA

So . . . I'm not too concerned with long-term plans.

BEN

Don't you think you'll get a little bored living with a
drunk?

SERA

That is what I want. Why don't you go and get your stuff?

BEN

You haven't seen the worst of it. These last few days I've been very controlled. I knock things over . . . I throw up all the time.

(*looks at her*)

Now I feel really good . . . You're like some kind of anti-dote that mixes with the liquor and keeps me in balance, but that won't last for ever. You'll get tired of it really quickly. Believe me.

*They sit in silence for a while.*

SERA

OK, you go back to your hotel and I'll go back to my glamorous life of being alone.

*She walks out of the room and into the bathroom, where she sits on the toilet to pee.*

(*to herself*)

The only thing I have to come home to is a bottle of Listerine to wash the taste of come out of my mouth. I'm tired of being alone . . . that's what I'm tired of.

*She finishes, wipes herself and flushes the toilet. Pulling up her panties, she walks back into the bedroom, where Ben is putting on his shoes.*

Don't you like me, Ben?

BEN

(*devastated*)

Don't be silly.

*Ben is unable to deal with the fact that he is absolutely in love with her. He walks out of the room. She follows.*

SERA

We gotta decide this . . . right now. Before we go any further. You either stay here with me or . . .

*Ben turns to look at her.*

> . . . we can't see each other any more.

*Ben and Sera look at each other for a long time.*

BEN

Sera . . . what you don't understand is . . .

SERA

What?

*Ben is deeply troubled. He comes to a decision.*

BEN

You can never . . . never . . . ask me to stop drinking. Do
you understand?

SERA
(*dead serious*)

I do. I really do.
(*smiles*)

OK. I have to do some shopping alone. You go out for a
few drinks and then pick up your things. Don't hurry and
I'll be back before you to let you in.

*Sera grabs him in a big embrace that knocks him off his balance
and into the wall. She kisses him all over his face and squeezes his
skinny frame.*

CUT TO:

84 INT. BEN'S ROOM AT THE MOTEL — DAY

*Ben is packing his liquor into his suitcase. The almost-empty bottles
he pours into a large cup, which he drinks from. The suitcase is now
full and Ben suddenly realizes that he hasn't packed any clothes.
They are all in a pile on the bed. He talks to himself.*

BEN

Maybe this isn't a good idea after all.

*He tries to put clothes in with the bottles, but the lid won't close. He
sits on the bed and has an imaginary conversation with Sera.*

Listen, angel . . . the thing is that I'm nuts about you and
this is a bad thing . . . because my real plan is to die here
and you were never even part of my plan . . . but like I
said, I am nuts about you . . . wait a minute, I have an
idea, angel.

*And he opens the closet and finds some plastic laundry bags, which
he puts his clothes in.*

85 SCENE CUT.

   CUT TO:

86 EXT. SERA'S HOUSE — DAY

*Sera's neighbours, a husband and wife, are standing outside her
house. They stop her. They are also her landlords.*

                          HUSBAND
We didn't know whether to call the police or not.

*And they indicate the sleeping figure of Ben, in the doorway, clutch-
ing a bottle of bourbon, using his suitcase as a pillow.*

                           WIFE
He's been there for about half an hour. My husband
thought he'd seen you two together, but I thought it best
to wait until you got home.

                           SERA
Yes, he's my friend. I guess he had just a little too much to
drink.
                 (*smiling uncomfortably*)
I'll help him inside.
                 (*puts down her packages*)
Thanks for your concern. Sorry to trouble you.

                         HUSBAND
                      (*gallantly*)
Well, call me if there's anything I can do.

*They go to their own house. Sera opens the front door, kneels down next to Ben and shakes him gently.*

> SERA

Can you wake up?

*Ben opens his eyes and looks around with a pleasant, cheerful expression.*

> BEN

Hi!

> SERA

Why don't you go in and sit down. I have some gifts for you.

> BEN

Right . . . OK . . .

*Ben stands and almost loses his balance. He picks up his suitcase and attempts to pick up her packages as well, but she stops him.*

> SERA

Don't worry . . . I got 'em.

*Ben staggers in with his case. As Sera enters, she looks around and sees the husband and wife at the window, still watching.*

> BEN (O.S.)

Want a drink? Great nap. Wanna go out tonight?

> SERA

Seriously, Ben . . . I need to keep pretty low-key around here. Maybe next time you could nap this side of the door. That was the landlord.

> BEN

Oh, I always do. Don't worry. I'm sorry about that, but I got back too early and the door was locked.

> SERA

Of course . . .

*She reaches into her purse.*

Gift number one.

*And she gives him a newly cut key. He takes it and tries it in the
lock, then drops it into his pocket.*

> BEN
>
> I used to carry a lot of keys, but one by one they all fell
> victim to the great condensation. Now I have just this one
> . . . which is . . .

*And he tails off and stares at the floor. She waits for him to continue
and then comes to him and touches him on the arm.*

87 INT. SERA'S HOUSE — DAY

> SERA
>
> Ben?

> BEN
>
> Sorry.

*He shakes his head.*

> I was miles away.

*He sees the parcels.*

> Ah . . . more gifts. I have to sit down for this.

*He strides into the living room and flops on to the sofa. She follows.*

> Sera, I love that name . . . S-E-R-A. Before we proceed
> onwards, there is something I need to say. OK?

> SERA
>
> OK.

> BEN
>
> I've come this far . . . here I am, in your house. I want you
> to let me pay your rent for this month. All right?

*And he stares at her as if to say that nothing can happen until this
matter is resolved.*

> SERA
>
> Why?

BEN

Because . . . it's better for me that way. OK?

SERA

Well . . . OK . . .

*She is uncomfortable.*

*They sit in silence for a while.*

BEN

Sera . . . I hope that you understand how I feel about this.
First of all, you're welcome to my money. We can buy a
couple of cases of liquor and you can have the rest. But I
don't think you're talking to me right now about money.

SERA
(*smiling*)

No?

BEN

No. I think you're talking about you. I'll tell you right now
that I'm in love with you . . . but, be that as it may, I'm not
here to force my twisted life into your soul.

SERA

I know that . . .

BEN

. . . and I'm not here to demand your attention to the
point where it changes your life. We know I'm a drunk . . .
but that seems to be all right with you. And I know that
you're a hooker. I hope you understand that I'm a person
who is totally at ease with this . . . which is not to say that
I'm indifferent or that I don't care . . . I do . . . it simply
means that I trust and accept your judgement. What I'm
saying is . . . that I hope you understand that I understand.

SERA

Thanks, I do understand. I was worried about how that
would be . . . but now I'm not. And you should know that

included with the rent around here is a complimentary
blow job.

BEN

Ah, yes . . . I suppose sooner or later we ought to fuck.

SERA

Whatever that means. Open your presents.

*She hands him the larger of the two parcels.*

Open this one first.

*Ben awkwardly unwraps the present, a large, colourful shirt. A gen-
uine smile comes on to his face.*

BEN

Very nice.

*He holds the shirt against himself.*

This should work very nicely with my suit, which, by the
way, is the only item of clothing I brought over from the
motel with me.

*Sera raises an eyebrow.*

SERA

Right . . . the suitcase was clinking. So what did you do
with your clothes?

BEN
(*laughing*)

I threw them into the garbage, which was perhaps immoral,
but I wanted to come to you clean, so to speak. I thought
we could go shopping and pick up a pair of jeans and forty-
five pairs of underwear and just throw them out each day.

SERA
(*smiling*)

Nice talk, Ben. Keep drinking. In between the hundred
and one proof breath and the occasional drool, some
interesting words fall from your mouth.

*She hands him the last present.*

Now, try this one.

*Ben unwraps the smaller gift. It is a silver hip flask. He is very touched and a little tear trickles down his cheek.*

BEN

Well . . . looks like I'm with the right girl.

*He turns it in his hands.*

I must say that I'm very impressed that you would buy this for me. I know you wouldn't do this without thinking about it. Funny . . . you did just what I would have done.

*Ben stands and tries the flask in his pocket for fit. It is fine. He walks to the door.*

I'm going to fill it right now.

SERA

Do you want to go gambling tonight? We could go out and play for a few hours.

*Ben comes back into the room, takes the flask out of his suit pocket and has a drink.*

BEN

I hadn't planned to gamble . . . but if you would keep the bulk of my money here, then I could safely blow a couple of hundred bucks.

*He takes out all of his money, peels off a few hundreds and then gives her the rest.*

Giving you money makes me want to come.

SERA

Then come.
                          (*pause*)
I'm going to change. Watch TV. I'll be half an hour.

*And she leaves. There is a slight edge to her voice and Ben is not*

*sure if he offended her or not. He watches through the small angle of
the door as she changes.*

I am planning to go out and do some work.

> BEN

When?

> SERA

Tomorrow night as a matter of fact.

88 EXT. THE STRIP — NIGHT

*Ben and Sera walking. The camera follows them. He is wearing his
new shirt and looks good in it. She is wearing a green dress and mismatched earrings and looks great. They walk and talk.*

> BEN

I like your earrings.

*He changes sides.*

I like women who wear mismatched earrings.

> SERA

Well, then . . . I hope we don't run into any tonight.

> BEN
> (*laughs*)

What do you mean?

> SERA

I expect some kind of loyalty here. Just because I fuck for
money doesn't give you cause to start picking up women
and leaving me looking silly.

*And she stops and looks at him, smiling but serious.*

> BEN

And I only have eyes for you. And we both know that you
would never become romantically involved with a trick,
right?

89 INT. CASINO – NIGHT

*They walk around the huge space, which is full of people and
energy, and suddenly Ben grabs Sera and pushes her against a slot
machine and kisses her deeply. At first she resists and then she gives
in to him and responds. They knock over some change, which falls to
the floor, and Ben pulls away from her for a beat to bend down and
scoop up all the change and hand it to the bemused player, before
returning to Sera's mouth for more. They break for air and then Ben
leads her towards the bar. As he waves to attract the barman's attention, she squeezes his arm.*

                           SERA
                         (*quietly*)
        I love you.

*But he doesn't hear her.*

ANGLE ON CASINO ACTIVITY

*On long lens we see Ben and Sera at the bar. Suddenly Ben seems to
fall asleep. Sera tries to wake him and then he goes crazy and falls
backwards off his stool, knocking a waitress and her drinks over.
Security guards appear and begin arguing with Sera.*

        CUT TO:

90 INT. SERA'S HOUSE – NIGHT

*Ben wakes up on the sofa, fully dressed. A night-light gives a soft
glow. He rolls off the sofa, landing on all fours on the floor. He
crawls to the kitchen, opens the fridge door and takes out a vodka
bottle and carton of orange juice. With difficulty he gets to his feet,
finds a glass and pours a drink. He swallows the mix and then
stands over the sink just in case he has to vomit.*

91 INT. SERA'S BEDROOM – NIGHT

*Sera wakes and Ben comes in and gets into bed with her.*

                           SERA
        How are you doing?

BEN

Very well . . . umm . . . I never expected to have to ask this
again . . . but how did our evening go? I remember getting
to the casino . . . I remember kissing you . . . that was
really nice but everything after that is a blank.

SERA

Well – I was prepared for worse, but it wasn't so bad. We
were sitting at the bar, talking about blackjack. You
seemed just fine, a little drunker than usual, but nothing
really strange, but then your head started to droop and I
put my arm on your shoulder and then, wham, you swung
your arm at me, and fell backwards off your stool into a
cocktail waitress. You smashed everything on her tray, it
was a real mess. You kept yelling and yelling.

BEN

Oh. What did you do?

SERA

I tried to shut you up and help you to your feet but you
kept swinging at me – not like you wanted to hit me, but
more just waving me away. Security came and when you
saw them you stopped yelling. They wanted to carry you
out and dump you on the street, but I talked them into
letting me walk you out.

BEN

That's impressive. How did you do that?

SERA

I told them you were an alcoholic and I would take you
home. I also promised that we would never come in there
again.

BEN

We?

SERA

Yes, we.

BEN
(*holds her hand*)
What happened then?

SERA
You were OK for a while, so we walked for about a block
and then you said you wanted to go home and fuck, but I
think even you knew that wasn't going to happen. We got
a cab and you asked him to stop at a liquor store, even
though I told you that we had plenty at home. In the store
you gave the kid a hundred and told him to keep the
change. I asked you if you knew it was a hundred. You said
you did, so I let you do it. We got here, you fell asleep on
the couch and I covered you up and came to bed.

BEN
I warned you . . .
(*kisses her hand*)
. . . but I'm sorry.

SERA
Here's my speech . . .
(*kisses his hand*)
. . . I know this shouldn't be acceptable to me, but it is.
Don't ask my why. I sense that your trouble is very big . . .
and I'm scared for you . . . and so I'm doing what I think
you need me to do. Falling down in casinos is little stuff.
It doesn't bother me. It has nothing to do with us.

BEN
That's amazing. What are you? Some sort of angel visiting
me from one of my drunk fantasies? How can you be so
good?

*She turns away to the wall and curls up like a small girl.*

SERA
I don't know what you're saying. I'm just using you. I
need you. Can we not talk about it any more, please. Not
another word.

*He thinks about this. He gently pushes her until she is lying on her front and then he pulls up her nightdress and strokes her naked back. He kisses her in the small of her back.*

                          BEN
Why don't you go back to sleep. I'll go out and buy us some breakfast.

                          SERA
Be careful.

*He stands and goes to the door.*

                          BEN
Don't worry.

*As he leaves the room, she calls after him.*

                          SERA
Ben, I'm working tonight.

*He opens the door and smiles at her.*

                          BEN
I know.

CUT TO:


92 EXT. SIDEWALK — EARLY MORNING

*Ben gets out of his cab and walks up to the doorway of a grocery store. It is locked. Ben looks at his wrist and then remembers that he no longer has a watch. He looks around, sees something and exits frame.*

CUT TO:


93 INT. ROUGH ENGLISH BAR — EARLY MORNING

*Ben enters and makes his way to the bar. This is a dirty, dark place. An aging blonde in leather hot pants is dancing by herself at the juke-box. A very drunk biker couple argue noisily in a corner, slurring their words. There is not much gambling taking place at the eight slot machines. Ben sits at the bar and the bartender slaps down a paper napkin.*

BEN

A beer and a double kamikaze, please.

BARTENDER

Sure thing. Anything to eat?

BEN

Not quite yet. First I have to drink myself sober, then . . .
a few crackers, maybe an egg and toast . . .

*The bartender walks away to get Ben's drinks. Ben continues any-
way.*

. . . then I'll go home with the groceries and we'll have
breakfast together, and that'll make her feel better about
my condition . . .

*Ben is interrupted by the arrival of the biker girl. She is young,
tough and pretty. She puts an arm around him and presses against
him.*

BIKER GIRL

Who the fuck are you talking to, mister?
(*laughing*)
Why are you all dressed up, honey? My, don't you look
fine.

*She runs her tongue around her mouth.*

I am very bored with my date. Would you like to buy me a
drink?

*Ben looks around and sees the biker staring at the two of them.*

BEN
(*loudly*)
Do you mind if I buy her a drink?

BIKER

Fuck her. I don't care what the fuck you do with her.

BEN

Maybe I could buy you both a drink?

                              BIKER

Fuck you. Don't fuck with me, motherfucker. Fuck off.
Go to it, she's waiting for her drink.

*The biker walks over to the slot machines and begins dropping in
quarters, never taking his eyes off Ben and the girl.*

                          BIKER GIRL

See what an asshole he is.
                          (*big smile*)
I'll have a rum and Coke.

                              BEN

Barman? A rum and Coke, please.

*The girl leans with her back to the bar, closer to Ben, who is facing
the bar on a stool. She brings her face closer to his.*

                          BIKER GIRL

Can I stay with you for a while?

                              BEN

You mean move in with me? Isn't this a bit sudden?

                          BIKER GIRL

Oh, I don't have a lot of stuff.

                              BEN

                          (*smiling*)

I don't think my wife would dig it too much.

*She moves to his ear to whisper.*

                          BIKER GIRL

Maybe we could just go find a room and fuck all day. You
wouldn't have to tell your wife about that, would you? I
could suck you like this.

*And she begins sucking on his lobe. Behind them, at the slot machine,
the biker is still watching. His face fills with a drunken rage.*

                              BEN

See, the thing is . . . fucking you would be wonderful, but I
am deeply in love with Sera . . .

*The biker throws down his beer can and walks towards the bar.*

. . . and it's almost impossible for me to imagine being
with someone else . . .

*The biker arrives at the bar and grabs Ben.*

#### BIKER
Now listen, asshole, I'm not gonna just sit around and
watch her suck on your ear.

*The biker is about to hit Ben, then holds back. He leans in and puts
his face next to Ben's.*

Now, I know that she came over to you, like she does, so
I'm gonna pretend that you're innocent and give you one
chance to walk out of this place . . . right now.

#### BIKER GIRL
(*to biker*)

Get lost, jerk.

*The biker slaps her and then grabs Ben by the collar.*

#### BIKER
What do you say?

*Ben shakes his arm free from the biker's grip. He thinks about it for
a couple of beats and then decides.*

#### BEN
I'm sorry . . . but she and I have decided to spend a few
hours together in a mo–

*The biker headbutts Ben in the face, sending him crashing off his
stool to the floor. His head cracks against the tiled floor. The biker
walks over to him, picks him up by his shirt front and punches him
in the nose. Blood sprays on to his face. The biker walks out of the
bar. The girl follows him quickly. The bartender takes a wet towel
and walks over to where Ben is struggling to get up, holding his face.*

#### BARTENDER
You're quite a fighter.

*He gives him the towel.*

> This may sound silly, but I'm going to have to ask you to
> leave. It's what we do around here when there's a fight.
> Men's room is around the back.

CUT TO:

## 94 EXT. SERA'S HOUSE – MORNING

*Ben lets himself in with his key. He is carrying a big bag of groceries.*
*His clothes are bloodstained. The landlady watches from poolside.*

> BEN
>
> I'm back.

*He walks into the living room and finds Sera reading on the couch.*
*She looks up and sees his face and his bloodstained shirt.*

> SERA
>
> Oh, no! Oh, fuck, Ben, look at your face. You get in a
> fight? I thought you didn't fight. Goddamnit. How do you
> feel? Wait here. Sit down.

*She goes to the bathroom and we hear her rummaging in the medi-*
*cine cabinet.*

> *(off-screen)*
>
> Did you stop at a bar?

*She comes back into the room, armed with bottles and cotton wool.*

> Did you say something stupid to someone stupid?

*She goes to work on his face, dabbing an open cut with some mer-*
*curochrome.*

> BEN
>
> Absolutely not . . . ow . . . I was defending the honour of
> some poor wayward maiden.

*She thinks about this for a moment and then kisses him on the fore-*
*head.*

> SERA

Why don't you go and finish this in the bathroom. Take a shower and put on your other shirt. I'll fix breakfast and then we'll go shopping and get some new clothes. I think this suit must be unlucky.

CUT TO:

95 INT. MALL – DAY

*Ben and Sera come out of a clothing store. Ben is wearing black jeans, red socks and a white dress shirt. They go up the 'up' escalator.*

> SERA

Very creative. Now we can get you a black bow tie and you can look like one of those casino dealers.

> BEN

OK, but remember that they wear it because they have to. I wear it because I want to. That'll make me look different. Let's get a drink.

*Ben somehow gets on to the 'down' escalator, leaving Sera on the higher level.*

> SERA

Ben?

CUT TO:

96 INT. SHOPPING MALL BAR – DAY

*Ben needs a drink badly but this is not the best place. Mothers with children, old people and a waitress with attitude. Ben tries to order but becomes angry when she doesn't bring it straight away. People begin staring. At the next table a dignified older man sits alone.*

*Ben hands Sera a small package.*

CLOSE ANGLE

> BEN

There was no time for me to write a card, with you

breathing down my neck all day, so you'll just have to
wing it, baby.

*He laughs and this induces a coughing fit. He downs his drink and
holds up the empty glass to let the waitress know she should bring
another.*

Open it.

*She does so. It is a pair of onyx earrings. Black onyx set in white
gold.*

#### SERA
#### (*pleased*)

Your colour.

#### BEN

I think you should wear one at a time. One of these . . .
and one of your others. In fact, I was going to buy just
one, but I didn't think it would fly . . . as a gift, I mean.

*His new drink arrives and he takes a swallow straight away.*

#### SERA

I'll wear them tonight . . . one of them.

*She looks at him, aware of what she has said, wondering how he is
reacting. She smiles and Ben takes a deep swallow, finishing his
drink. His mood suddenly changes.*

#### BEN

Yes . . . tonight. Put it on.

*She does so. Ben helps her, bringing his face down close to hers.*

You'll be able to feel it, sharp and hot under your ear, as
one of the brothers is driving your head, face down into
one of the penthouse pillows.

*They are both suddenly deeply shocked by what he has said. They sit
in silence for a while. Sera is close to tears. Ben gets up suddenly,
puts down a couple of bills and walks away from the table. When he
is almost at the door, Sera gets up and quickly tries to gather up all
of the packages.*

                              SERA
        Ben, wait . . . please wait for me.

ANGLE ON THE DOOR

*The dignified older man stands in Ben's path and places his hands*
*on Ben's shoulders.*

                              MAN
        Maybe you should wait for her, sir.

                              BEN
        Why?

                              MAN
        Because . . . you can hear in her voice that she really wants
        you to.

*Sera catches up and the man lets go of Ben. Ben takes the packages*
*from Sera and the two of them step out into the mall.*

97 INT. MALL – DAY

*They walk together.*

                              SERA
        What was that all about?

                              BEN
        Can we just forget it?

                              SERA
        I don't understand any of that.

                              BEN
        Can we just ignore it?

*They stop and look at each other. The PA system gives out an inane*
*message.*

        Please!

                              SERA
        Yes . . . I'll give you that.

> BEN

Thank you, Sera.

> SERA

Do you want me not to go tonight?

> BEN

No . . . we already talked about that.

CUT TO:

98 INT. SERA'S BEDROOM — NIGHT

*Sera is preparing for work. In the background we can hear the TV next door. She dresses carefully. Black underwear, stockings, heels, a tight black skirt.*

99 INT. LIVING ROOM — NIGHT

*Ben is watching TV and drinking.*

100 INT. SERA'S BEDROOM — NIGHT

*Sera at the mirror, putting on her make-up. Her make-up is more pronounced than we have seen it before. Everything is more extreme.*

101 INT. LIVING ROOM — NIGHT

*Sera comes into the room. Ben looks up at her and sucks in his breath.*

> BEN

Wow.

*She walks over to him and takes his head and places it between her breasts and kisses the top of his head.*

Maybe I should follow you around and ask one of your tricks what it's like to sleep with you.

> SERA

They wouldn't know.

*She comes on to him.*

Maybe you should ask me sometime. I'd be happy to show you.

*She goes to the door.*

I'll be back home around three. If you're back by then we can watch TV or something . . . I guess what I'm saying is . . . that I hope you are back when I get home. Please be careful.

> BEN

You be careful too. I'm going to miss you.

> SERA

Shall we go away for a couple of days?

> BEN

Yeah . . . I'd like that.

CUT TO:

102 INT. SMART HOTEL — NIGHT

*Sera walks through the lobby, looking for business.*

103 EXT. A STREET — NIGHT

*Ben lying down with people walking past and over him.*

ANGLE ON BEN'S FACE

*A big smile appears on his face. He starts to laugh.*

FADE OUT.

FADE IN:

104 EXT. DESERT — DAY

*A blue car drives across frame. The sun is bright.*

105 EXT. DESERT MOTEL — POOL — DAY

*Sera is a very good swimmer and we see that Ben must have been quite an athlete. They look at each other under water. They're under water for a long time. Ben exhales. Sera pushes him towards the sur-face.*

*Ben and Sera come to the surface. Ben has swallowed water and has a coughing fit. Sera hugs him until the fit passes. The camera moves in tighter on them and music gives the moment a strange chill.*

> SERA
>
> Don't do that to me. Don't frighten me like that.

CUT TO:

106 EXT. POOL — NIGHT

*Ben and Sera are watching the TV next to the pool. They are sitting in reclining chairs. In the distance a coyote howls.*

> SERA
>
> Years ago, in LA, I turned a trick on Sunset and Western. The guy was polite and didn't argue about the price. He parked his car and I took him to a house that I had an arrangement with. A fat Mexican woman was watching a TV and I told him to give her the twenty for the room. There were three or four small naked children playing on the floor and we had to step over them to get into the room. The room had a bed and a dresser. He lay on his back on the bed and I put a rubber on him and sucked him for a while until he was hard and then I eased on to him. About twenty minutes later there was a knock on the door and it was the woman saying our time was up. I felt kind of guilty because he hadn't come and I offered to reason with the woman and get another ten minutes, but he said it was all right and began dressing. When we were ready to leave the room he stopped me and . . . hugged me and kissed me on the cheek. He gave me an extra hundred as a tip and went back to his car. I remember being relieved that I wouldn't have to work again that evening.

> BEN
>
> Last spring I happened to walk past a house that I had once patronized. There was a cool breeze blowing off the

ocean and through the window I could see a bare leg. The girl must have been taking a break between customers. It was a strange moment for me because it reminded me of my mother and despite the fact that I was late for something already I just stayed there, loving the atmosphere of it and my memory and . . . the reason I'm telling you this epilogue is that I felt that I'd come full circle.

                    SERA

Where was that house? The one in LA, I mean.

                    BEN

Fifth and Mayflower. You know it?

                    SERA

Yes. One of my friends was there. I wonder if you ever clipped her.

*They watch the TV in silence for a while. Sera holds his hand.*

                    BEN

I like it here with you.

                    SERA

Let's stay for a while.

                    BEN

OK.

CUT TO:

107 INT. MOTEL ROOM – DAY

*Ben mixes a cocktail for himself, then one for Sera. The camera follows him as he goes . . .*

108 EXT. POOL-SIDE – DAY

*. . . to the side of the pool, where Sera is sunbathing. He lowers himself unsteadily into the chair but avoids spilling a drop of the drinks, which he puts down on to a glass-topped table. He is pretty loaded. Sera turns over and moves out of his shadow.*

SERA

I've missed the best sun. Why did you have to pawn your
watch?

BEN

I didn't know I'd ever need it again.

*Sera gets up, takes a drink and then walks to the diving board. As
she takes a position at the end, she pulls the bathing suit out from
her bottom, does a very natural dive into the pool, swims a length
under water and then comes out near Ben, pulls herself out of the
pool in one move and bends down and kisses Ben for a long time.
Ben responds and kisses her back. There is no one else around the
pool.*

*The kiss becomes heated and urgent and Sera sits on Ben, making
him wet from her. He pushes the top of her suit down and kisses her
breasts. She picks up the glass and drinks, letting the alcohol spill
from her mouth, over her breasts. Ben drinks from her.*

Take this off.

*He tries to pull her swimsuit down.*

SERA

Maybe we should go inside. Come on.

*She stands up, covering herself. Ben stands up, laughing, loses his
balance and slips on the wet concrete. He falls backwards, half on to
the chair, which breaks, and then on to the glass table. The table goes
over and it and the glasses all shatter on the concrete. Ben falls on to
the broken glass and cuts himself all over his back and his arms.
Glass goes into the pool. Blood mingles with the water on the steam-
ing cement.*

BEN

Whoops.

*Sera picks up her towel and lays it down next to him. She kneels
and helps him up, trying to pull out the little bits of glass sticking to
him. Ben stands unsteadily.*

I'll go and clean up. Perhaps you could take care of this.

*He indicates the mess, then walks to their room. Sera begins carefully picking up the broken glass. The desk clerk appears with a broom and a dustpan.*

> DESK CLERK
> (*cheerfully*)

Everybody OK?

> SERA

Yes, fine. Don't worry. We'll pay for the chair, and I'll clean all this up, the pool too.

> DESK CLERK

Don't worry.

*He begins sweeping the broken glass into the pan, cheerfully ignoring Sera.*

> SERA

You seem prepared for accidents.

> DESK CLERK
> (*still smiling*)

Yeah . . . we get a lot of screw-ups here.

*He looks directly at Sera.*

Now, you two keep your loud talk and your liquor to your room. Check out first thing tomorrow and after that I don't want to see either of you here again. I don't need you paying for the chair or cutting your pretty hands on the glass. Let's leave it at that.

*Nodding firmly, he goes back to the mess, indicating that the conversation is over.*

See ya in the morning.

CUT TO:

109 INT. MOTEL ROOM — DAY

*Sera comes into the room.*

                                    SERA

  Ben?

*She sees that he is already asleep on the bed, his half-naked body
covered with countless bits of bloodstained tissue. The image has an
almost religious feel to it. The TV is on and a sitcom is playing.*

*Something funny catches Sera's attention. She laughs and sits on
the bed next to Ben.*

                              (*voice-over*)
  I think we realized that we didn't have long and accepted
  it. My charm, for him, was that I accepted him exactly as
  he was and didn't expect him to change. I think we both
  realized that about each other. Ben needed me and I liked
  his drama. I loved him.

  CUT TO:


110 EXT. DESERT LANDSCAPE — DUSK

*We see Las Vegas lighting up. The blue rental car passes through
frame and drives towards the town.*

  FADE OUT.

  FADE UP ON:


111 INT. SERA'S BEDROOM — LAS VEGAS — NIGHT

*Ben wakes from a dream. He is fully clothed and very agitated.*

                                    BEN

  Sera?


112 INT. KITCHEN — NIGHT

*Sera is cooking.*

                                    SERA
  I'm in here. You probably don't want to hear about it right
  now, but I bought some plain rice. I thought it might be
  something you could eat. So if you get hungry later on,
  just let me know.

*Ben comes in from the kitchen and takes vodka bottles from the fridge.*

113 SCENE CUT.

114 SCENE CUT.

115 INT. BATHROOM — NIGHT

*Ben's hands are sweating and it is difficult for him to keep hold of the bottle as he drinks. He gets most of it down and then he hunches over the sink and immediately vomits. He takes the second bottle and tries again.*

    CUT TO:

116 INT. SHOWER — NIGHT

*Still holding the bottle, Ben stands in the shower. He drinks some more and closes his eyes.*

    CUT TO:

117 INT. KITCHEN — NIGHT

*Ben enters, smartly dressed and smiling.*

BEN

I think I'm ready for the rice!

    CUT TO:

118 INT. DINING ROOM — LATER THAT NIGHT

*Ben and Sera sitting opposite each other. He has a bowl of rice, which he is pretending to eat in between sips of vodka. She has a bowl of vegetables and rice. She sits, silently for a while, and then puts down her chopsticks.*

SERA

You're pretty sick.

*Ben looks away.*

What are you going to do?

*She folds her arms.*

I want you to go see a doctor.

*He thinks for a while and then turns to meet her gaze. They look right into each other's eyes.*

                              BEN
Sera . . . I'm not going to see a doctor.

*Sera continues to look at him almost defiantly.*

Maybe it's time I moved to a hotel.

                              SERA
And do what . . . rot away in a room?
                         (*becoming angry*)
We're not going to talk about that. Fuck you! I will not
talk about that. You're staying here. You are not moving to
a hotel.

                              BEN
Will you lighten up, please?

                              SERA
                         (*close to tears*)
One thing . . . one thing . . . this is one thing you can do
for me. I've given you gallons of free will here! You can do
this for me.

*She leans right forward.*

Let's face it. Sick as you are, I'm probably the only thing
that's keeping you alive.

*She stands up.*

I have to go to work now.

*Ben doesn't say anything. He just stares a hole in his bowl of rice.*

CUT TO:

119 INT. CASINO — NIGHT

*Ben walks by himself. He is deep in thought.*

    CUT TO:

120 INT. CASINO — NIGHT

*Ben recklessly bets $200 at the craps table . . . and wins. As he leans
forward to collect his winnings, he sees . . .*

ANGLE:

*. . . a blonde in a very low-cut outfit. She smiles at Ben and walks
around the table to pick him up. Ben puts all of his winnings on one
bet and wins again. This pattern repeats a few times and drinks are
on the house.*

                        BLONDE
    Hey . . . that was quite a play. You in for the convention?

*Ben gets to the point.*

                         BEN
    I'd like to fuck you.

*A few people hear Ben and the blonde is almost put off, but he does
have about $8,000 in winnings and so she leans in very close so that
she can talk quietly.*

                        BLONDE
    I'm very expensive.

                         BEN
    How mush to lick your pussy?

*The blonde picks up a sizeable stack of chips and looks at Ben.*

    CUT TO:

121 INT. SERA'S HOUSE — LATER THAT NIGHT

*Sera lets herself in, looks around and opens the bedroom door.*

ANGLE:

*In one fluid movement the naked blonde gets off the semi-conscious
Ben, pulls her dress over her head and walks past Sera. Moments
later we hear the front door slam. Ben comes to and looks at Sera.
He is more or less unaware of what has just happened.*

BEN

Hello . . .

ANGLE ON SERA

*Her eyes are wet.*

SERA

There are limits.

BEN<br>(remembering)

Yes . . . I guess I knew that.

*He gets out of the bed. He picks up the bottle on the bedside table
and stands.*

Perhaps I could crash on the couch for a few hours . . .
and then I'll leave.

*He walks out of the room and closes the door. Camera moves in on
Sera. She covers her face with her hands. She drops her purse and
slides down the wall to the floor, weeping quietly.*

SERA (V.O.)

I heard the door slam a couple of hours later and he was
gone.

FADE OUT.

FADE IN:

122 EXT. STREET — DAY

*Ben coming out of a liquor store with a large brown bag.*

CUT TO:

123 EXT. STREET — NIGHT

*Sera getting out of a car. The car drives off. Sera examines her face in a pocket mirror. Puts on more lipstick.*

CUT TO:

124 INT. MOTEL ROOM — DAY

*Ben is on all fours in the bathroom trying to vomit. His thin frame is heaving. Bottles are everywhere.*

CUT TO:

125 EXT. THE STRIP — NIGHT

*Three college boys with beer bottles walk The Strip. They are all wearing the same numbered jersey. Nice middle-class boys looking for an adventure. They see Sera and go into a huddle before walking over to her.*

> TALLEST COLLEGE BOY
> How much will it cost us to fuck you?

*The other two college boys titter. Sera starts to walk away and then hesitates.*

> SERA
> Sorry, guys, but I don't know what you mean. Anyway, I never date more than one guy at a time.

> SMALLEST COLLEGE BOY
> Come on . . . we got money . . . show her the money.

*The other college boy gets out his wallet and opens it to show her. Sera hesitates, not somehow comfortable with the situation, then goes ahead.*

> SERA
> How much of that money did you guys want to spend?

> TALLEST COLLEGE BOY
> How much you want? How about two hundred for an hour?

> SERA
> (*becoming annoyed with them*)

Don't your friends talk?

> (*no answer*)

Try three hundred for a half-hour.

> OTHER COLLEGE BOY
> (*nervous*)

Three hundred for the hour.

> SERA

OK . . . three . . . and we'll see how it goes. Where are you staying?

> TALLEST COLLEGE BOY

The Yukon, room twenty-four.

> SERA

I'll see you there in fifteen minutes. You can pay me then. Why don't you all take a shower while you're waiting.

> OTHER COLLEGE BOY

A shower? In fifteen minutes?

> SERA

Look . . . I'll only need one of you at a time. RIGHT? UNDERSTOOD? So . . . the other two can shower while I'm there. OK?

*They walk off in a huddle, giggling – three small boys.*

CUT TO:

126 EXT. YUKON MOTEL – NIGHT

*Sera drinks from a beer bottle as she approaches their room. She talks to herself.*

> SERA

Where are the boys this weekend, Frank? Why, hell, Charlie, I sent 'em off to learn the one thing I couldn't teach 'em.

*She looks at the numbers and finds the room. She knocks and a moment later the tallest college boy opens the door in his jockey shorts.*

127 INT. MOTEL ROOM – NIGHT

*Sera steps in. One boy is coming out of the bathroom wearing a towel and the third is sitting in a chair smoking a cigarette, which he passes to the boy in the towel. The other boy is fooling around with a video camera. The atmosphere is weird and Sera is suddenly alert.*

*The tallest college boy hands her the money. He is very well built, a football player. Sera hesitates, holding the money. The tallest college boy closes the door and then leans against it. They are all staring at her now. No one says anything. Sera smiles suddenly and puts the money in her purse. All business.*

> SERA
>
> OK . . . where's the bedroom, and who's first?

*They all look at each other.*

> SMALLEST COLLEGE BOY
>
> I want to fuck her in the butt . . .

*He looks at the other.*

> . . . you too, right?

> SERA
>
> Forget that. No one's doing that. You'll all go one at a time. If you want I'll suck you instead, but that's all. Then I'm out of here.

> SMALLEST COLLEGE BOY
> *(looking at tallest)*
>
> You said I could fuck her in the butt.

> OTHER COLLEGE BOY
>
> Shut up.

> SMALLEST COLLEGE BOY
> *(shouting)*
>
> It's my fucking money.

SERA

That's it . . . Take your money back. I'm leaving.

*The smallest college boy gets off the bed and comes over to Sera.*

SMALLEST COLLEGE BOY

No . . . don't go.

*The tallest college boy is still standing in front of the door and things are getting strange. The other boy turns on the video camera. Sera loses her cool.*

SERA
(*to the smallest college boy*)

Maybe you'd like to fuck one of your friends in the butt instead.

*The room goes very quiet. The kid tears up. Sera tries to back-pedal.*

Hey . . . I'm sorry . . .

*The kid punches her hard in the stomach, knocking her to the ground.*

CUT TO BLACK.

QUICK FADE IN:

*Close-up on Sera's face pushed into a bloodstained pillow, her body being pounded from behind. The naked legs of two of the boys behind her. We hear voices, filtered, from a long way off.*

VOICE

Go on . . . fuck her ass . . .

OTHER VOICE

Look at me . . . look at me . . . look at me.

*A hand comes into frame and pulls her head up by the hair. A pair of legs moves in. There is the sound of a punch.*

FADE OUT.

FADE IN:

*Sera's body on the floor. In the background trousers being hastily pulled on to legs. The boys exit with sport bags.*

*The last one turns out the lights and closes the door.*

    FADE OUT.

    FADE IN:

128 INT. MOTEL ROOM – DAWN

*In the half-light Sera gets up and walks with difficulty to the bathroom.*

129 INT. BATHROOM – DAWN

*She clicks on the mirror light. Her face is awful. One eye is swollen almost shut. Her top lip is cut.*

    CUT TO BLACK.

130 INT. CAB – EARLY MORNING

*Sera gets into the cab with considerable difficulty. The cab driver is a cynic.*

                CAB DRIVER
    What's the matter, honey, get a back-door delivery you
    weren't expecting? You gonna be able to pay the fare?

*Without speaking she takes out a twenty, leans forward and drops it on the front passenger seat. He drives. Looks at her in the mirror.*

    Oh, don't wanna talk to me, unh? Well, don't take it out
    on me, I'm just covering my ass. What the hell do you
    expect, sluttin' around like that . . . dressed like that? You
    oughta be glad the creep didn't nail ya.

    CUT TO:

131 EXT. SERA'S HOUSE – MORNING

*As the cab drives off, Sera walks slowly to the door.*

*Her landlord's wife passes and takes in her face.*

    CUT TO:

132 INT. SERA'S SHOWER — DAY

*Sera is slumped on the floor of the shower, her arms hugging her legs, the water pounding down on her.*

    CUT TO:

133 INT. SERA'S HOUSE — DAY

*Sera opens the door and we see the landlord. Behind him, on the sidewalk, we can see his wife. He is embarrassed.*

ANGLE

*Sera, wearing dark glasses. She looks terrible. Her mouth is swollen and some of the bruising around her eye is visible.*

                LANDLADY
I'm sorry . . . but we'd like you out by the end of the week.

    CUT TO:

134 EXT. WHOLE YEAR INN — DAY

*Sera gets out of a cab and goes into reception. She is wearing huge dark glasses to hide the black eye and the bruising.*

    CUT TO:

135 INT. HOTEL — DAY

*The desk clerk is wearing a shirt of Ben's that we recognize from an earlier scene.*

                DESK CLERK
I'm sorry, ma'am. He never checked back in.

    CUT TO:

136 EXT. THE STRIP — NIGHT

*Sera walks alone. She's dejected as she looks for Ben.*

137 INT. CASINO — NIGHT

*Sera comes to an elevator and waits. She is wearing a thin black top without a bra. Her bruised face makes her suddenly very conspicuous and vulnerable. A big man in a white stetson stands next to her. He looks at her and grins. She smiles, coldly. He takes from his pocket two black hundred-dollar chips, places one in each hand and deliberately places each one against her nipples. Other people see this and stop and watch. Sera looks down at his hands and stares until the man becomes uncomfortable.*

> STETSON MAN
> What's the problem, honey? . . . You on strike?

*And he walks away laughing.*

> CUT TO:

138 EXT. 7-ELEVEN — DAY

*Sera is sitting on a freshly painted red kerb. She smokes a cigarette and doesn't give a damn that her short skirt is somewhat revealing. Opposite her a bum is sleeping on the pavement. For a moment it looks like Ben. The camera comes in tight on to her face. She looks more lost that we've ever seen her. She drinks coffee from a styrofoam cup. The sun is bright and hot and traffic is noisy.*

139 INT. DOCTOR'S OFFICE — DAY

*Improvised scene.*[*]

140 INT. CASINO — NIGHT

*Sera comes in and the camera follows her as she makes her way to the bar. She has covered up much of the bruising with make-up but it is still pretty obvious. In wide shot we see her strike up a conversation with the man next to her at the bar.*

CLOSE SHOT — THE BAR

*A hand comes into shot and grips her arm firmly. We see that it*

[*]See Afterword.

*is a casino security guard.*

SERA
Let go. What's the problem?

SECURITY GUARD
We don't want you in here, that's the problem. Let's go.

*And he jerks her arm. People are watching now.*

SERA
Don't worry . . . If you don't want me in here, then I don't want to be in here. Just let go of my arm and I'll walk out of here.

SECURITY GUARD
Yeah . . . we'll both walk out now.

*He steers her firmly across the floor.*

CUT TO:

141 EXT. CASINO — NIGHT

*They reach the sidewalk and, without relaxing his grip, he grabs her between the legs with his free hand and says in her ear:*

SECURITY GUARD
Next time it won't be so fucking easy.

*And he pushes her towards the street and walks back into the casino. Sera is shocked. She looks around and the group of people who have stopped to watch the event move away.*

142 INT. SERA'S HOUSE — DAY

*Sera is throwing clothes into a suitcase. The phone rings. She thinks about it for a long time and then it stops. She carries on packing and then the phone rings again. She picks it up.*

SERA
Hello . . . hello . . .
                (*suddenly alert*)
Ben? Where the fuck are you? Give me the address.

CUT TO:

143 INT. CAB — LATE AFTERNOON

*The driver is black and friendly. The radio drones quietly – a religious program. The Rev. Ike is taking listeners' calls.*

#### BLACK DRIVER
What in hell happened to you, Miss?

#### SERA
Oh . . . it was an argument.

#### BLACK DRIVER
Leave him, Miss. Pretty girl like you could get any man that you wanted.

144 INT. BEN'S MOTEL ROOM — DUSK

*The door opens. Ben is naked. His body looks bad. Leaving the door open, he retreats to the bed.*

145 INT. BEN'S MOTEL ROOM — NIGHT

*Sera comes in, closing the door behind her. The shades are drawn and the room is gloomy. Ben has got back into bed. She comes to the bed and sits.*

#### SERA
Ben . . . I've been looking for you. Have you been here since you left? It smells bad in here. It's so dark.

*She clicks on the bedside light and is truly shocked by his face.*

#### BEN
I wanted to see you . . .

#### SERA
Oh, Ben . . . you look so very sick . . . my love . . . you're so pale.

*She goes to the bathroom and returns with a wet face-cloth. She wipes his face.*

> BEN
>
> I wanted to see you . . . you're my angel.

*He sits up painfully and finds a bottle, summoning up some last strength to drink. His entire body shudders as he drains the bottle. He puts it down and focuses on her for the first time. He sees her damaged face, touches her face, looks at her questioningly.*

> SERA
>
> Something went wrong . . . I'm OK.

*Ben begins to cry and that sets her off.*

> BEN
>
> I'm sorry I put us assunder.

*She shakes her head, unable to speak for the moment. She gets into bed with him, kissing his face. She caresses his whole body, which is shaking, possessed by an uncontrollable fever.*

> See how hard you make me, angel.

*She excites him with her hand, kissing his face gently. When he is about to come, she straddles him and brings him inside. As he comes, he opens his eyes wide and looks at her.*

> You know I love you . . . yeah?

> SERA
> (*she comes*)
>
> Yes.

SLOW FADE TO BLACK.

FADE IN:

*Sera is sleeping. A sudden gasp wakes her. Ben is having a spasm. Suddenly his body relaxes. He turns his head, opens his eyes wide and looks straight at her.*

> BEN
>
> Oh . . . I'm so sorry . . .

*He smiles and turns his head away. He is very still.*

SERA

Ben . . . Ben . . . Ben?

CUT TO:

146 INT. BEN'S MOTEL ROOM – NIGHT

*In the darkened room we can just make out Sera sitting on the bed, looking at the still form of Ben.*

CUT TO:

147 EXT. STREET NEAR MOTEL – DAWN

*Sera walking. A paramedic van goes past with its lights flashing. The soundtrack is empty – silent. We slowly fade in theme music and titles start to roll.*

PUBLISHER'S NOTE

This text is based on the shooting script of September 1994, which was redefined substantially in the editing process (see Afterword).

# AFTERWORD

I thought it might be interesting to talk about how the film redefined itself in the editing room. The Editor was John Smith and this is his first feature. I met John because he had cut the five commercials that I have shot. I like his work and asked him one day if he had ever considered cutting a feature. It seemed no one had ever asked him. So I did. He came to the film with none of the preconceptions or rules that pervade feature editing and he was prepared to try anything. We've also worked together on art documentaries on Vivienne Westwood and William Forsythe, the American choreographer who heads the Frankfurt Ballet.

## FINAL CUT SEQUENCE

Note: first number denotes position of scene in completed film; the number in square brackets denotes position of scene in the original shooting script.

1 [56] Ben in a liquor store filling a trolley and whistling. Originally designed for a much later sequence. We dropped it altogether from the film and then, quite late in the day, I put it back in as the opening shot because it so clearly states something about Ben's character.

2 [1] Ben comes into smart LA restaurant and bums some money from his ex-agent.
This is the first time Nic improvised the expression 'outstanding', which is the trade mark of a well-known agent in LA. The two actors playing the agents, Steven Weber and Richard Lewis, based their performances on other well-known agents.

3 [26] Ben in an LA bar drinking heavily. Tries to pick up Teri (Valeria Golino).
We got into a bit of trouble here because Nic (with my

approval) sang a song called 'You Turn Me On'. He'd heard this in a famous strip club in Paris and recorded it on a voice recorder. When it came to clearing the song in post-production, the club refused to let us use it. The writer of the song was dead, the owner of the club was dead and the estate was in litigation. Up until the last minute it seemed as if we were going to have to take it out and I had no cover at all. And then they relented.

One of the shots of the barman in this scene is completely out of focus but the bottles behind him are sharp, so I felt OK about using the shot because I could rationalize to myself that it was a drunk's POV. I think we went through three focus pullers on the shoot.

4 [*13, 27*] Ben, drinking and driving, is buzzed by a cop on a motorbike.

5 [*28*] Ben in a strip club. Drinks bottle of Scotch.
This was supposed to be a much longer scene with dialogue, but it was too slow and literal. The dancer was very beautiful and had a slightly eerie quality. We found her in a trendy strip club in LA. Nic took Lisa Shue and I out on the town in the rehearsal period. We set off in a Bentley with a driver, drank expensive Scotch and listened to *Kind of Blue* by Miles Davis. We arrived at the club, which was full of agents and producers having bachelor parties. Lots of blondes with huge breasts paraded on the stage and it became clear that the gig involved choosing a girl who would then dance exclusively for her patron of the moment. One of the girls was stunning and I made the mistake of saying this aloud. Minutes later she approached our table, introduced herself to me (we actually shook hands), and began dancing. The next day I asked the production office to call her and offer her the job.

The older man who Ben sits next to in the strip club is the actor Al Henderson. I used him on *Mr Jones*. He plays a sound mixer in the film *Modern Romance* and has the line, 'You saved the movie.'

I tried something new here. When Ben drinks the bottle of Scotch and then goes into shock, I pull out the sound, every-

thing – the music, the atmos, the effects. I have always wanted
to do it but in the past have been talked out of it by engineers
and mixers who told me that something has to be left on the
track, even if it is only white noise. I enjoy watching this
sequence with an audience because it does have an unnerving
effect. The cinema goes quiet, a rare thing. When the sound
comes back Ben's voice is distanced but the music is not and it
is not until he crosses the street in traffic that things come back
to normal.

6 [*31*] Ben picks up a young prostitute on Sunset.

7 [*32, 34, 36*] Ben and prostitute behind motel on Sunset.
Ben's one line here is as much back-story as we need: 'Can't
remember if I started drinking because my wife left me . . . or
my wife left me because I started drinking, but fuckitanyway.'

8 [*33, 35, 37, 39*] Ben wakes up on his kitchen floor.
I am very happy with the sound on the film. I went back to a
style of mixing that has always interested me. For example, in
this scene as Ben wakes we hear the sound of the refrigerator.
Then we hear the sound of his watch as he brings his hand to
his face. As the prostitute takes his ring there is the sound of
teeth on metal and a distant siren. Never do we hear Ben's
breathing, or the movement of his clothes.

9 [*38*] Flashback to prostitute stealing his ring.

10 [*40*] Ben goes to the bank but is shaking too much to sign
the back of the cheque.

11 [*41*] Ben has a drink in a bar. Barman ticks him off for being
a drunk.
There was no coverage on this scene because we were in such
a hurry that I decided to risk it and shoot the complete scene
in one take. This means that it is very difficult to shorten the
performance in the editing. The barman is played by Graham
Beckel, a fine actor with whom I worked on *Liebestraum*. Our
claim to fame on that film was that he performed the longest
screen piss of all time.

12 [*42*] Ben back at the bank. Recites erotic poem and signs his cheque.

One of the scenes that I cut (scene 10) involved a drunken fantasy of Ben's in which he is in the bar and a game show is playing on the TV. Carry Lowel, the actress who plays the bank teller, also played the part of the game-show hostess. I liked the scene very much because it reminded me of a section of one of my favourite books of all time, *A Fan's Notes* by Frederick Exley. In Exley's book his hero has a fantasy that a soap becomes more than real and all the characters start talking dirty and fornicating. Alas, my game-show sequence slowed the narrative down and it had to hit the floor.

13 [*11*] Ben at work faking phone calls, faking deals.

In John O'Brien's book, on which the script is based, it was never made clear what Ben did for a living. It was my idea to make him a film person. People have asked me to define his job but I cannot. Like so many people making a handsome living in what is known as Hollywood, Ben has an office, several hundred scripts and makes phone calls in which as many names are dropped as possible. But I still don't know what Ben, or indeed they, do for a living. It was Nic's idea to hold the phone upside down.

The sympathetic woman who gives him his messages is played by the actress Susan Lange. I've known her for a long time. We first met at the La Mama Theater in New York and later at the Mickery Theatre in Amsterdam where we were both with performance-art groups. She has been in most of my films. In *Liebestraum* she played dual roles of nurse and hooker. In *Mr Jones* she played a therapist. Even though this was a small part, I raised the money to fly her in from New York.

14 [*12*] Ben is fired by his boss, Bill, and given a cheque. Says he's moving to Vegas.

Bill is played by Tom Kopache. Kopache was in the same performance group as Susan Lange. He also performed in *Liebestraum* and *Mr Jones*, in which he gave an incredible performance as a mental patient. So convincing that when the

Tri-Star executives came to visit the set they steered well clear of him in the food line.

When I'd finished the first draft of the script I gave it to Bill Tennent to read. Bill is an ex-alcoholic. At one stage in his career he was one of the most successful of American agents but fell from grace and re-emerged five years later clean and sober. I met him when he was one of the producers on *Stormy Monday*, and we became friends. An active member of AA, Bill gave me some stiff advice about the morality of glamorizing drinking, which I took to heart and made changes (see scene 55). There is something of Bill in the scene with Tom Kopache.

15 [*2, 3, 5, 6, 9*] Title sequence intercut with Sera and Yuri in hotel suite with clients.

The first cut was fairly representational of the shooting script. But John Smith and I found that the story was too disjointed and it was taking a very long time to get Ben out of LA and on his way to Vegas. I also found after the first cut that the real strength of the film lay in the relationship between Ben and Sera, and I wanted their relationship to start as soon as possible. So, we decided to try to create one long drinking session with Ben in LA and then get him out and on his way to Vegas. We changed the sequence around and it worked, although it did create a big continuity problem. Ben has his wedding ring stolen by the prostitute, but a couple of scenes later, as he is being fired, the ring is back on his finger because in the shooting script the scenes are the other way around. It would have been possible to go to a digital company and have the ring removed, but having shot on 16mm, and with very little money to play with, it seemed silly. Money did have to be spent on digital cleansing, though. In the title sequence a woman is seen doing a line of coke. Also in the shot was a bottle of vodka and we had to change the label because no booze company wants to be associated with the idea of alcoholism. (One very famous beer company offered us free booze *not* to put their label in the film.) So, we had to go into the image and redesign the label. It's an amazing process but costs thousands of dollars a second.

I made big cuts in the LA sequence, including most of the stuff with Ben and his house, the small boy next door, and Ben following a girl walking her dog and having thoughts about the colour of her underwear. They were all great scenes and I was sad to see them go, but in a sense they all repeated the idea that Ben is a poetic drunk. After a certain time they become tedious and self-indulgent. With earlier films I would have found it difficult to lose such well-acted scenes, but with this one it was a joy to find the rhythm by being this tough. Maybe they will find their way into the documentary that we shot at the same time.

The flying shots of Vegas by night were a late thought. When it became clear that we were not going to get the permissions to shoot much of the film in Vegas, I became concerned that we would not see enough of it and the film would start to feel low-budget – by which I mean there were too many interiors, etc. Marc Fischer, the Line Producer, agreed with me and we managed to scrape up enough money for three hours in a helicopter. It was exciting. At one point I asked the pilot (ex-Vietnam, of course) to do a tight circle around the glass pyramid of the Luxor Hotel. This pyramid has the most powerful light in the world coming out of its pinnacle and on a clear day it is visible to pilots in LA. I wanted a shot looking down into the light (like looking into hell). The pilot obliged and we went into the tightest of circles with cameraman Declan Quinn's eye glued to the camera monitor in the back and mine to the monitor in the front. Suddenly, the image span and I said: Wow, great move, sir.' He looked at me and said: 'Sorry, sometimes it's difficult to control those rising thermals coming off the desert.' The hot air had spun us around 360 degrees in a very short space of time. I used part of the shot, though, in scene 79.

16 [54] Sera talks to her shrink (#1).

SERA

You know, I bring out the best in the men who fuck me. I mean . . . it's not easy, but I'm very good, I mean, it's amazing, it's like . . . if I haven't worked for a really long time then . . . boom, I can just turn on a dime. I can just

be who they want me to be. I walk into that room . . . and
I know right away . . . this is their fantasy and I become it.
I'm that service, you know, I just . . . I perform it and I
perform it well. I mean, I'm an equation most of the time.
It's like thirty minutes of my body is . . . costs $300 . . .
well, that's just to get into the room and then it's about
$500 after that . . . you know . . . we negotiate but . . . uhh
. . . it's a performance, it's definitely a performance.

In pre-production I took a tough look at the script. This is
always a crucial moment on a film because the actors are in
place and practical decisions are being made about locations
and so on. The story starts to be real. I liked the script but I
had a nagging worry that Sera didn't have enough of a voice in
the story. In the book there is a lot of internal thought from
her, but in the script it was difficult to find a way of expressing
those ideas. Her thoughts are about her job as well as about
Ben and they are not the kind of ideas that could be expressed
in the context of dialogue to him. Ben, on the other hand, is a
drunk and has licence to be as expressive as he likes. For
example, his thoughts in the bank are recorded on a portable
tape machine and we learn something about him. Sera's character does not have that freedom. So I came up with the idea
of her talking to a therapist (not a new device – I remember it
in *Klute*). I went back to the book and found all the interesting
stuff about her and put it into the script as therapy sessions. I
reasoned that she would have plenty of cash and if everyone
else in the US is talking to a shrink, why wouldn't a prostitute?
Lila Cazès (the Producer from Lumière pictures) didn't like
these changes at all and asked me to take them out of the
script again, which I did. However, I was still concerned about
the imbalance, so I did a sneaky thing. We shot a camera test
the week before the shoot and I asked Elisabeth to wear her
costume. I gave her all the deleted text to read and then, on
camera, I interviewed her in her character as Sera and she
improvised her answers based on the material from the book.
Some other things came out of the sessions which had a lot
more emotion in them, and I think these elements were crucial

to her character. She told me afterwards that it was a great way of getting into character. I asked her about her life as a prostitute, about her feelings towards Ben when she first met him. Then she changed costume and we jumped forward in the script to where Ben has moved in with her, then we moved to the end and used the past tense as she talked about her feelings for him. A couple of days later I saw the results and was pleased. The Lumière folk were not happy that I'd done this, but I told them that it had cost them nothing and we should think of it as insurance and probably wouldn't use it. They calmed down, but in my heart I knew it would end up in the film.

Towards the end of the shoot I remembered the footage and thought I should take another look at it because, after all, on the day we did it Lisa hadn't even done a scene with Nic and hadn't really formed her character. I had in mind the idea of stealing an hour one night to do some more therapy. I asked Waldemar Kalinowski (Production Designer) to get the couch ready. I viewed the footage again and was blown away by how accurate her emotions were. I was moved to tears by the last scene and cancelled the extra 'illegal' shoot.

None of these therapy scenes appeared in the first cut of the film. This was deliberate. I wanted to be absolutely sure that they were needed. Afterwards we quickly made a second pass and added everything. I particularly liked the speech about the fat hairy man. Interestingly enough, so did the American censors and they asked me to make significant cuts in this text for the US release. I'm beginning to realize the power of the word in film. Someone talking about sex is stronger than seeing sex. The same is true about death.

17 [*22, 24*] Sera and Yuri have breakfast together.

18 [*20*] Yuri and Sera in bed together.
The US censor asked for cuts here. They felt that Julian Sands' buttocks were too strong for the scene. Julian Sands is a great performer. This is the second of many films that I hope to make with him. I remember walking out of *Gothic* when it first came out, and then watching it again when I was making *The*

*Browning Version* (sitting next to Julian). I loved it second time
around. He is a great actor to work with, frightened of nothing.
After the great LA earthquake, in the week of the 2,000
tremors which followed the big one, Julian decided to inspect
the foundations of his Hollywood house. To do this he had to
inch his way around the crawl space at the bottom of the
house. (Imagine potholing!) He's a man I'd choose to be in a
trench with if a hostile army was advancing. (I think of film-
making as trench warfare.)

19 [*43*] Ben in the supermarket buying garbage bags and firelighters.

20 [*40, 45–8*] Montage as Ben clears his house and burns personal things.

21 [*49–50*] Montage as Ben drives to Vegas.
A couple of interesting stories about this sequence. When we
were shooting the scenes in Ben's house, we ran out of time.
We'd budgeted and scheduled a day for everything. Most of
the day had been used up on all the scenes that later got cut
from the film. Gary Marcus, the First AD, came to me and
said that we had an hour left to shoot all of the scenes that
involve Ben packing and clearing his house. After that our per-
mit would run out and, as it was a residential area, we would
be in trouble with the police if we carried on. In his opinion it
was not possible to finish, so what did I want to do? It seemed
that the only option was to come back, find some money from
somewhere to pay for it (or sacrifice another couple of scenes
as a trade-off). This upset me because up until then we had
stayed in budget and on schedule and with something as tight
as this film I felt it was important to be on top.

Something else was bothering me. Things had slowed up.
Because we were in a house for a whole day, equipment had
started to appear and things were cluttering up the space:
cable everywhere, lights everywhere, people everywhere making little camps of folding chairs and boxes and coffee cups. I
hate all that stuff because I know equipment slows a film down
and on this shoot I'd decreed that we'd have as little as possi-

ble. Nearly all the scenes were either hand-held or off a tripod.

I gathered everyone together and told them that we were going to finish the scenes in the remaining hour. I asked Declan if he could shoot on fast stock with available light and he said that he could. We cleared all the equipment out of the house and he put bright bulbs in all of the practical lights. The art department set up the props in all of the rooms. I talked to Nic and told him that we were going to shoot the whole sequence in one continuous take. He was delighted with the challenge. We put a radio mike on him so that we'd have a guide track in case he decided to speak or sing – this way we'd at least have a chance to replace the track in post-production. I quickly went over the route that he and Declan would have to take, discussed the pace and feel of the scene and then told them that from then on in they were on their own.

Within about twenty minutes the house was ready. Everyone except Nic, Declan and his assistant left the house and began packing up the trucks. I went out as well and had a cup of coffee and a cigarette, confident that great things were happening inside. This was confirmed a few days later when I saw the dailies. We finished on time and completed the day's shoot. I've never felt happier. The crew got away on time and the energy was still intact the next day because everybody felt that they had achieved something special. Despite the subject matter this was an immensely happy shoot.

The first cut of the film dealt with the journey to Vegas in real time. It was too slow and lacked urgency. Whilst reviewing the dailies on video at high speed I was struck by how much more interesting it looked at pace and asked John to consider cutting the whole sequence like that to the song 'Lonely Teardrops'. The Michael McDonald track had always been in my mind as a Ben song. It's that rare thing, a very sad song that has great energy and pace. I had some very scary moments trying to buy the rights and I'm very pissed off that it didn't end up on the album.

John went to work and when I saw his cut a few days later I was amazed. (I think there is a device like this in *After Hours*.) The film was cut on an Avid; a sequence like this would have been inconceivable on the traditional Steenbeck. On a computer you can see the finished effect straight away. Editing is going through its biggest revolution because of this new development.

22 [51] Ben stops at the gas station and sees three Polish gangsters who discuss Yuri.
Waldemar Kalinowski has been my production designer on every film I've made in America. We hit it off when we met on *Internal Affairs* and quickly discovered we had many things in common. Waldemar trained as a rocket scientist in Poland, came to the US as a young man, and worked as a photographer and an actor (*Heaven's Gate* and *Breathless*) before becoming a production designer. Rocket science had eluded me, but everything else was parallel. I thought it would be nice (and cheap) for us both to be Polish gangsters. On the first day of shooting I went off to the bathroom to slick down my hair and change, and when I came back on to the set I realized that the strange looks I was getting from the crew were because no one recognized me.

23 [52] Ben arrives in Vegas at night.

24 [52A] Ben almost runs Sera over.
As we were shooting this I decided to give them some dialogue. Something that would inform an audience that there was some kind of chemistry between them. I'm glad I did. This was also their first scene together.

25 [55] Ben checks in at the 'Hole You're In' motel.

26 [57] Sera and shrink (#2). Talks about the fat hairy man.

SERA
I walked into the room and he was lying on the bed. He had his arms behind his head. There was hair everywhere. He was really really fat and he had a large erection . . . I remember he was so proud of his large erection.* And I asked him where my money was and he pointed at the dresser. And then I asked him what he wanted and he said, 'Lie down . . . I'm on top.' And he started pounding me really hard. I remember I had to bite my tongue to

keep from crying. And then he did that for a while . . . and then I started to get up and he pushed me back down and he held my hair . . . he was pulling it and then he . . . stuck his penis in my mouth and it really hurt. So I tried to get up again and he said, 'Stay there, baby, I'm gonna come on your face.' So he did . . . and then he rubbed his semen all over my face and in my hair.* Then he kicked me off the bed and told me to leave.

27 [58–59] Sera on the streets. Ben picks her up.
When we were editing this sequence I felt we needed a shot of her by herself on the street before she bumps into Ben. We didn't have one. Then I remembered that we'd shot a camera test with Lisa walking along Sunset. No one could find the shot or the negative. We searched and searched, to no avail. Eventually we gave up, but John Smith did find a video of the shot and we had that transferred to film. It has to be one of the darkest shots I've ever seen and if it wasn't for the fact that she's lighting a cigarette you wouldn't know anyone was there. But it does the trick. There's a lesson there.

28 [61, 64] Ben and Sera go back to Ben's motel room. They don't have sex. She falls asleep.
US censors asked for cuts in this scene. They felt her head movements during the blow job were too realistic. It was diffi-cult for us to recut the scene with as much power and I wasn't happy with the result. I'd argued that his singing here took away the perverse element of watching two people have sex. The singing came about because in the rehearsal Nic sang and, although I liked it, I was not about to get into a legal cor-ner afterwards negotiating the rights to a song, as happened with 'You Turn Me On'. He then told me that he was the writer and that I could use it. I love the use of this song and I think it illustrates Cage's brilliance perfectly.

29 Road cleaning truck passes through frame. Sera wakes and exits.

*The references to erect penis and coming on her face were deleted in the US release.

It gave me great pleasure to use the road-cleaning shot. It's a snip from a beautiful sequence that was designed to be the last shot in the film but got replaced because it was too dark.

30 [65A] Sera hurries back to her house at dawn.
This was quite a late thought. I suddenly realized there were no 'establishing shots' of where she lives and, while I am not a fan of this kind of film-making, sometimes it is necessary to give the audience this kind of information. I was keen to show that she lives in a nice place and to get away from the clichés about prostitutes.

31 [66] Yuri hits Sera for not earning enough money in the night.

32 [8, 23] Flashback: Yuri cuts Sera with a knife.
Shot on slow colour film – pushed – printed as black and white. I've come to the conclusion that quite a lot of rubbish is talked about black and white. It's been my experience that the best results come from shooting on colour and then going to black and white. I think *Manhattan* was shot this way, but perhaps this is a myth.

33 [21] Sera with shrink (#3). Talks about Yuri being paranoid.

> SERA
> Yeah . . . he cut me a couple of times. I mean . . . he'd always say, never on the face, so he cut me right here (indicates her bottom). He cried and I . . . I felt sorry for him. Well, in his mind I'd done something wrong but in my mind I . . . hadn't done anything bad. He's kind of paranoid.

34 [68] Yuri on the streets of Vegas followed by Polish gangsters.

35 [67] As Yuri tries to pawn his jewellery, Ben comes in and sells his Rolex Daytona.
Dialogue was created on the spot. In the book they never meet, but I love coincidences that go nowhere.

36 [70] Sera fails to pick up a conventioneer. She is observed by another prostitute.

R. Lee Ermey, who plays the conventioneer, was also the drill sergeant in Kubrick's *Full Metal Jacket*. He came in for the evening to shoot this scene and we kept him waiting until about five in the morning, by which time everyone was punch drunk with fatigue. I felt bad about this. Mariska Hargitay, Jayne Mansfield's daughter, kindly agreed to come and play the other prostitute at very short notice when Naomi Campbell dropped out to promote her record.

37 [71] Sera gets out of a car, spits on the street and lights a cigarette.

38 [65, 69] Sera talks to her shrink (#4) about Ben, and how she was looking for him.

> SERA
>
> I don't know . . . it's just . . . I really like this guy. I mean . . . I've never felt anything for anyone that I've ever been with . . . as a trick . . . and it's . . . weird. I feel kind of confused about it. We were with each other for only one night but I felt like the relationship . . . you know . . . I felt like there was a relationship being formed and it was . . . I . . . I was kind of scared. No . . . I don't think I should see him again. But I look for him. I went out last night and I was looking for him.

39 [74] Ben and Sera meet on the street. She declines his offer of dinner.
I loved this location. In the background of the wide shot we see Bally's casino, which has a constantly changing light show outside. We had no traffic control so the actors had to really push their voices to be heard. I am totally in favour of this. I hate it when the traffic is stopped and the voices get quiet and then in post-production the traffic is put back on again but somehow never sounds natural.

The ending was a Nic improv: 'We could get prime rib . . . they've got it on offer for $2.99 . . . I love that dress.'

I wrote a musical theme for *The Browning Version*. I'd negotiated a deal with Paramount and Ridley Scott (Producer), which gave me the right to compose the score. It became clear to me as soon as the editing started that this was not part of any master plan and at the earliest possible legal date I was replaced by Mark Isham. The same thing had happened on *Mr Jones* and a small picture I made with Juliette Binoche for HBO called *Mara*, based on a short story by Henry Miller. By the time *Leaving Las Vegas* came along I was more than a little insecure about my ability to compose. Annie Stewart suggested that maybe the *Browning* theme would work in *Leaving Las Vegas*. So, during the rehearsal week I played it to Nic and Lisa and also to Declan and Waldemar. Encouraged by their enthusiasm I included it in the ideas for the new score. It appears first in the motel room when Ben asks Sera to stay. It was used again here, as Ben says he wants to see her again. Part of the discarded *Mara* score also appears in the film.

40 [75] Sera goes to a hotel to pay Yuri.
Without wanting to name-drop, Pedro Almodóvar says that this is his favourite scene because of the sound her skirt makes as she walks.

41 [76] Yuri, paranoid at hearing voices through the wall mumbling in Russian, tells Sera he will never see her again. Tells her to leave.
Yuri's character was a real problem (and the result on film is a real credit to Sands) because he couldn't be too strong as he would then need to be paid off in a more dynamic way. Film language is very unforgiving. If you see a bad guy who uses violence then you expect to see him paid off with that violence. I had to avoid creating a scenario where the audience expects Yuri to jump out and be a threat to Ben's and Sera's love affair. This was not the nature of the story. On the other hand, he has to be strong enough to be believable as her pimp. I didn't want to show him being killed and I dropped the sequence where we see the gangsters' car driving into the desert with the body (scene 82 in original). By bringing in Sting's version of 'My One and Only Love' as Yuri looks up at the gangsters at the door, we have already crossed over into the love story and never give him a second thought. The other thing I loved about Yuri's tale was that it reminded me of Hemingway's *The*

*Killers*, which is one of my favourite American stories. I made him more philosophical than John O'Brien had and suggested to Julian that he accept his fate.

43 [*stolen from 75*] Sera on the street looking for Ben.
I had no scripted shot here, but looking at the cut I realized that we needed some air in the story otherwise we'd be in hotel rooms and restaurants for a long time. The shot was borrowed from the scene when Ben asks Sera to dinner.

44 [*77*] Sera arrives at Ben's motel and agrees to have dinner with him.

45 [*80*] Over dinner Sera asks him why he is a drunk.

46 [*79–8*] Ben and Sera on the street, walking. She asks him to stay with her.
The dialogue here was moved from the restaurant. I felt the developing love story needed as much time as possible. I notice, though, that in other films couples fall in love within minutes (with a great deal of help from the score).

47 [*78*] Sera's apartment. He tells her she 'looks extremely beautiful'.
These scenes were shuffled around because I wanted them to get on with their dialogue, get on with their relationship. After all, this is almost the halfway mark in the story.

48 Sera talks to her shrink (#5).

> SERA
>
> I mean . . . it's really weird because . . . um . . . you know, it's just like this thing's happening really quickly, you know . . . um . . . I just don't know what's going on. I mean . . . just the second I met him and the way I . . . I said my name . . . you know . . . I just said, hi, my name's Sera. And that's not what I do and . . . uhh . . . it's just it's all happening really quickly. I just felt like we were . . . we've been together for a long time. You know . . . it just felt so . . . easy . . . and . . . I felt like . . . um . . . I felt like . . . um . . . I felt like I was me. I didn't feel like I was . . . trying to be somebody else.

The therapy stuff was particularly useful here. Sera tells us she is in love.

It was strange for me. I've spent my whole life thus far being convinced of the power of the visual image over the spoken word. Now I realize how powerful a short sentence can be and how it can sometimes get to the point far quicker than a visual image. Subtitles also have great power. The ending of *Montenegro* has an amazing subtitle.

The entire sequence from the end of scenes 42 to 48 is linked together by Sting's version of 'My One and Only Love'.

49 [*83*] Ben wakes up in Sera's apartment. She suggests that he move in with her. He tells her that she can never ask him to stop drinking.

I can't remember any more if it was my intention, but many people have pointed out that when Ben asks her if she understands that she can never ask him to stop drinking, her answer, 'I do, I really do,' sounds like a wedding vow.

50 [*84*] Back at the motel Ben packs his case with booze. Talks to the camera.

51 [*86*] Sera returns to her apartment to find Ben drunk at the gate with her landlady.

Laurie Metcalf kindly agreed to come and do a day's work. I first met her on *Internal Affairs* and agreed with John Malkovich's remark that she is the finest actress around. She is amazing to watch. Any section of her work could be used to illustrate acting technique to students. Within minutes of scene 51 starting she had everyone rolling in the aisles and I was very sad to see her go. I'd love to find a meaty role for her in the future. Meanwhile it's nice that *Roseanne* pays the bills.

52 [*87*] Sera gives Ben two presents. They discuss the relationship. She suggests they go gambling.

John O'Brien's family turned up on the set while we were shooting this scene. It became difficult to continue working. I was aware of a wave of grief coming off them. I was also aware of how painful the experience must have been for them, given the autobiographical nature of the story. Much later they wrote

to me and confirmed my suspicions, but added that in a
strange way it had been a kind of a ceremony as well and had
given them a sort of closure. His book has now gone into
reprint and he is getting the kind of attention that I feel he
deserves.

53 [*88*] Ben and Sera walking on the streets.

54 [*89*] In a casino Ben and Sera kiss.
We slowed this shot up and I used a little echo of the theme to
play up the romance while still keeping it sad.

55 [*89*] Ben has a violent fit in the casino and has to be
restrained by security guards.
We shot two cameras nearly all the time and I operated the B
camera. The shots leading up to the attack (where Ben is
drunk but still cheerful) are running slightly slow because of a
mistake that I made. We used my camera, an older Aaton, to
film the underwater sequence (new scene 66), and Declan
thought it would be interesting to run at thirty frames per second instead of the usual twenty-four. We were so exhausted
that the speed was not reset until we'd been shooting for quite
a while the next day. However, we liked the results here; I think
they accentuate the drunkenness. I like mistakes. At first I had
no focus puller, there being not enough money in the budget. I
did have a trailer, though, which I used twice a day to pee. I
asked Marc Fischer whether I could trade my trailer for a
focus puller and a day later Bonnie Blake turned up.

   In the first draft, the scene in the casino was described by
Sera to Ben in answer to his question the next morning: 'What
happened?' After my conversation with Bill Tennent I decided
to show the scene to illustrate the fact that drunks behave
badly.

56 [*90*] Ben wakes on Sera's sofa and has DTs. Tries to hold
down some vodka and orange juice.
This scene evolved out of some research I did. I discovered
that the stomach of an alcoholic contracts to about half of its
normal size during the withdrawal state. As soon as any alcohol
hits the stomach lining it relaxes to its normal size. The prob-

lem is that it is very difficult to hold alcohol in the stomach when it is contracted and so it is necessary to mix the orange juice with the vodka.

57 [91] Ben gets into bed with Sera and he asks her to tell him about the previous night.
I would say that as much as anything the voice of Maggie Nicols was the key to the emotion of these last two scenes. She came into the recording studio and watched the section of film, listened to the underscore that I had already prepared, and then went straight into the booth and improvised. I think her work is outstanding. I first used her on *The House* (Channel 4, 1984).

58 [92] Ben goes to buy some food but the store is closed.

59 [93] Ben goes into a biker bar and gets into a fight. Gets head-butted.
Julian Lennon does a cameo here. We'd talked a few months earlier about his desire to get out of pop music and into drama, so I suggested he do a small role and see how he felt about the business afterwards. The day he came on the set the radio seemed to be playing John Lennon songs all day.

60 [94] Ben meets the landlady on his way back to Sera.
The 'sexy, sexy' line is entirely Nic's.

61 [94] Ben surprises Sera in the kitchen.
The only time on the film that Nic and I had a disagreement. I was a bit taken aback when he came in full of energy and strangeness and he misread my confusion for criticism. He did a subdued take, but it was not as good so we stayed with his interpretation. The quote 'Kling klang king of the rim ram room,' Nic assures me, is from an early Sinatra song.

62 [95] Ben and Sera in a mall. He is wearing new clothes. He goes down the escalator.
The great thing about shopping malls in America is that they are all identical. This one is somewhere in LA and had huge cracks everywhere from the earthquake.

63 [*96*] Ben gives Sera earrings. She says she will wear them at work. He reacts badly. He gets up to leave, but is persuaded not to by a stranger.

This cameo is by Bob Rafelson, director of one of my favourite films, *Five Easy Pieces*. I have known him for a few years and he has always been supportive and very entertaining with his stories of film-making. A very good man.

The first mix of this scene had some emotional music on it, but I tried it without and realized that it wasn't necessary. I had some mall muzak in the background instead.

64 [*101*] Sera leaves for work while Ben watches TV and drinks.

They agree to go on a short vacation together.

65 [*106*] At a desert motel they sit by the pool at night and watch *The Third Man* on TV.

Why *The Third Man*? It's one of my favourites but the real reason is a low-budget reason. I wanted them to watch a film. Lumière pictures sent me a list of all the films they own the rights to. This was one of them. I also loved the idea of that zither theme in the desert mixing with crickets and coyotes.

66 Next day by the pool. Ben goes underwater and Sera is concerned. She dives in and sees him drinking on the bottom of the pool. They kiss.

67 [*108*] Sera pours Scotch over her breasts and Ben kisses them. They get up to go inside, but Ben falls and cuts himself on a glass table.

68 [*108*] Sera attempts to clean up the glass. The desk clerk tells her to check out with Ben.

69 [*110*] Sera drives Ben back to Vegas.

70 Night-time shot of Vegas.

This whole sequence (scenes 65–70) went through several versions both as script and then as edited footage. An earlier draft of the script had a scene on the way to the desert motel where Ben and Sera stopped the car and went for a swim in a lake.

They both swam underwater but Ben was reluctant to swim up
to the surface again and Sera had to persuade him. In pre-
production we realized that this would be an expensive and
time-consuming sequence so, reluctantly, I let it go from the
script. When we were shooting in Vegas, Annie Stewart (Producer) told me that she'd spotted a perfect swimming pool for
the scene. It was raised up above ground level and had windows on the side so that you could see the swimmers. I put it
to the actors and they agreed to go for it. So, after a full night's
shooting, on our way to the next location we stopped: just me,
the actors, Declan and a few people to help us out. We were
helped by the fact that Lisa is a brilliant athlete and could
really control her movements underwater. We shot at thirty
frames per second and, as I've already mentioned, later forgot
to reset the camera. I saw *Casino* the other day and noticed
that Scorsese had used the same pool.

At the desert motel location I shot a scene where they come
to the surface of the pool gasping for breath and Sera tells Ben
that he'd frightened her. In the editing room I realized that it
was redundant because we know what Ben's agenda is and
don't need to be constantly reminded. The desk clerk (Susan
Barnes) gives a chilling performance. I see this as the real turning point in the film. Any hope that Ben may be cured or saved
has to be abandoned after this scene.

71 [*111–14*] Ben wakes in the dark and goes to the fridge for
vodka.
I had enough confidence in Declan to suggest going hand-held
and shooting these three scenes in one. I'm very happy with
the results.

72 [*115–16*] Ben drinking vodka in the shower.
I did shoot the scene with him throwing up, but it was very
upsetting and almost unwatchable.

73 Ben and Sera sit down for food. Sera wants him to see a
doctor.
At the end of this scene Ben uses his chopsticks to pick up a
piece of ice. It struck me as the sort of thing that a drunk

would do. It is the only time we see a solid pass his lips and the crunch of the ice as we fade to black is very strong. I can remember being immensely moved by Lisa's performance as we shot it. I looked around the set and could see that I was not alone in my opinion. It was interesting to see how she over-came everyone's preconceptions about her ability as an actress.

74 [*98, 100*] Sera dresses for work.
Borrowed from an earlier sequence.

75 [*119–20*] Ben at a casino table. Black-haired woman tries to pick him up.
The same woman who earlier observed Sera failing to pick up the conventioneer. I like trying to integrate the smaller charac-ters as much as possible.

76 Flashback to photo burning, Sera kissing him, dice rolling. Electric billboard saying 'unfinished business'.

77 [*121*] Sera comes home from work. Ben is with the other woman. Sera tells him to leave. She cries.

78 [*123, 125*] Three college boys proposition Sera.

79 Dark, sinister shot of the glass pyramid.

80 [*127*] Sera is raped by the boys in a motel.
A horrible scene to shoot for everyone involved. Lisa was fine until the physical stuff began, then she lost it. Every move was worked out with her before we shot and I decided beforehand that nudity was not necessary, neither was simulated sex.

81 [*129*] Sera surveys herself in the motel mirror.

82 Sera hails a cab, standing next to huge fake waterfall.

83 Cabby is cynical with Sera.
Xander Berkeley has a great reputation among younger Ameri-can film-makers. He worked with me on *Internal Affairs*. He came in for a couple of hours to do this role and clearly he wasn't concerned about appearing to be unsympathetic. A very good actor.

84 [*131*] Landlady observes Sera limping home.

85 [*132*] Sera bleeding in the shower has flashbacks to the rape.

86 [*133*] Sera is evicted by the landlady and landlord.
David Brisbin (landlord) is another actor who I know from
performance art rather than cinema. He worked with Mabu
Mimes and I met him doing a solo piece at the Mickery Thea-
tre in Amsterdam which I filmed (*Rembrandt and Hitler or Me*).
He also worked on *Mr Jones*.

87 [*138*] Sera sits on the kerb as traffic goes by, drinking a coffee and smoking.
I changed this shot and I'm sorry that I did. In the first version, we see Ben in the background staggering past with a bag
full of booze. Neither of them is aware of the other.

88 [*122*] Slow-motion montage of Ben drinking and walking.
I like this effect – shooting straight into the sun but exposing for
the shadow – and I used it in *Mr Jones*, but I think it got cut.

89 [*138*] Back to Sera and traffic.

90 [*134*] Sera goes looking for Ben at the 'Hole You're In' motel.

91 Sera on the streets looking for Ben. Blue night sky.
This was a comic moment in the Las Vegas shoot. A pair of
security guards came out to stop us filming. I tried to reason
with them, pointing out that the sidewalk was public domain.
They disagreed and insisted that the casino owned the sidewalk. Seeing that this was a no-win situation I asked them if
they felt that the casino owned the road in front of the sidewalk.
They thought long and hard about that one and then decided
that they probably didn't. My next question was whether it was
OK for Lisa to walk on 'their' sidewalk. They said it was OK for
her, but not the camera. So we put the camera in a car, opened
the window and kerb-crawled next to Lisa. I am learning. A
gypsy woman once told me that I should not confront situations but swim around them like the Piscean that I am.

92 [*137*] Sera in a casino is insulted by an Italian man in a
white suit.

93 [*140–41*] Sera is evicted from the casino by security guard.

94 [*143*] A sympathetic cab driver asks her what happened. Lou Rawls is an actor as well as a singer, and I jumped at the chance to work with him. I also had the nerve to ask him to sing 'Stormy Monday' in the cab before he talked to Sera. However, some months later, in the cutting room, it seemed very self-indulgent and I removed the singing.

95 [*142*] Sera packs her bags and the phone rings twice. It is Ben.

96 [*145*] Sera arrives at Ben's new motel. He is dying. They make love.
This was the last scene that we shot and everyone began to dread it. Nic lay on a bed of ice to get his body in spasm but it made a lot of noise so he got rid of it. I think it probably helped to get him ready, though.
   When I adapted the book I had a big problem with the ending. In the book they do not make love; she masturbates him. This would be very difficult to do in a film without alienating a lot of the audience. The film was already a tough story. I kept it but then added the scene of her climbing on top and consummating their love. I expected a bad reaction to the masturbating, but so far it has not even been referred to.

97 [*145*] Sera sleeps, and Ben wakes and then dies.

98 [*146*] Sera sits on the side of the bed next to Ben's body. Voice-over begins.

99 Sera in therapy (#6). Tells how she really loved Ben.

> SERA
> I think the thing is . . . we both realized that we didn't have that much time and . . . I accepted him for who he was. And I didn't expect him to change. And I think he felt that for me too. I liked his drama and he needed me. And I loved him. I really loved him.

100 Slow-motion clip of Ben which goes into freeze-frame. End titles. Sting sings 'My One and Only Love'.